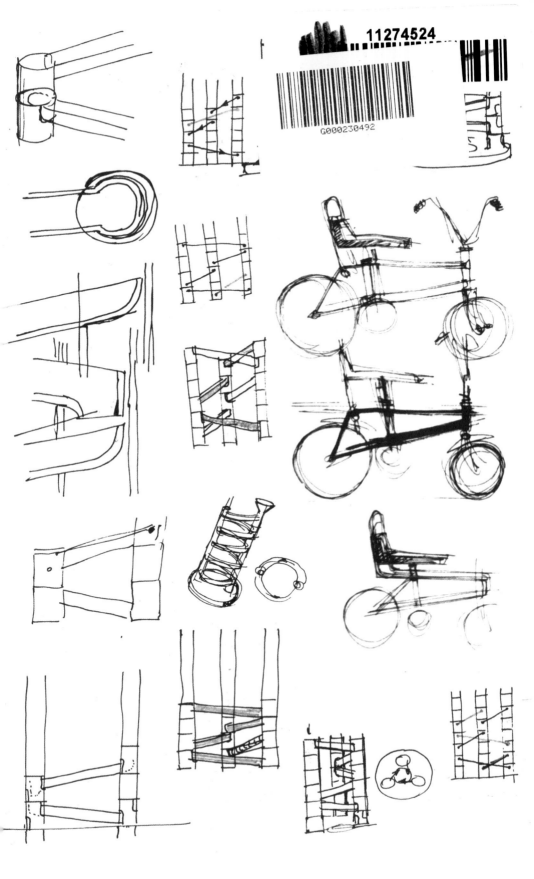

TOYMAKER

TOYMAKER

MY JOURNEY FROM
WAR TO WONDER

BY
TOM KAREN

WITH
RICHARD ASKWITH

First published in the UK by 535
An imprint of Bonnier Books UK
Wimpole Street, London, W1G 9RE
Owned by Bonnier Books
Sveavägen 56, Stockholm, Sweden

Hardback – 978–1–788700–86–3
Ebook – 978–1–788700–87–0

A CIP catalogue of this book is available from the British Library.

Designed by IDSUK (Data Connection) Ltd

All chapter heading images unless stated © Tom Karen
P. 283 image © Alamy
P. 369 illustration © Mark Wearne
All sketches © Tom Karen
With thanks to the V&A Archive for providing the sketches.

Printed and bound by Clays Ltd, Elcograf S.p.A

1 3 5 7 9 10 8 6 4 2

535 is an imprint of Bonnier Books UK
www.bonnierbooks.co.uk

To my grandchildren:

Theo

Louis

Roob

Arlo

(Aalia)

Maia

Zachery

CONTENTS

1

HOME THOUGHTS

AH, THERE you are. Come in. You found the place all right? Most people do. I'm told it's obvious which door is mine, even if you've forgotten the number. It's just an ordinary terraced house, but there is something distinctive in its appearance. All those flying beings dangling in the bay window – the angel; the broom-borne witch; the sitting birds on either side – or the tree silhouette with birds in its branches, or the three wooden penguins. You don't see such objects in every window; nor do you often see front doors decorated, as mine is, with exuberantly handwritten notes. And where else would you see a windowsill inside that's crowded with a wooden Noah's Ark, a big pottery badger, a fleet of hand-made rockets and a wooden-spoon-based rocket-launcher?

It must look rather bewildering at first; chaotic, even. In fact, there's a rhyme and reason to it all. These are my memories, and the further you come inside, the more of them you'll see.

Take a look in my front room: it's an Aladdin's cave of objects, products, artworks and souvenirs. Most are things I made myself, but not all. Above my little fireplace, for example, there's a deep-orange mantelpiece (formerly a steel girder; converted into a fireplace). On it are five objects: a little bronze blackbird (sculpted by me); a pleasingly shaped piece of slate (found); a large pine cone (from Portugal); a beautiful wooden hippopotamus (from Denmark); and a little 'ladies in waiting' laser-cut (model designed by me), which I'll tell you about later. I don't actually need any of them. But why would I ever get rid of any of them? Each one pleases me in its different way: to look at, to pick up, even to smell. To me, they're precious.

It's the same all through my home: models, pictures, toys, things. Why do I have a panel of tiles showing various animals' bottoms? It's a long story – I'll explain later – but the main reason is that it makes people smile. It's the same with that Marble Run toy on the table, or the vintage radio, or all those model cars. Pleasing objects are what I live for. I make them, imagine them, collect them; and they, in turn, reflect me. Each one tells you something about me.

Even the books on my shelves – a seemingly random collection covering history, art, aircraft, wildlife, motoring, architecture, design, toys – offer a broad brushstroke sketch of their owner. If you want to get to know me, wander through my home. This is where I store my memories.

I'm usually to be found in the big room at the back. Let's take a look. Strictly speaking, this is my kitchen. As you can see, though, little that's in here has anything to do with food: it's more of a storeroom, my studio and my office. That's the sink, over there, behind that box. But it's a lovely place to sit and work, or just to gaze out into the garden. There's plenty of sun, especially in the afternoon, and there's a nice amount of shelving. You can fit many memories in here. This lovely table – made by the Devon craftsman Paul Anderson from the oak of old ships – I use mostly as a desk. And my office chair has castors, so if I want anything from a shelf I can just roll over and get it.

Sometimes I think about having a clear-out, but I never get much beyond thinking about it. Where would I start? Where would I stop? If I got rid of every object that isn't strictly necessary for daily life, I'd need a skip the size of this house. If I kept everything that was capable of bringing a smile to my lips just by being what it is, I wouldn't get rid of anything. Objects have meaning, messages, value. You can't just throw them away.

In any case, I have other priorities. My instinct is to create, not to cull. You see that garage down there, at the far end of the garden? That's my workshop. It's one of my favourite places, although it gets a bit cold in winter. Come on, I'll show you. Mind the step – and watch out for Rusty, too. He's that big laser-cut dog, made of steel and then salted to make him rust, next to the garden path. There's a smaller Rusty at the other end, as you'll see, as well as a bigger version of that 'ladies in waiting' laser-cut I mentioned earlier.

I have to take the path carefully these days, but it's worth the effort. Time in my workshop keeps me sane. Making things always has. I set myself a practical task, settle down to doing it, and all my other cares disappear.

It's a bit cluttered, but there are ways of getting from one side of the room to the other, if you know the routes through the maze of memorabilia. I think of it as a creative warm-up. I had the whole place done up soon after I moved here, but things have been gathering in it ever since. Some of the objects are there because I've nowhere else to put them: that great big bicycle, for example, or the wooden marble run by the door, which I made with my grandchildren (I did the carpentry, they painted the animals).

But most of this stuff is here because it is needed. If you make things, you require materials, and tools. All those things on the shelves are related to my craft activities: paints, glues, varnishes. So are all these things on the floor: tiles, wood, hardboard, cardboard, modelling clay, plastics, fabrics – you can make things out of almost any material. And then, as you can see, I have any number of specialist tools: drill, bandsaw, sander and so on. I can hardly start getting rid of *those*. I suppose you could make a case against keeping quite so many offcuts, but you never know when they'll come in useful.

The real problem comes from all the career memorabilia that have settled around the craft materials – again, because I've nowhere else to put them. There are folders full of slides, big binders full of newspaper cuttings, boxes of obscure correspondence and old diaries. I'm not sure how it all got here, but it's here now, and I can hardly get rid of it. These, too, are objects that carry the story of my life.

The trouble is, there's now so much clutter in the workshop that it's impossible to clean. So the dirt and the sawdust keep accumulating, and the idea of sorting it all out becomes less and less attractive. Sometimes I think I'll have a go, but life's too short. I'm 94. How many active days do I have left? And why would I want to waste any of them on tidying, when I could be making things?

In any case, where would I start? What I really need is some kind of anthropological archaeologist, or perhaps a brilliant detective, to go through my home and my workshop systematically, layer by layer. They could label and catalogue each object, assign each one to a different period; and perhaps, finally, amaze onlookers by describing me and my life in vivid and comprehensive detail.

Actually, that's not such a crazy idea; or, at least, it could be distilled into a viable form. (Many of my best ideas start out like this.) I have had a rich and remarkable life. I would like to tell my story, while I can. But I'm no writer, and the things that matter most about me cannot easily be expressed through a conventional narrative.

But physical *stuff*? That's a different matter. Three-dimensional objects – designed, man-made objects – have been the one constant theme of my existence; in a sense, they have been my life. I don't mean that they are the only things I have lived for, but they are the things I have lived *through*. I'm a designer. All the stages that matter in my journey through life can be described in terms of man-made objects. Some were designed and made by me; others came into my life in other ways. And most can be found (or at least are represented in some form) in my house.

If I reconstruct my past through the prism of physical souvenirs, I think I can tell you my whole life story – or all the interesting bits, anyway.

You don't believe me? Come on, let's give it a try.

2

THE LOST BOY

I DON'T much like this picture. I haven't even bothered to hang it. It usually just leans against a bookshelf behind my sofa, year after year, along with some other forgotten pictures. But it's a good point from which to begin my story. Its journey has been almost as long as mine.

It was painted more than 80 years ago. It's oil on canvas, about 330mm by 430mm, with a plain wooden frame that was added several decades later. The well-dressed, well-scrubbed boy it depicts is me, not long after my 12th birthday. I don't recognise myself. But visitors who notice the portrait among the jumble of objects and memorabilia in my front room insist that it looks just like me, and surviving members of my family agree. The artist ought to have known what he was doing. He was my grandfather.

Actually, Arthur von Ferraris was more than that. In the early 20th century, he was one of Europe's most fashionable portrait painters. Perhaps that sounds grand. Well, my childhood was grand.

I was born in a sanatorium in Vienna, on 20 March 1926. Our home, however, was in Brno, a prosperous, industrial city, 120 miles south-east of Prague, in Moravia, in what was then Czechoslovakia. We lived in Hlinky, a broad, curving, tree-lined avenue in the south-west of the city, far from most of the industry. Locals called it 'millionnaires' row'. Our house, known as the Kohn Villa, was one of its larger buildings.

I was born Thomas Joseph Derrick Paul Kohn. We weren't a very happy family, but we were rich. I think I would have preferred it if it had been the other way round.

The wealth came from my father's side. His grand-father, Gottlieb Kohn, had done military service in the Austrian Imperial Guard and had used the resulting bounty to start a brick factory in Brno, back in the 1880s. Gottlieb's son Max – my father's father – trained as a geologist and later had the brilliant idea of supplement-ing the factory with a cement works. The local land was rich in the necessary raw materials, and the plant became the biggest in Czechoslovakia, employing 500 people. It made the family very wealthy. Max Kohn was also an astute investor in property, but he lived a simple life in a flat and enjoyed lavishing his wealth on my father and his sisters.

My mother's side of the family was more exotic. Her father, Arthur von Ferraris, was originally from Galicia (in what is now Poland). After training at art schools in Vienna and Paris and earning a modest living as a painter of Egyptian scenes, he fell in love (via her portrait) with a beautiful red-haired Hungarian woman named Ottilie Kállay,[1] married her and settled in Austria. Guided by his accomplished wife, he carved out a lucrative new career for himself as a portrait painter. Franz Joseph, the penultimate Habsburg emperor, Carol I, king of Romania, and Wilhelm II, the last German Kaiser, were among his subjects; so, much later, were US president Franklin D Roosevelt and US tycoon John D Rockefeller – although by that time the First World War had wiped out most of Arthur's wealth.

My mother, Margaret, was the least glamorous of Arthur's children and knew it. Her brother, Stephen, was educated at Harrow and relied on his old school tie and his smooth English manners to charm and muddle his way through life. Her sister, Mimi, was radiantly beautiful (red-haired also) – although an unfortunate love affair led her to suicide. My mother, the youngest by seven years, was unremarkable, home-educated and apparently uncherished. She did receive one offer of marriage as a teenager, during a family trip to the US, but her parents rejected it. In 1923, she found herself sitting near a thin-lipped young man at a dinner in Vienna. This was my father, Paul Kohn. She barely noticed him. He, however, was taken with her innocence. This, he decided, was the kind of woman he needed as a wife. His family had

---

[1] Ottilie Kállay's mother was born in Pogranice, Slovakia.

warned him against falling into the clutches of a gold-digger. Margaret seemed a safe, sensible choice. They were married three weeks later.

It doesn't sound like a recipe for a successful marriage. It wasn't. Each of my parents was unfulfilled in a different way. My father, tall, handsome and brilliant, realised too late the disadvantages of sharing his life with someone who did not share his intellectual flair. My mother, short, shy, spoiled and lacking intellectual curiosity, failed to appreciate his gifts. She was barely 20 when she married, apparently just to please her parents, and I don't think she was really ready to leave the family home in Vienna. She clearly felt little enthusiasm for living in Brno and was not ready to have children – the two things to which marriage destined her. In short: husband and wife both felt trapped. I don't think they quarrelled; but I never saw them laughing together, or even looking relaxed.

My father's loneliness was compounded by his father's insistence that he take over the family business. Not everyone would have considered this a hardship. He did. He was an intellectual: a man of ideas. He loved to read, or to talk to other intellectuals. From time to time, high-powered visitors would appear in our house: including the Bishop of Brno.[2] At other times – rare moments when his time was his own – my father would

---

[2] My daughter Eugenie recently reminded me we are distantly related to the former Archbishop of Olomouc but that was before this time.

read. He had a vast collection of books, including dozens of cheap English paperbacks, which he kept in our big, wood-panelled library. But he had never been allowed to go to university (because his father intended him to take over the family business), and by the time he had thrown off the burden of his parents' expectations there were other family pressures to consider.

Had he lived as he had chosen, my father might have been a man of letters – perhaps an academic or an inventor. Instead, most of his life was spent playing a supporting role to his own father's story, helping the family make bricks and cement.

My mother was equally dissatisfied with her allotted roles. She had three children – I was the second – but nothing in her upbringing had prepared her for parent-hood. She had been brought up by nannies and tutors, and I don't think she had ever felt loved by her own parents. So perhaps it is not surprising that, when she became a mother herself, she had no example of motherhood to aspire to. I don't think she ever changed a nappy or bathed a baby or read a bedtime story or gave hugs and kisses. It doesn't seem to have been obvious to her to make us feel loved or valued. She was more concerned with what impression we might make in good society. I suppose you could say that she craved the love and admiration of the outside world. She insisted on giving birth to each of her three children in Vienna: an Austrian birth certificate seemed more prestigious to her than a Czechoslovak one.

And although she was a good linguist – she spoke German, Hungarian, English and French – she never bothered to learn Czech, which until 1918 had been considered the language of servants and working people.[3]

By any normal standards I was fabulously fortunate in my early years. Our home was called a villa but was really a grand town house. Wide and low, with ornate stucco bas-reliefs under the main windows, it would not have looked out of place in grounds designed by Capability Brown. Instead, its neo-Renaissance frontage dominated one of Brno's most opulent streets. The main entrance was in a gated courtyard at one end, where visitors could – theoretically – disembark from their carriages.

Inside, there was a wide wooden staircase and high ceilings, stuccoed or inlaid. There were parquet floors and many dark, panelled walls. In one corridor there was a piano, and there was a full-size billiard table in the hall. A huge garden at the back included a tennis court and a 20-metre swimming pool, a kitchen garden, a big green-house, a landscaped wooded area, a stream and a pond.

And then there were the servants. We had a staff of 17. Many worked in the garden, and there was also a uniformed butler called Petr (my father's valet), a live-in nanny, maids, several kitchen staff, and a chauffeur to

---

[3] Roughly a third of Brno's population had German as their first language. Brno was closer to Vienna than Prague so this was not a major issue in the early days of the Czech Republic.

drive my father's car. My mother had a Bugatti and for long trips we used an enormous Hispano Suiza. The changing room by the swimming pool had its own telephone, which my mother used for calling the house to say that we were ready for afternoon tea. Petr would appear shortly afterwards, carrying a silver tray in white-gloved hands.

The head gardener had his own flat on the ground floor. Other servants lived on the top floor, in rooms with little, arched dormer windows. We lived on the first floor, where you could look out on the chestnut trees on the far side of the avenue and, beyond that, at Brno's new exhibition centre. (The city liked to think of itself as a grand regional capital, and the architecture reflected this.) Yet the upstairs space wasn't very well arranged: it was built for entertaining rather than living. Many rooms could be reached only by walking through other rooms. My parents' bedroom was vast. I, on the other hand, had to share a room with my younger sister, and we both used to walk through her nanny's room in order to get to our bathroom.

Arthur's portraits were everywhere, but the painting I loved was an Impressionist work hanging in the entrance hall. The scene was set in a village with men drinking wine in the foreground and a hay cart pulled by oxen in the background. The colours were beautifully bright and it had made a big impact on me.

You'll have got the idea by now. We had everything money could buy, and we could not possibly have been considered deprived in any material sense. We always ate well, and we children had plenty of fresh air and exercise: my mother even arranged for us to have what would now be called a personal trainer, a humourless man called Mr Kussi, while our enormous playroom was equipped like a gym. But there is a difference between having what others might consider enviable and having what you actually want or really need.

Normal children would have ridden their bicycles in the park with friends. We had no friends. Our cycling was mostly restricted to circuits of the path around our garden. On the one occasion I did try riding my little red bike outside in the street, some other boys laughed loudly at me. I was so upset that, on our next Sunday visit to our grandfather Max (my father's father), I cadged some money from him and secretly spent it on a big new bicycle. My father wasn't pleased when he found out: he thought the shop was likely to have overcharged me because they knew how rich we were. Meanwhile, riding a larger bike proved more challenging than expected. I had several painful falls before I could ride it and faced similar problems mastering dismounting.

We wore smarter clothes than other children. I liked my lederhosen but only wore them in Austria. Our family holidays took us to exotic locations – skiing in winter, Venice or Lake Garda in the summer – but there were no shared experiences with our parents. Instead, we were supervised by a nanny, or, on skiing holidays, by Mr Kussi. On one of these trips, by an Austrian lake, Nazi troublemakers had a shoot-out with loyal forces. My sister was distraught, but I kept hoping that the Austrian navy would appear. I have no idea where my brother or parents were.

Every Christmas and every birthday, each child would receive lavish presents chosen by my mother without any thought as to what we might actually want. At different times I was given a toy fortress, a set of model soldiers, an electric railway – and I barely touched any of them. What I longed for instead were pencils, paper, paints and brushes, but the question of what I was interested in was never discussed. There was no conversation at family meals: just relentless oversight of our manners. I spent long hours detained at the dinner table until I had finished the last of my vegetables. But I don't remember being asked what I had done at school that day or what I thought about something.

It seems wrong to complain, but it really wouldn't have taken much effort to work out that my talents and interests related to the shapes and appearances of things. When I was two, I could recognise 12 different makes of car. I know this because my nanny noticed, and won a bet about it with a friend who refused to believe it. My mother, however, was oblivious to this unusual aptitude. And so, at the stage in life when I was most capable of learning, I was never taken to galleries or museums, or encouraged to draw or paint, or given any kind of creative start in life. Even now, in the tenth decade of a life that has been full of success and creative fulfilment, it frustrates me to think of the lost opportunities. I got no benefit from Grandfather Arthur von Ferraris's artistic expertise, for example; nor did anyone think to take advantage of our frequent visits to Vienna to expose us to the city's wonderful cultural heritage. As for my father, who had a phenomenal brain, I could have learnt so much from him, given the chance. But instead of discussing things as a family, we spent our mealtimes being trained to use cutlery correctly, to put our free hand on the table and to sit up straight without touching the back of the chair.

When we did speak, we spoke German: the language of the ruling classes of the defunct Austro-Hungarian Empire. At first we went to German-speaking schools, and we were imbued with Roman Catholic traditions. My father's side of the family were Jewish, but he had rebelled against the heavily Jewish milieu in which he was raised. I don't think I ever saw the inside of a synagogue. Then again, I can't remember going to church, either. My mother, a Catholic, was concerned with appearances, not the well-being of our souls.

One day, when I was about ten, the chauffeur who usually took me to school took me instead to a building that I had never seen before. It turned out that this was a big Czech-speaking Gymnasium, or middle school. No one had thought to mention this to me. I was just expected to knock on the door and introduce myself – without knowing a word of Czech. I refused point-blank – a rare rebellion – and in due course was introduced, more gently, to a much smaller school, where I was able to pick up Czech without too much difficulty. Picking up friends, however, was a different matter. I just didn't know how it was done.

Looking back, I can see that my childhood was very lonely. At the time, I hardly realised. There was nothing to compare it with. But I never learnt how to form or maintain friendships, and, as a result, have never developed the social skills that most people take for granted. When my mother organised a birthday party for me once, she invited a whole crowd of children – none of whom I knew. That awkward feeling has never quite left me.

I didn't even socialise much with my siblings. My elder brother, Felix, was two years older than me, and for some reason we failed to get on; we didn't actually fight, but we had nothing in common. One of the few toys I liked was an electric replica of the Bugatti Type 35 racing car that you could actually sit in. But Felix had most use of it and, of course, we used to quarrel over who used it. My relationship with my sister, Bettina, was less fraught, but she was four years younger than me and a girl, and so was a useless playmate.

As for my mother, I barely saw her, especially when – to general amazement – she learnt to fly. I don't know why, but when I was about eight she and my father took lessons, using decrepit French biplanes left over from the First World War. My mother proved particularly adept and in due course became an accomplished pilot, flying competitively on a number of flights. My father even had a plane made for her, eventually: a little high-winged Hadimrška. I think she found in flying a sense of fulfilment and self-esteem that she had never experienced in childhood or motherhood. I admire her for this, but it did not make our relationship closer.

I did enjoy my father's company, when the opportunity arose. He had a brilliant mind and a kind heart. I think his marriage made him miserable. But life had allotted him a role, and he seemed stuck in it. He was always beautifully dressed – he wore monogrammed shirts, and his suits were made of English cloth by Knize, the best tailor in Vienna – but the suave appearance was undermined by an air of persecution. He rarely radiated happiness.

He liked his children, of course, and was fond of animals. But work always came first. He shared my enthusiasm for cars, and sometimes he would take us on drives through the countryside, for no particular reason. But when it came to the annual Grand Prix at the Masarykring – a 19-mile circuit of public roads near Brno that was occasionally used for motor sport – it was always the chauffeur, not him, who took us. I loved these events: I can still remember the drivers (Louis Chiron, Hans Stuck, Rudolf Caracciola), and I could draw their winning cars today: the Bugatti, the Alfa Romeo, and later the Auto Union and the Mercedes-Benz. But it would have been nice to have been able to share the excitement with my father.

In the right mood, at the right time, he was great, but all too often he was busy and frustrated. It seemed to me that his wealth was a burden for him. Every facet of his life was weighed down by it. When my sister was little, for example, he was terrified that someone might kidnap her for a ransom – like the baby of the wealthy American aviator Charles Lindbergh, whose abduction and murder had made global headlines in 1932. (For some reason, he wasn't so worried about his sons.) Even his love of animals made him a target. The local pet shop owner seemed to have worked out that he would buy any animal that he thought had been ill-treated. We had many dogs – up to eight at a time with three in the house, the others in the greenhouse – but we regularly found space for rescue animals as well. At one point we had a pair of raccoons, which had a special raccoon house built for them, and there was also a strange incident when my father rescued a lot of swallows that had been left in distress by the unexpected early onset of winter. Having restored them to health indoors, he had them flown to southern Italy by plane. His love of animals had no limit. For the pet shop owner, my father's soft heart and deep pockets represented a valuable source of income; as it did, I imagine, for the local vet, who was a regular guest in our home. I wonder if my father would have been happier if it hadn't been so easy for him to buy whatever he wanted, but he had instead been free to live his life as he chose.

I used to look forward to Sunday mornings when, finally, he would get a little time to be himself. He would sit cross-legged on the floor of our playroom, surrounded by newspapers, reading each one from cover to cover while we ate our breakfast. His persecuted air vanished, and he seemed instead like the bright, curious, enthusiastic man that he was. Those were the moments I loved.

But those happy interludes were rare, and as I grew older they became rarer. The rise of the Third Reich cast a shadow over our home, as it did over most of Europe. In 1936, my father took me and Felix on a cruise holiday that was supposed to call in at Barcelona; the Spanish Civil War broke out just before we arrived, and we were diverted to the Côte d'Azur. By 1938, when the Nazis annexed Austria, my parents were visibly anxious about what might happen if – as seemed almost certain – Czechoslovakia was Hitler's next target.

I understand that the portrait with which I have chosen to begin my story was painted with this threat in mind, along with similar portraits of my brother and sister. My parents were considering the possibility of escape, and there might not have been another opportunity for my grandfather to capture our likenesses. I think, however, that he painted us in a hurry. He would certainly have been preoccupied. After the Nazi occupation of Austria, he had made an urgent alteration to his portrait of President Roosevelt, which he had painted in 1935 but which by 1938 had for some reason come back to Arthur's studio in Vienna. Word had reached him that the Gestapo, who were looking for his Anglophile son, Stephen, were about to raid his studio. With no time to hide the large portrait, Arthur hastily painted a swastika brooch on to FDR's lapel, then persuaded his unwanted visitors that the portrait depicted a leading Nazi. (The brooch was removed 40 years later when the portrait, after a convoluted journey, was auctioned by Christie's in London.)

In such a climate of fear, it is understandable that Arthur might not have been able to give his fidgeting grandson his full attention. Then again, I didn't have much expectation of being the focus of adult attention. At home, I may have spent more time with our pets than with either parent. We even had a tame jackdaw, called Kako, who killed the odd mouse and stole little silver items which he carried off to a hollow in a big tree in the garden. For some reason he was very fond of me and when I scratched his head gently he would flutter his wings. He identified the window to my bedroom, which was one of a dozen on the front of the house and always open (my mother believed in fresh air). Kako would fly in and sit beside my pillow when I woke up. I can also remember at least one occasion when, feeling sad about something, I curled up with my favourite dog, a German shepherd called Beno, hoping that he might console me.

It never occurred to me to seek comfort from my mother. Actually, I can't remember her ever hugging me.

Such was my start in life. I was lost in the world. I couldn't make friends. I didn't know what I was or where I was going. We were rich in luxury and unnecessary wealth, yet impoverished when it came to affection or meaningful stimulation. Looking today at my grandfather's portrait of me, I am surprised how cheerful I look. Perhaps that is why I don't recognise myself.

3

THE JOURNEY

FOR REASONS that will become clear, I no longer have my Water Line warships. But when I think of the next chapter of my life, it is always those models that come to mind. The episode began five days before my 13th birthday, when I was in bed with a cold. I think it was late evening. I was asleep. All I remember is being roused by my sister's nanny. She seemed agitated. She told me that I had to get dressed – quickly.

News had reached my parents that Nazi troops had begun to cross the Czechoslovak border. By 6:00am, a full-scale invasion would be in progress, with Czechoslovak forces ordered to offer no resistance. I knew that my parents had been worrying for some time that such a catastrophe might occur: my father would get terribly upset listening to Hitler's speeches on the radio. We already knew what Arthur von Ferraris and his family had experienced under Nazi rule; and we knew that, unlike them, we would be targeted as Jews. But I had no real sense of what all this might mean in practice. My parents did, and the staff were already packing. Within an hour, we would be fleeing for our lives to Prague.

I was told to choose a favourite toy to take with me. I grabbed a few Water Line warships. I was getting a bit old for such playthings, but these ones were special. Designed and die-cast in Germany by a company called Viking, they were exquisitely detailed, with every last gun turret and porthole faithfully reproduced. Each model came with extensive notes, on tonnage, armaments, speed – the details fascinated me. I can still remember some of them: for example, the *Émile Bertin*, a French light cruiser and minelayer, carried 200 mines; while HMS *Nelson* had three gun turrets for its 16in guns, all positioned at the front of the battleship, with the third one only firing sideways.

The neat thing about Water Line ships was the fact that each vessel was cut off at the bottom, at the level where the waterline would have been. So you could put the flat-bottomed models on the floor and they would look as though they were at sea. But the great thing about the Viking ones – as opposed to earlier Meccano versions – was their painstaking accuracy. Every detail was correct, including the paint; and each model came with notes telling you about the ship's capacity and capabilities. I still enjoy remembering those details, and I wish more of today's toymakers understood how much children appreciate such authenticity. I treasured my ships not because they were playthings but because they represented the cutting edge of military technology and design.

Even now, if you asked me to draw the *Nelson* or the *Émile Bertin*, I could do so. That night, however, there were other things to think about. The ships were stuffed into the boot of the Hispano with the other luggage, and I was stuffed into the back seat. I was now wide awake as we drove through the night to Prague. There was a sprinkling of snow on the roads, and the night seemed strangely white and still. Nobody spoke. Gryc, our Czech chauffeur, sped along the empty roads. The big engine barely hummed. Everyone was preoccupied with fears and uncertainties – including Gryc, who had served the family devotedly for years. Yet no one broke the silence, and as long as it remained unbroken it felt as though the life we were leaving hadn't quite come to an end.

We reached the capital around daybreak. My father checked us into one of the best hotels. Soon afterwards, we went to his lawyer's office, which, like the hotel, was near Wenceslas Square. So we were well placed that afternoon to see Adolf Hitler's motorcade arriving, followed by a vast, triumphant, military parade through the square. The columns of soldiers and helmets, glinting in the March sunlight, seemed to go on forever. The roar of aircraft overhead was as awesome as it was deafening. Bettina, who was nine, laughed at the way the soldiers goose-stepped. I was more struck by a sense of brutal, mechanised military force. I was familiar in the abstract with much of the machinery of modern warfare – my Water Line ships were just part of my collection. But those were just models. There was nothing imaginary about this invasion.

Yet my family, whose Jewish name made them likely to be among the invaders' earliest victims, seemed outwardly calm. During the following days we found time for some sightseeing, and I think my mother took Bettina shopping. We also moved to a smaller hotel. One day Gryc decided to let me drive my father's little Škoda. (I am not sure how or why, but this had turned up in Prague.) Gryc had often let me sit behind the steering wheel while he drove. Now, for the first time, he let me drive unaided through the countryside near Prague. I did so without problems. The security forces, old and new, had other things on their minds than the menace of 13-year-old drivers.

But these were diversions, intended, I suppose, to distract us from the danger of our situation while my parents tried to find a way out. My 13th birthday passed unnoticed, even by me. At some point, although not immediately, my father was arrested by the Gestapo, who detained him in an improvised prison (actually a bank vault) for several days. At another point, possibly before that and probably in the lawyer's office, my parents completed divorce proceedings, which I imagine they must have initiated in advance. My mother could be classed as an Aryan and reverted to her name of Margaret Ferraris. As far as we knew, it was only my father's side of the family that was Jewish. (In fact, this wasn't altogether true.) So the idea was that the rest of us would stand a better chance of escape if my mother reverted to her previous 'Aryan' identity as Margaret von Ferraris, a Vienna-born Roman Catholic from Austria.

Somehow, after three days, my father's release was arranged. The Gestapo kept his passport, but he quickly made arrangements with contacts in the Czechoslovak Air Force to have a new one made. He then escaped to Poland on foot, before flying first to Sweden and then to the UK. There were no goodbyes. One day he was with us; the next, he wasn't. It never occurred to me to worry that I might never see him again. Everything just seemed to happen, for unseen reasons, as if in a dream. I went along with it passively, assuming that – as usual – our problems would somehow be sorted out.

Luckily, a wonderful Belgian family came to our aid. Their daughter was married to one of my father's employees, Walter Rosenberg. We had met both the daughter and her mother – we called her Tante Rose – in Brno. Now they were all safely in Brussels, where we were able to contact them. They invited us to join them, and Tante Rose worked tirelessly to arrange entry visas for us.

Extensive string-pulling was required. Most of it went over my head, but I think Tante Rose was able to call in a favour from a friend in the Belgian Ministry of Justice. I had no idea of the danger we were in, but I realise with hindsight how concerned my mother must have been. Outwardly, she was the same: her air of anxiety and her constant smoking were no different from her usual comportment. But she now had sole responsibility for the survival of her three children. She must have known that the odds were stacked against her.

Eventually, we children got Belgian visas and exit permits from Czechoslovakia. Felix, for some reason, was sent to Brussels first, by train. Bettina and I were sent by plane to Vienna to say goodbye to our grandfather and uncle. I hope it meant more to him than it did to us at the time. We never saw my grandfather again. (Years later, we learnt that he died in poverty in Hungary – probably shot by the Russians – just after the end of the war.)

We then flew to Frankfurt in a beautiful Focke-Wulf Condor, later used for maritime surveillance. After some tense moments going through passport control, we flew on to Brussels. I presume that a journey via Austria and Germany was considered less likely to run into difficulties than one from Czechoslovakia, but that is just a guess. If anyone had explained the thinking behind our movements, I hadn't been listening. I just went where I was sent. Yet I did feel a chill of apprehension when we showed our passports. There seemed to be swastikas everywhere, and men with guns. Our name was still Kohn. Even I knew that this might not go down very well.

Eventually, Bettina and I arrived in Brussels, a few days after Felix. Tante Rose lived in an old, narrow-fronted house with dark rooms, which she shared with her daughter and son-in-law. It felt cramped, compared with what we were used to, but she looked after us brilliantly. She was strict, but, unlike my mother, she had some sense of what bringing up children involved. She was a brilliant teacher, motivating us to work hard without ever bullying us. I was enrolled in a local school, the École Moyenne de Schaerbeek, and with Tante Rose's expert encouragement I learnt French quickly. I also enjoyed art lessons, where, for the first time in my life, I was encouraged to draw. The school itself did not take art very seriously, but the art teacher did, and his delight in my pictures was a great boost to my enthusiasm.

In the summer, Tante Rose took us for a short seaside holiday in Middlekerke. The North Sea coast seemed cold and grey compared with the Venice Lido, but we spent a lot of time on the beach, and I enjoyed the sense of wide, empty spaces. Brussels could feel claustrophobic, especially in the narrow streets where Tante Rose lived. (I'm told that the rue Gallait, where her home was, is now part of the red light district.)

In all this time, I don't remember worrying at all about what would happen to my mother. This was partly the callousness of youth and partly a symptom of our lack of closeness, but I think it also reflected a naïve confidence that, if my mother said she would join us in Brussels, she would. There had been no tearful embraces when we left her in Prague, and we assumed – as did thousands of other children sent away by their parents in 1939 – that we were being sent on a journey that was within the bounds of normality. The true context did not become clear until much later.

As it happened, our family was among the lucky ones. Eventually, months after sending us away, my mother reached Belgium. The divorce ruse had turned out to be of little use when it came to getting a visa; or when it came to extricating the family's wealth from the country. Our home in Brno had been taken over by German officers. Some of the staff remained loyal, rescuing possessions that, much later, they returned to us. (These included my grandfather's portrait of me, mentioned in the previous chapter.) Others, notably the head gardener, declared themselves ardent Nazis.

It must have been distressing for my mother to hear about this. Whatever her other failings, however, she did not lack courage, and she was determined to rejoin her children. She still had some jewellery and access to some money, and in the end she was able to bribe a Gestapo official with an expensive new Leica camera for a permit to leave the country. Her train journey to Brussels was agonisingly slow: it took about three days. At one point, exhausted, she decided that she wanted to get out for a break. A fellow passenger persuaded her not to. When she reached Belgium, Germany had already begun to invade Poland. The world was at war.

We stayed in Brussels for about six months. Tante Rose's home was cramped, and my mother's presence made it harder to ignore the overcrowding. She had no experience of life without servants, and although I think she did her best to fit in, tensions emerged between her and our hosts. Yet Tante Rose, to her immense credit, made no attempt to get rid of us. When we did move on, in March 1940, it was for a more pressing reason. Hitler was turning his attention to the west; Belgium was unlikely to remain safe much longer. The fact that we had probably outstayed our welcome made it easier to make the decision to be among the first to flee. So we got on another train and travelled to the south of France.

We found lodgings in Nice, in a comfortable guest house on the Boulevard Carnot, not far from the seafront. We remained here, on and off, for two years. It was a strange place and grew stranger. Its fabric was still that of one of the French Riviera's most desirable seaside destinations. The air was clear; the light was soft; the architecture was grand. Palm trees and luxury hotels overlooked a long, pebbled beach. But beneath the genteel surface a subculture of hardship and desperation was taking root.

France capitulated to the Nazis in June 1940, shortly after Belgium's surrender. But Nice was far to the south of the line that subsequently divided Occupied France (in the north and west) from the notionally independent 'zone libre' administered from Vichy by Marshal Pétain. So refugees like us continued to drift into Nice from all over Central and Eastern Europe.

We went to school, spoke French and, on the whole, lived comfortably. The Pension Floréal, run by a mother and her daughter, had a garden, a terrace, and reasonably congenial fellow guests, including a youth of about my own age called André Mallard. He came from Normandy, trained to be a telegrapher on merchant ships, and subsequently jumped ship to fight for the Allies. We met again in Britain during the war and became lifelong friends.

As the war continued, food became scarcer. We went months without seeing a potato, and the daily bread ration – 350g for a child – was strictly enforced. If the baker accidentally cut you a chunk of baguette that was a gram or two too heavy, the excess would be ruthlessly sliced off. We were hungry from morning until night; and, given our upbringing, the discomfort was hard to bear. We got used to it, of course – just as millions of hungry people do today. But hunger always gnawed at our minds.

My mother's cash and jewellery took a while to run out. She was also in touch, somehow, with my father in England, and every now and then he was able to send her money, which was a huge relief. Once, Felix and I hired bicycles and rode off westward down the coast, then wound our way back along little inland lanes, looking for farms. We were rewarded with some extra bread and, wonderfully, a rabbit each – which we then had to smuggle through a police roadblock in Nice. Luckily, they thought us too young to merit more than a cursory search. I can still remember the delicious joy of our rabbit feast that night.

Such moments of indulgence were rare. Usually, we scraped by on rations, and for long periods cash was scarce. One day, in desperation, I sold my collection of Water Line ships to a French boy – another reason why, in my mind today, those toys have become emblematic of this period of my life. At the time, however, I gave little thought to their loss. I should have felt sad, but I was too busy looking for food to buy with the proceeds.

Sometimes, it got worse. Not long after our arrival, rumours swept the city that Mussolini was about to invade southern France. (In fact, the Italian army didn't get much beyond the Alps in 1940.) We tried to get on board a ship taking refugees to the UK but, instead, found ourselves trying to follow it westward down the coast. It was a dreadful journey. At one point they stopped all the trains, and we were stranded. Some kind French people at the station went round giving out cups of hot coffee. I had never drunk coffee before, or accepted charity, so I asked my mother for permission before saying yes.

We then continued the journey by bus, in torrential rain, with our luggage on the roof. Many of our things were damaged. We stayed briefly in Aimargues, in the Département du Gard, 200 miles west of Nice, where a lovely family sheltered us in a house with beautiful vaulted ceilings. Then we were moved to a nearby village called Aigues-Vives. The place accommodated lots of Belgian soldiers and was overwhelmed with several thousand refugees: two for every villager. We found rooms above the café. The owners were kind, but it was the most unhygienic place imaginable. The walls were black with flies: I still flinch when I think of them. The water was filthy; and my brother claimed that there were only two proper toilets in the whole village.

After five or six weeks, the rumours of invasion subsided. We returned with relief to Nice. It seemed unlikely, however, that we would be safe there indefinitely. Yet what could we do? Joining my father in England – the obvious solution – required exit visas from Vichy France, entrance visas for the UK, visas for passing through Spain and Portugal en route; all had to be validated at the same time. It was a formidable bureaucratic obstacle course. Both parents made desperate attempts to secure the necessary paperwork.

Looking back, I can imagine my mother's rising sense of panic as she and my father struggled to get all our 'ducks in a row'. Yet we children still seemed to drift on through our education, with a mixture of fatalism and apathy. In the end, we spent around two years in Nice, interrupted by a brief interlude when Bettina was sent to a convent in the Haute-Loire, while I spent a few weeks helping on a farm nearby. I proved hopelessly inept as a cowhand and was soon sent back. I was then enlisted into the École du Navigation Maritime (where André Mallard was also studying).

Had we stayed longer, I might eventually have acquired some seafaring skills, but that phase of my education proved brief. We were clearly in danger in Nice. The Vichy regime had already begun to round up Jews, and an Italian invasion was once again rumoured to be imminent. We needed to get out before it was too late. Our sense of urgency might have been greater had we known that, back in Czechoslovakia, my 84-year-old grandfather, Max Kohn, had already been incarcerated in Terezín, the ghetto-cum-prison-camp that the Nazis had created in northern Czechoslovakia for the country's remaining Jews. He was taken there that April. Six months later, he was transported to Treblinka in Poland, where he was soon killed – one of more than 77,000 Czechoslovak Jews murdered in the Holocaust. As with my other grandfather, we did not learn of his fate until many years later. All we had to guide us in Nice was the pervasive and increasingly intense sense of fear.

Eventually, in June 1942, all the visa paperwork fell into place. We travelled by train along the coast into neutral Spain: I remember my relief when we crossed the frontier safely. In Madrid, food was plentiful, and for the first time in years we ate until we had had enough.

We resumed our travels, with a slow, much-interrupted train journey to Lisbon. It was a steam train, and by the time we reached Lisbon we were black from the smoke. Finally, after a wait of about a fortnight, we were able to board a plane to the UK. It was an ex-KLM Douglas DC-2, with an extra petrol tank in the cabin so that it could take a wide detour around Brest rather than risk being shot down (as had recently happened to another such flight). It was a modern plane: just a twin-engined 14-seater, the 737 of the day. But it was hard not to feel a deep affection for it as it lifted off from Portuguese soil, and we allowed the relief to flood through us. Continental Europe was murdering its Jews, and now, at last, we were escaping.

Several hours later, on a summer afternoon, we touched down at Whitchurch Airport in Bristol. For the first time in three and a half years, we could stop running away. My mother, whatever her other shortcomings as a parent, had got her children to safety. I am grateful to her. I have always wished, however, that I had kept one of my Water Line ships – but at least it made another boy happy.

4

FLIGHTS OF FANCY

Y OU CAN'T spend long in my house without realising that it is full of flying objects. They aren't all flying, but they are things whose essence is flight. The angel and the witch in the front window are just tasters. They share that room with, at my last count, 26 birds of various sizes, all made by me; plus assorted rockets and aeroplane designs. In my kitchen I can see from my chair six more birds and four more aeroplanes. The plane that comes nearest to actually being in flight is a little white 'spy plane', dangling from an orange beam. (It's actually an overhead girder that was installed as an RSJ when I had the room extended.) I like the way that it seems to be flying towards me when I glance upwards. But my favourite winged object of all, suspended near the other end of the girder, is flying in the opposite direction. It is a flying pig.

This creature is often the first thing people notice when they enter the room. It's big, it's cheerful, and it seems to have a strong sense of what it is and where it is going. Its body is papier mâché, built around a wire frame and coloured a warm pink. Darker, flesh-pink spots, nose and tail add character, while the big, cream-painted cardboard wings on its back look pleasingly light by comparison. The wings are hinged where they join the body, and there's a string hanging down from its belly. The slightest draught makes the wings flap: slowly, smoothly and for a surprisingly long time. I love that pig. There's a strange sense of power in those wide wings, and a confidence in the slow way they flap, like a great eagle setting out on a long journey. Even when the wings are still, it somehow appears to be gliding, serenely, on its way to some delightful adventure.

I can't remember exactly when I made it, but it must have been within the past ten years – probably when my grandchildren were starting to visit. Yet when I look at that pig my mind tends to drift to a much earlier stage in my life. It does so, I think, because it is hard to look at it without various aeronautical questions suggesting them- selves. Have I got the wing-to-pig ratio approximately right? Would my wing design, quite straight at the front, with curves at the back, provide as much lift in actual flight as the aesthetics suggest?

These are idle speculations, but they tell you some- thing important about me; as does the fact that, when I make them, my memory draws me back to a period more than 70 years ago, when I first arrived in this country. It was then that I first began to wrestle seriously with concepts such as aerodynamics.

Those were strange, bewildered years. I was 16 when we arrived in Bristol in the summer of 1942, passed through immigration, then caught a train to London and, eventually, tracked down my father to a small flat in a tall, red-brick mansion block in Maida Vale called Clive Court. The flat belonged to a friend and was not suitable for a family of five. For a single occupant it would have been very pleasant. Our arrival was, to put it mildly, awkward. Our clothes were little better than rags by now; we had grown out of those that came with us from Brno. We moved to a nearby hotel. Despite rationing, food was plentiful and those hungry days were quickly forgotten. We could also replace our poor-quality worn-out clothes, although my mother had to accept that she could no longer shop as extravagantly as she had on previous visits to London.

I'm not sure how my father was earning a living. None of us were. (This may just have been lack of curiosity on our part.) He appears to have had access to a modest income: I think he had transferred a lump sum to a British bank before the war, some of which he had been able to wire to my mother while we were in Nice. But I suspect that he was also borrowing money, against the promise of generous repayment once the world was put to rights. Whatever the truth, our short-term state can't have been penniless, because we sometimes ate out at one of the Lyons Corner Houses, which were exempt from rationing restrictions; and I remember vividly that, for the first time in ages, I experienced life without the constant ache of hunger.

Yet compared with my early years in Brno we were poor. As soon as we could, we moved to a house in Hanger Hill, in north London. Bettina was sent to a boarding school in Northamptonshire. My mother, who had never worked, started learning how to cook and carry out domestic work. But my brother and I, at least, needed to find useful roles for ourselves. Felix got a job in a factory making Bofors anti-aircraft guns; then, following his 18th birthday in September 1942, he enlisted with the Czechoslovak armed forces in exile, eventually joining a Czechoslovak squadron in the RAF. I was too young for that. So I was sent to study aeronautical engineering at Loughborough.

I am not sure whose decision this was, but there was obvious logic to it. My education was incomplete. I loved aeroplanes and fast vehicles. Even my parents were by now not entirely oblivious to my fascination with the shapes, designs and workings of things. Aircraft design was a hot topic, and the war meant that aeronautical engineers were in demand. So I was signed up for a three-year course in aeronautical engineering at Loughborough in Leicestershire, starting in the autumn of 1942. In the remaining weeks of the summer, I stayed at the home of a headmaster whom my parents had hired to teach me English. He taught me next to nothing: he was a spectacularly disturbed individual who I am sure would not have been allowed to teach in today's less brutalised world. Luckily, I had grown quite adept at picking up languages – this was my third change of country in less than four years – and by the time I arrived at Loughborough I could communicate reasonably well.

That is to say: I could speak English reasonably well. Communication was trickier. I lived in a big house called Barrow Hall, about four miles outside Loughborough, with 16 other students. I was foreign, socially awkward and much younger than everyone else. Most of them came from the same kind of English private school – in some cases from the very same schools. They had so much in common with one another, it felt as though they had known one another for years. I, by contrast, was an obvious outsider. Yet my strangeness and my youth ended up working in my favour. These young men treated me with kindness and consideration; at times, they were almost protective. I think they may have seen me as a kind of exotic mascot. After all, I came from the land of Jan Kašpar, the pioneering aviator; and Czechoslovak pilots in the RAF were already making names for themselves with their bravery. My awkwardness was misinterpreted as linguistic incompetence, my shyness as modesty. As a result, people seemed to accept me. For the first time in my life I felt a slight sense of belonging.

The highlight of my time at Loughborough was being made captain of the Barrow Hall swimming team. I was a strong swimmer for my age, but they appointed me only out of kindness. I repaid them by arranging to get the 50-yard dash – our strongest event – made into a point-scoring discipline in the inter-house cup – which, as a result, we won.

After the upheavals of the previous few years, I am sure the stability I experienced at Loughborough did me good. The war was not forgotten: sometimes the skies were crowded with hundreds of bombers from various airfields, assembled before heading for Germany. An awesome sight. But there was no sense of imminent danger. On the contrary, there was an air of sleepy permanence about our village, Barrow upon Soar, and the Leicestershire countryside surrounding it. It was quite different from the landscape around Brno: greener, lusher and on a smaller, denser scale. Yet I soon began to think of it as *my* landscape, and the familiarity was reassuring. I knew there was still a war on, but I never for a moment felt that my life was in peril.

The one drawback of my time at Loughborough – quite a big one, now I think of it – was that I had limited aptitude for aeronautical engineering. I was fascinated by the broad ideas, but I never had the maths to be much good at stressing or aerodynamics; and, foolishly, I made no attempt to correct this shortcoming.

Instead, I relied on my existing aptitudes. I already knew quite a lot about aeroplanes. I had even been allowed to take the controls of one once, briefly, when I was 11 or 12. I could also distinguish between different aircraft types as confidently as I could with cars. Just before my sister and I had left Prague in 1939, we had been waiting at the airport with my mother, standing next to the airport commandant, who was a friend of hers. I got into an argument with him about whether an incoming plane was a Savoia-Marchetti or a Junkers. My mother urged me to keep my opinions to myself, but it soon became clear that I was right and the commandant was wrong.

This intuitive feel for aviation meant that, while I was an undistinguished student, I did not fall hopelessly behind. Much of the course was practical: weeks of academic study alternated with weeks in the pattern shop or foundry; and these, at least, I loved. I attended lectures dutifully, which I think counted in my favour, and some last-minute mugging up on metallurgy ensured that, somehow, I ended up with a diploma.

Then came a new set of challenges. By then it was the summer of 1945. My father, mother and sister had already taken advantage of the end of hostilities in Europe to return to Czechoslovakia. Their main aim was to recover some of the family property, and perhaps to rebuild the lives they had abandoned in 1939. They faced a long, tedious struggle. Our property had been recovered from the Nazis but much of it was then taken into administration by the restored Czechoslovak state. In December 1945, our industrial holdings were nationalised; the fate of everything else was in the balance. These were not matters that could be managed remotely. Felix had ended up in Czechoslovakia, too. Initially he was posted to Prague with his squadron; then, following his demobilisation, he was assigned a job in Moravia. This left me alone in England and, to all intents and purposes, alone in the world. All I had to help me was my diploma. I used it to find employment, at a company called Hunting Percival, based in Luton.

So began the most barren years of my life. The job, in the stressing office, entailed calculating the robustness of aircraft structures. I was useless at it. I had vaguely imagined that I might be allowed to design wonderful shapes, but instead I was being given tasks better suited for a mathematician. My boss knew of my shortcomings but I think he had a kind heart, so he didn't throw me out. I did love to sneak into the factory to watch aircraft being built.

It must have counted in my favour that I didn't cost the company much. I earned £5.15/- a week, of which £2 went in tax. I rented rooms in a series of digs: the one I remember best was on a big main road called Hitchin Road. There was an outside toilet, the bath didn't work and the rent cost me £1.3/4 a week.

This was a miserable period. I was bad at my job and I knew it. I was hopeless at life, too. I had no friends, no family. When I wasn't working, I just sat in my room. For the best part of five years, I don't think I even read a book – I just glanced every now and then at the *Daily Express*. My health began to suffer. With hindsight, this wasn't surprising; I was depressed. I tried going for long walks to keep myself sane, but that was all. I knew I had to get out of this rut, but where else could my studies and experience take me?

For a while I played football at lunchtimes. Then I broke my leg. This became the pattern of my life: good intentions repeatedly abandoned, with repeated break-downs in my health offering an escape from my work. It was hard not to associate this frailty with my wider lack of enthusiasm for my life. At one point, I caught pneumonia and was sent to a convalescent home in Brighton. (Luckily, such things were free in those days.) Another time, I had colitis, which required a long period in hospital and, later, another spell in a convalescent home. Yet this turned out to be a blessing. In hospital, I was offered the opportunity to do some occupational therapy. I chose basketwork and the staff seemed impressed with my output. Soon, when the matron made her daily inspections, she barely bothered to ask about my health: she would ask, 'How is the basket today?'

This provided a vital nudge, reminding me of a side of myself that I had forgotten. I carried on making things while I convalesced. Then, on returning to home and work, I started going to evening classes at a local adult education college. I think my boss assumed, or at least hoped, that I was studying mathematics. In fact, I was studying art and graphic design and going to life drawing sessions. They weren't the world's greatest classes, but they helped remove a block from my mind. My instincts were creative. I needed to create.

At around the same time, I acquired a new surname. I forget the date, but it must have been around February 1948. That was when I took out British citizenship, and the two steps were connected. The prospects for people like me seemed bleak in Czechoslovakia. (That month, the Communists seized total control.) In the UK, on the other hand, there was always the theoretical possibility that, if I worked hard enough and thought creatively enough, I might yet carve out a viable future for myself as a Briton. But I didn't think it was helpful having a surname that identified me as a foreigner and a Jew. I chose Karen instead because I remembered it from a time in Czechoslovakia when my mother had proposed changing the family name to make us seem less Jewish. Karen had been one of the names she considered, and I liked it.

I don't suppose this attempt at personal rebranding made the slightest practical difference. I had only to open my mouth for people to realise that I was not English-born. But it did boost my confidence and my determination as I attempted to fashion a new life in my adopted country.

With this sense of new identity in mind, I spent a lot of time drawing, developing my awareness of where my creative strengths lay. At one point, I drew some cartoons on themes relating to aviation. When I had done a few that I liked, I sent them off to an aircraft magazine called *Aeronautic*. I was pleased when they were used by the magazine. They paid me three guineas for each one – more than my weekly take-home pay for my 'real' job.

From then on, I knew. I had to get out of Luton. I became more desperate to get out of stressing. And I had to start earning my living in a more creative way. By great good luck, I didn't have to wait much longer. An organisation called the Air Registration Board (ARB), which looked after the safety of aircraft and produced various publications, advertised a vacancy for a technical illustrator. I decided to apply.

I had never done any technical drawing, I barely knew that such a thing existed. So I went to Luton library and copied out some technical drawings, then sent them off. Soon afterwards, the ARB asked me in. Their interviewer seemed very taken by the fact that, in addition to being able to do technical drawings (apparently), I had a diploma in aeronautical engineering. So they offered me the job – at twice my existing salary.

I don't think this was a great choice on their part: I was a competent if slow technical illustrator and did no more than cope with other duties at the office. Yet from my point of view it was a brilliant move. It got me out of Luton: the ARB was based at Croydon Airport. Best of all, I found digs in a lovely stockbroker-ish village called Chipstead.

It would be almost another five years before the aeronautical phase of my life came to an end. I was thrilled when it did so. Yet, looking back, I realise that these hard, early years gave me a vital grounding in the core disciplines of proper, rigorous industrial design. Every detail of an aircraft design can be a matter of life and death: it isn't just about broad brushstrokes. Designs have to work at every level, in every detail. That understanding has, I think, informed my work as a designer ever since.

Even now, long retired, I think about questions of flight almost daily. I have not stopped thinking about technical questions involving aeroplanes, as we shall see in due course. Mostly, however, my thoughts about flying are thoughts involving birds. I feel such admiration for birds, and for the brilliant natural designs that enable them to fly. I am constantly playing with the forms associated with flight in my craft activities.

And I think that this is why, when I look back on my years in the aviation industry, I do so with gratitude. I was miserable for much of the time, and there can't have been many aeronautical engineers who were worse at their jobs than I was. Yet those experiences equipped me for what was to follow. The technical understanding I developed then has never stopped proving useful; nor have the habitual disciplines of rigour and attention to detail. But those years also gave me something else. They awakened in me perhaps the most important and elusive of all the qualities you need as a designer: the courage to dream, and to let your dreams take wing. And that brings me back to the flying pig in my kitchen.

I have always loved the idea of flight – perhaps it goes back to my childhood friendship with Kako the jackdaw; or perhaps, unconsciously, I envied my mother's airborne adventures. That sense of adventure still excites me. But I think what excites me most is the sheer improbability of flying – and the improbable power of design to overcome that improbability.

No creature symbolises this paradox more neatly than the winged pig. 'Pigs might fly,' people say, when they want to pour scorn on a wild idea. But wild ideas are what make life worth living. John Moore-Brabazon, who in 1910 became the first person to receive a UK pilot's licence, actually took a small pig up with him on one of his early flights – in a wicker basket dangling from a wing – just to prove that, sometimes, pigs *can* fly. I know just how he felt.

5

THREE STYLE

NO longer have my Vimp: that's another flaw in my narrative plan. But I do have several photos – look, there are some in this folder here. Sorry about the dust. They're only black and white, but they're better than nothing. You can just about make it out in these 65-year-old newspaper cuttings, too. I wish I could show you the car itself, but I got rid of it. I had no choice: I could hardly have dragged it with me through the next six decades or so. Yet I'm sad that I don't have it now. Yes, that's right, the young man bending over it in the photograph is me, aged 28.

It wasn't my best car design, but it was my first. There are echoes of it in several of my later cars. What I cherish about it, though, is what it stood for: a new self-belief; a new determination; and a period in my life in which, finally, I began to blossom.

I made the Vimp in my spare time, in a workshop in Kingswood, Surrey, which belonged to a young friend called Andrew Waddicor. It was a tiny three-wheeler, with a light alloy stressed skin body. I just wanted to make a car: to take one of my ideas and to turn it into physical, three-dimensional, functioning reality.

I lived initially in some wonderful digs in the Surrey village of Chipstead, with an easy commute to Croydon Airport by train. The work at the ARB was less exciting than I had hoped. The village, on the other hand, changed my life.

I suppose you would have called it a typical commuter village, right in the middle of the stockbroker belt, with a population (then) of around 1,600 people. The countryside was charming, with mature trees and hedgerows, narrow lanes and an area of open common. But what made it special were its residents. It feels strange to write this. I still had no idea how to make friends. But there was a great deal of organised recreational activity in Chipstead, and I found that I could fit in, up to a point, by getting involved and making myself useful. For example, there was an amateur dramatic society. I threw myself into set design, prop-making and, later, other aspects of production. There was a tennis club. I played, reasonably well; and, as a result, was welcome.

Somebody started giving pottery classes, so I learnt to make pots. Handling the clay came naturally to me (perhaps my family background in brick-making helped) and I developed my own way of building with clay. Scottish dancing classes were less suited to my talents, but I signed up to those too, and enjoyed them. The clearly defined goals and activities meant that my awkwardness was not a handicap.

These cultural pursuits transformed my life, allowing me to throw myself into the community life of a quintessentially English Home Counties village. Perhaps it would be overstating things to say that I fitted in, but I was not a complete outsider. As a result, my self-belief grew. It grew even more as I learnt that, broadly speaking, creativity was what I was good at. For the first 25 years of my life, I don't think that thought had occurred to me.

The dramatic society – the Chipstead Players – was particularly valuable for me. At first it was just play readings, but before long I was throwing myself into every production, and I realised that, in addition to being good at set-making, I found everything about theatre extraordinarily interesting. In some ways it was easier to relate to than the more confusing world of real-life adults. I began to act a little; one of my performances even earned a favourable mention in the local paper. I also began to make regular trips to watch plays in London. This was a golden age of theatre, and I was lucky enough to see most of the great actors of the day, from Laurence Oliver to John Gielgud.

I also made an important discovery. The Chipstead Players liked to involve children and teenagers in their activities, but no one particularly wanted to take on responsibility for putting on young people's productions. I volunteered to help – and found that I was good at it. For all my lack of social skills when dealing with adults, with children I seemed to be able to establish an instant rapport. I don't really know how to explain this, but I know that it is an important part of who I am. Perhaps that lonely boy in Brno who never experienced the creative childhood he longed for has remained a part of me. Perhaps I have an inner child whose interest in childish things – such as toys and play – has informed my adult work. Meanwhile, this hitherto unsuspected quirk had the practical result that I soon found myself in charge of all the society's theatrical productions for children.

This gave me great pleasure. I was connecting, on a personal level, with fellow human beings with whom communication felt easy. I think the children enjoyed it, too. I was living by then with a family called the Peppers, whose son, Christopher, was away at boarding school but loved to take part in our productions during the holidays. Another boy, Jimmy Larkham, the butcher's son, felt so at home in the Chipstead Players that he took to trotting alongside me on my way to the railway station in the morning and chatting as we walked. Decades later – after hearing me give a public lecture at the Victoria & Albert Museum – Jimmy got in touch to tell me that, when he was growing up in Chipstead, I was the first person with whom he ever had an adult conversation.

But these connections were revelatory for me as well. In Croydon, at work, I wasn't learning much. In Chipstead, I was learning how to live. My discovery that there were ways in which I could connect constructively with the people around me coincided with a heightened awareness of my creative powers. The world seemed to glow with possibilities.

Between 1950 and 1954, I experienced an explosion of private creativity. It was almost like madness. My house is still littered with things I created during that blossoming: pictures, pieces of pottery, cane creatures – I just couldn't stop making things. When I bought my first car – a decrepit Austin 7 that cost me £50 – I decided that I didn't like the look of it. So I asked another young friend, the aforementioned Andrew Waddicor (whose mother was very active in the Chipstead Players) if I could borrow some space in his family's workshop in the nearby village of Kingswood. There I stripped off its bodywork and made it a new body of my own, using aluminium sheets on a wooden framework. The panels were all single curvature – it wasn't panel-beaten – and the visual effect was quite original. Mechanically, however, the car remained the disaster it had been when I bought it. You could start it only by bump-starting it as it rolled downhill – I had to remember to park it at the top of a slope – and the brakes were alarmingly unreliable. But those problems pre-dated my adjustments, and on balance I was proud of it. It was much lighter and more fuel-efficient than it had been before. And it was the nearest I had yet come to designing a functioning vehicle of my own.

With hindsight, I suspect that financial insecurity encouraged me to experiment. Despite my newfound sense of belonging as a villager, I felt acutely aware that I was alone in the world. There was no one to help me if things went wrong – only my own creativity. So I poured my energies into making things, in every spare minute I could find.

After a few years in Chipstead, I moved into new digs, in the village of Tadworth, a couple of stops further up the railway from Croydon. The house, which was called Orchards, was the home of a painter, John Livesey, and there was a powerfully artistic feel to the place. Creating things felt like the norm, not the exception. My blossoming continued.

At some point in late 1953 or early 1954, I got it into my head that I wanted to create a car with three wheels. I don't know what prompted this, beyond a desire to take my experimentation to the next level, but it was a significant step forward. Three-wheelers have a particular elegance, which has fascinated me for much of my career. In contrast to a four-wheeler, the chassis on a three-wheeler is never subjected to any twist. It has the stability of a three-legged stool, on which you can always sit firmly on any ground, however uneven. It also has the virtue of being a simplification: you can dispense with one wheel and a lot of suspension. For me, simplification is a great virtue in design, saving money, time and materials and, usually, resulting in more pleasing forms than more complex alternatives. But this new project was my first serious attempt to explore that idea with a real-life car.

Once again, I used Andrew Waddicor's garage, and he and his teenage friends happily mucked in. It was an exercise in innovation at many levels – that was the fun of it. Not only did I need my design to be coherent and functional, I also needed materials and parts that suited my minimal budget – and my relatively limited manufacturing skills.

I managed to acquire a small Villiers engine from a local motorbike shop, along with some old moped wheels. I made the framework from wood, which was easy enough. (I didn't have any training in carpentry, but I assumed – correctly – that I could do it.) I was able to buy some sheet aluminium locally, and the Waddicors, luckily, had some cutters and a pop-riveting machine. The metal was much harder to manipulate than the wood, but we worked it out eventually.

The aim was to economise by making everything as compact as possible. The single-cylinder air-cooled engine went in the rear. There were no side windows and no roof: you just climbed in and out by tilting the windscreen forward.

The resulting vehicle was not pretty: I wince when I look at the pictures. But its minimal bodywork made it fantastically light. As a three-wheeler it was classed as a motorcycle, and could legally have been driven by a 16-year-old. I'm not sure how road-legal it was in other respects, but nobody complained, and we did raise enough eyebrows to attract some interest from the media. It's name Vimp, a cross between Imp and Vamp, may have helped suggest a slightly mischievous image, to which journalists responded. *Motor* magazine's Laurence Pomeroy Jr – one of the leading motoring writers of the day – gave it a generous review, and a photograph of me sitting in the prototype appeared in several publications. 'Next year Earl's Court?' suggested *The Sketch* magazine – meaning the Motor Show. The same thought had crossed my own mind, but I lacked the connections or business know-how to take the project further. It felt wonderful to have created such a vehicle from scratch – to have taken my most complex design idea so far and turned it into physical, three-dimensional, functioning reality. For all its charm, however, the Vimp was a bit too much like a toy car to have a commercial future.

From a rational point of view, my own prospects were equally limited. It was late 1954. I was 28, and for all the ferment of my creative juices I remained a moderately competent technical illustrator, working in a dull job with the Air Registration Board from which I learnt nothing. Somehow, however, the frustration felt less soul-destroying than it had felt in Luton. I wasn't yet earning a living in a way that used my talents or brought me fulfilment. But now, at last, I knew what I wanted to do. I wanted to be an industrial designer.

6

LEARNING CURVES

MY FRENCH curves are among my most precious mementoes. I keep them in a big paper carrier bag, which usually hangs from a drawer handle near my kitchen sink. I like to keep them handy, because I still use them sometimes. I also feel an emotional attachment to them. They are old friends, who served me well through the ups and downs of my career.

Perhaps I should explain what a French curve is. Even professional designers are unlikely to have encountered such objects, unless they are already of retirement age or beyond. Yet before computers became ubiquitous it was impossible to design without them. Everything had to be sketched on paper, when I learnt my trade, exactly to scale, from every possible angle; and each curve had to be no less precise than each straight line. This was impossible to achieve unless you used the curved equivalent of a ruler: that is, a French curve. And, since designs without curves are almost unheard of, we used them constantly.

Each French curve is a solid template, typically made of wood or clear plastic, embodying a relatively small number of carefully crafted curves, with progressively varying gradients. You need quite a few of them, because – obviously – curves come in many forms. They can be more open, or more closed, depending on the shapes they describe. The arc of a circle's circumference is different from that of an ellipse or oval; and that's before you consider less regular shapes. In theory, the range of possibilities is infinite. Even a line that looks straight – in a car, for example – often turns out to be subtly curved. Yet designers need (or needed) to be able to trace accurately the contours of any variant their design might require. The genius of French curves is that they allow you to do just that.

Some of them have names: the Million Dollar curve, for example, which is almost straight but tightens up towards the end; or the Ram's Horn, which looks much as its name suggests. I have about 20 in my set, some so battered that their only value is sentimental. Of course, it doesn't matter how many you have if you don't know how to use them properly, but for designers of my generation they were the most trusted tools of our trade.

I grew adept at using mine, eventually. In 1954, I knew nothing about such matters. Actually, I still knew relatively little about anything. My tennis had improved while I had been working at the Air Registration Board, and I had become quite good at assembling my own cars. In terms of work, however, I had learnt next to nothing in four years. I wasn't unhappy. Professionally, however, I was going nowhere.

Then fate intervened, with a dollop of unexpected good fortune. For several years, various Western governments, including the UK and West Germany, had been negotiating with various Communist regimes in Eastern Europe, including Czechoslovakia, about, on the one hand, compensation for exiled citizens whose property those new regimes had seized; and, on the other, the possible return of Eastern assets that had been frozen in Western banks. I won't attempt to explain this tortuous process; I didn't understand it even at the time. But a distant relative of my family, a lawyer called Fritz Karsten, had been in contact with the relevant bodies in the hope of securing us some kind of compensation for our lost wealth. Around the end of the year, he finally succeeded in doing so – although as the only British citizen among us, I was the only member of our family to benefit at that point. The payout was modest, relative to what had been taken from us; but it was big enough to transform my life. Suddenly I had room to manoeuvre, because I could afford a period without paid employment.

I handed in my notice at the ARB almost immediately. I knew exactly what I needed to do. I wanted to be an industrial designer, but I lacked the training that would turn me into one. So I turned up one day at the Central School of Arts and Crafts in London – I think it was the only such school I had heard of – and asked if I could study there. For some reason they accepted me. Perhaps they were impressed by my eagerness, or by the fact that, in addition to being able to draw, I had worked in the aviation industry. Industrial design was still a relatively new discipline, but it was growing fast. Anyone who could bring to it a bit of practical know-how as well as artistic flair was welcome. I had missed the beginning of the academic year but nobody seemed bothered. I was allowed to attend on a not-quite-full-time basis without even being formally attached to a specific course. There were, of course, no tuition fees. How innocent that long-lost age seems.

My studies began in early 1955. The school was in Southampton Row, in a big old building just off High Holborn. I commuted daily from Tadworth – a far easier journey than it would be today. If there was inconvenience, I barely noticed it. I was too thrilled to be going to the Central. Perhaps the passage of time has rose-tinted my memories, but when I cast my thoughts back to that slice of my past, the main thing that comes back to me is an almost incredulous sense of privilege.

This was heaven: the kind of creative environment I had yearned for all my life. There were painters and sculptors; furniture makers, glass makers and potters; and all their facilities were at my fingertips. I loved being there: it felt like where I belonged. In fact, my studies – what some people spoke of as 'work' – were as close to pure happiness as I could then imagine.

I was exposed to all the right tutors. I particularly remember Douglas Scott, who designed the Routemaster bus and the AGA cooker. There was also a lovely drawing teacher, called Mr Patchett if I remember rightly, whose most valuable lesson was in believing in my own abilities.

The head of the school, William Johnstone, encouraged me, too. His profile was usually low, but he wandered around quietly, keeping an eye on what was going on, and for some reason he noticed my work. I became aware that he approved of what I was doing.

I think he liked the idea that I could draw and could make models in clay and other materials, yet also had this technical background. No doubt he also appreciated the fact I was a mature student and didn't mess about. The school made me feel valued, at all events; and, as a result, I picked things up quickly. I have never forgotten Mr Johnstone's enthusiasm when I made a little model of a toaster, which among other things involved ceramics. It was a nice piece of work, but his delight surprised me. It also provided a huge boost to my morale, convincing me that I wasn't failing but, on the contrary, really could hope to get ahead and, one day, do something worthwhile in industrial design.

I wasn't sure how I should go about making this happen, but before I had completed my third term, fate intervened again. A man called Terence Beckett, head of the Ford Motor Company's product planning department in Dagenham, came to Central on a recruitment visit. This was an annual occurrence. There was no such thing, in those days, as a properly trained car designer:

the discipline didn't exist. So a motor manufacturer that took design seriously, as Ford had begun to do, had to seek talent from the broader fields of art and design. Central was a prime recruiting ground.

Mr Beckett, whose department included a highly regarded Design Studio, looked at everyone's work, chatted to us, and I presume he studied our CVs, too. He then gave a very persuasive talk. I forget his words but I remember the feeling they left me with: a vivid and thrilling sense that, for an aspiring industrial designer, Ford – and specifically its Design Studio – was a dream workplace.

Not long afterwards, Ford offered three of us jobs. It seemed like a wonderful opportunity, even though it meant cutting our education short. Just to be sure, I consulted a strange and important figure who had recently appeared in my life: a lady from the Council of Industrial Design (CID) called Mrs Cycill Tomrley. A former art student and activist at the Design and Industries Association, Mrs Tomrley worked as a secretary at the CID but had somehow also taken on – officially or unofficially – a significant behind-the-scenes role as one of Britain's leading spotters of design talent. She made it her business to keep an eye on promising students and novice designers and to put them in touch with appropriate employers and projects. I would be surprised if anyone who wasn't personally affected by this process had heard of her, yet she must have been an astonishingly influential figure in the development of British design in the post-war decades. She had made contact with me at some point while I was studying at Central, and in due course I came to think of her as a kind of fairy godmother. She wasn't a showy person: on the contrary, she was businesslike and matter-of-fact to the point of invisibility. But she must have been shrewd, and she was certainly well connected. In the years to come she would advise me repeatedly, always in a constructive way. I accepted each of her suggestions without question.

On this occasion she confirmed my sense that this job offer was an opportunity to be seized with both hands. I had loved cars all my life, and here, at last, was a chance to work on their design. And so it was, that in mid-1955, my formal training in industrial design came to an end, and I began a new life at Ford.

It was a great place to work in those days. The location wasn't ideal – at the drab works of Briggs, Ford's body-making subsidiary in Dagenham. But the company itself could hardly have been more exciting. Its managing director – soon to be chairman – was an Irish-born industrialist called Sir Patrick Hennessy, who had done great work in manufacturing during the war. Under his inspired guidance Ford had become probably the only well-run motor company in the UK. Sir Patrick placed particular emphasis on the product planning unit, and recruited some ultra-bright people to work there, notably Terence Beckett (who would later become chairman himself). The Design Studio existed to turn this brilliance into attractive, marketable products.

I was an inexperienced designer in a big room full of designers – 15 in all. We each had a unit where we could sit, with a drawing board and some storage space, plus the means for airbrushing our sketches. There was a lovely model shop on-site, which could make models for us, big or small. Part of the excitement came simply from being in that environment; and, gradually, from becoming a functional part of the whole, extraordinarily complex design process.

A motor car is made up of hundreds of components. Everything from the badge at the front to the 'shutlines' on the passenger door or the bulbs in the brake lights or the grip on the rim of the steering wheel: each detail is a part, just like the chassis or the engine; and each one has to be designed to be appropriate to the model in question. None of this happens by accident.

This meant that, even in a mighty, long-established organisation like Ford, there was an awful lot of creative work that had to be done, designing the bits and pieces in a way that satisfied all the interested parties.

I worked on the exteriors at first then moved to interiors – things like instruments and dashboards – which I found more interesting than I expected. The product planning people would say, 'We want to facelift this instrument panel,' and so you'd draw some variations – all of which were expected to conform to their very rigorous specifications. I might spend weeks on such an assignment, sweating blood over every detail. Then the bosses and the production people would examine my designs, and if I was lucky they would see something that pleased them. So at the end of the day someone might say, 'OK, you've done this little shelf for putting things in by the glove compartment. We quite like that. We'll take that . . .' And everything else was wasted.

Despite such frustrations, it was an exciting environment. I didn't think highly of my immediate boss, Roy Haynes, but the man in overall charge, a young designer called Colin Neale, was something of a visionary, and the sense of high expectations was both inspiring and empowering.

I loved the atmosphere. Nobody taught you. You learnt by watching what other people did – and they were a strange bunch of people. None of them had trained in automotive design: there were no courses available, in those days. So there were people who had trained as artists, people who had done industrial design courses, someone who had been a retoucher – anyone who had visual flair and loved cars. Some of the designers could draw brilliantly. One, a Welshman known only as Dai, was a positive genius. It came to him so naturally that his first reaction to skidding off the road in his car one winter was to draw a beautiful picture of the accident scene. My friend Peter Cambridge, who also had a background in the aircraft industry, had come from Central at the same time as me and became a lifelong friend.

I realised that I had a lot of catching up to do before I could start asking for my work to be taken more seriously. Among other things, I had to persuade more experienced colleagues to lend me their French curves, as templates from which to make my own. But in other ways I think I was perhaps more profound than many of my colleagues about what I was trying to achieve as a designer. I cared about looks and about function. I also understood quite a lot about the manufacturing process. I wanted to create designs that worked at every level. And for all my short-comings, I did have one advantage: I think I worked harder than the others.

We were all fairly industrious, and creating little shelves that might or might not be used in a glove compartment was more absorbing than I have made it sound. But it didn't leave me feeling that I was really stretching myself as a designer. Sometimes, admittedly, we were asked to think the unthinkable: for example, what if steering wheels were square? But this blue-sky aspect of our work never seemed to lead anywhere. It was diverting but not fulfilling. I knew that, ultimately, I wanted more.

This growing restlessness may partially explain the fact that, within about a year, I abandoned my digs in Dagenham and moved back to London. Dagenham was tolerable, but it was bleak. Meanwhile, I still had a few thousand pounds of compensation money left over. I invested this, prudently, in a house in Bloomsbury. I had grown to love the area during my time at the Central. The address, Doughty Street, is now highly desirable and expensive, but in those days it was little better than a bomb site: the fire brigade used to get water from a big crater at the end of the road. Most of this house was let out, but there were a couple of empty flats at the top. My sister (now back from Czechoslovakia) began to live in one of them, while I lived in the other. I didn't have much furniture, but I was back in my favourite part of London. And, in contrast to Dagenham, I now had a base from which, if I chose, I could do things outside working hours.

I was still desperately short of social skills, but I was not quite the recluse I had been in Luton. It must have been around this time that I first came into contact with a loose network of other non-Britons living in central London: Australians, South Africans, French people, even Russians. In those days, to be a foreigner of any kind marked you out as, at the very least, exotic. So we tended to congregate together, in a milieu that could almost have been described as Bohemian.

I wouldn't say that I became sociable. But I had worked out that it wasn't good for me just to sit at home by myself every evening, and I found that I felt more at ease among fellow exiles than in more traditionally English circles. At some point, probably in 1957, I noticed that one of them – a young woman from Mauritius called Nicole Lagesse – was taking a particular interest in me.

We got on quite well: we could both speak French, and sometimes we did so to one another. After a while, she began to invite me round to meals in her bedsit in Earl's Court. Sometimes, too, we would go to the theatre together. Initially, it was the theatre that made the deepest impression on me. I will never forget the evening we went to see John Osborne's *Look Back in Anger* at the Royal Court. The play had opened more than a year earlier, but the waves of its initial impact had failed to reach Dagenham. Now it hit me with all the explosive power that had scandalised the theatre-going public at its premiere. This incoherent cry of a young man's rage at establishment complacency felt as though it had been written with me in mind. I saw it repeatedly, and sometimes I felt like standing up and punching the air in support.

If you had asked me what I was angry about, I am not sure that I could have articulated my frustration. I certainly couldn't explain it now. Life had treated me kindly, compared with what millions had suffered in wartime. Britain had treated me kindly. I had been extremely lucky in material terms. I had made a good start on a career path that made use of my talents. I had a home I liked, and I was even learning to form friendly relationships. What did I have to complain about?

Yet I was restless, even so. I had – and still have – a deep-seated instinct that tells me that things could be *better*. This makes me hostile to the establishment's default idea that things are fine as they are. I am always looking for better ways of doing things. Often – in terms of design, at least – I find them. But that's only half the battle. A good idea needs a receptive audience. Otherwise, it risks being lost and forgotten. I hated the thought of that happening to my ideas. To ensure that it didn't, I needed to change something.

When I look at my sketchbooks from my Ford days, I am struck by how high-powered most of my work seems. Every sketch is astonishingly detailed and precise; each design works functionally as well as aesthetically. Similarly, when I look at my collection of curves, I am reminded of how much I learnt in those years. This was when I came to appreciate the full complexity of automobile design. A car body is like a sculpture: every line, in every dimension, contributes to the whole. Barely any of these lines are straight, although some may seem straight at first glance. Instead, they are nearly all curves: sharp bends on corners, or long, flat sweeps – arcs from circles with vast radii – or tight or tightening curls. Each line and each form has to have a logical beginning and end. So the sweep of the roof, for example, might be almost flat, but at the end it would have to be tightened up. Nowadays, it is all done with computers. We did it all by hand, helped by our precious curves.

I wasn't the best at drawing at Ford, although I wasn't bad. But what I did have was an instinctive sense of form, which meant that I could pick up the use of curves very quickly. Within a year or two, it was all second nature. I still feel privileged to have been introduced to this crucial aspect of design in such an immersive way, at such a centre of excellence. And I still feel a deep attachment to the collection of curves that I acquired – mostly by making them myself – during those years. They are such beautiful objects, and everything I know about their use I learnt at Ford.

I also learnt to take pride in my calling. In previous jobs I had been a shabby dresser, wearing some hand-me-downs from my father. But one or two of my colleagues at Ford had decided that work as important as ours merited a more ambitious sartorial approach. They initiated a tradition that was the opposite of 'dress-down Fridays': for one day each week, you were expected to dress as elegantly as you could. So I had a smart suit made, and began to adopt the immaculately tailored look that I associated with my father. It was a habit that stayed with me for the rest of my career.

All in all, it was the most exciting workplace I had ever had. But there was one drawback to the job: no matter how much I learnt and how conscientiously I tried to live up to the Design Studio's exacting standards, my attempts at more advanced styling rarely made it beyond my sketchbook.

Very occasionally, I would make a small breakthrough. Once, I was asked to prepare some lettering for the badge on the front of the Ford Anglia 105E. The specification was for six separate chrome letters spelling out the word

Anglia. Each would be die-cast in chrome and fitted with a clip. This struck me as wasteful. So, without being asked, I designed the lettering as a single one-word die-cast badge with a plastic insert. I had a model made, and presented it to the product planning people, who weren't sure whether to be annoyed or delighted. On the one hand, it wasn't what they asked for. On the other, it looked much nicer than the separate letters, and it would obviously be easier to fit. They scratched their heads for a while. Then they costed it, and the decision made itself. My version was significantly cheaper – and so my badge ended up going on the front of the Anglia.

If that sounds like a tiny thing, all I can say is that it was probably the most successful design I did for Ford. I suppose that explains why I was frustrated. My potential was starting to be appreciated, at least by Colin Neale: I was eventually promoted to the rank of advanced stylist. But I really didn't feel that I was contributing as much as I could.

Then, in 1958, some colleagues began to talk about the annual design competition organised by the Institute of British Carriage and Automobile Manufacturers (IBCAM). This was one of the industry's most prestigious prizes, and Ford set great store by it; previous winners included Colin Neale. Anyone could enter: all you had to do was come up with a new car design. Several of us considered submitting designs, and four of us eventually did so. One was Roy Haynes, who had come second the previous year and was absolutely determined that this time he would win. It meant so much to him that he even did research into the judges' personal colour preferences.

But I was determined, too. I worked on mine for months.

It was a fairly radical concept for what was called the 'baby car' class. It was a four-wheeler, but some of its compactness derived from ideas I had first explored in the three-wheeled Vimp. It had a flat, twin-cylinder, air-cooled 600cc engine, mounted at the back. A partly transparent roof and a wide, deep windscreen ensured exceptional visibility. There were no doors in the conventional sense. Instead, the windscreen, which was split by a hinged central line down the middle, swung open on either side, allowing you to climb in and out without stooping.

The unusual colour scheme – brown outside with a green interior – emphasised the car's slightly crazy, iconoclastic spirit, as did the name I gave it: the 'Rascal'. But there was nothing reckless about the way I presented the concept. Instead, I worked painstakingly to create the required three design boards. I knew that the idea was original. I also knew that the design needed to be brilliantly executed. That meant presenting the judges with three perfect presentation boards, using airbrushing and hand-lettering that left no room for vagueness or error. Each tiny detail had to be rigorously worked out, just as it would have been for a project for Ford. So, evening after evening, I worked on the design in my primitively furnished flat. I would sit and draw with my feet under the bed and my drawing board on my knees. Then, when that became intolerable, I would sit on the bed and draw with the board propped up on a chair.

I was fairly conscientious about doing it all outside working hours, although I did make occasional use of facilities such as airbrushing. But I must have thought about the project many times while I was in the office, and there were quite a few mornings, especially as the deadline approached, when I came into work exhausted as a result of those sessions at the drawing board.

The effort paid off. Rascal was declared the winner in its class. I won £60 and a medal; and, more importantly, the right to say that I had won what was arguably the UK's most prestigious car design contest. Colin Neale called me in and told me that I could expect to be promoted before long. I was also sent off to the Paris Motor Show, from which IBCAM required me to file a report.

But that wasn't quite the end of the story. All four of us who had entered from the Ford Design Studio had submitted designs for baby cars, and we took the first four places in that category. Ron Hickman, who came fourth, later designed and patented what became the Black & Decker Workmate, making him a multi-millionaire. So I don't think the disappointment did him any harm. More problematic for me was the fact that my immediate boss, Roy Haynes, came second. He was clearly far from pleased at what must have felt like a public humiliation. It was a strange position to be in. I had achieved the big goal I had set myself, yet my immediate prospects at Ford suddenly didn't look so bright – especially when Colin Neale announced that he was moving to the US.

My competition win emboldened me to apply for membership of the SIAD, the Society of Industrial Artists and Designers. They turned me down. But many years later, I received a letter from Misha Black, the head of Design Research Unit and professor at the RCA, who invited me to become a Fellow of the Chartered Society of Designers. I didn't need to be a member and wasn't required to submit examples of my work – it was considered well known enough. I accepted. I had come a long way. Now all I needed was my next big breakthrough.

7

WHITE HEAT

My award-winning Hotpoint washing
machine sketch, now in the collection of the
Victoria & Albert Museum, made in 1958.

MY HOME may seem cluttered today, but you should have seen it five years ago. In those days, in addition to all my objects, artworks and souvenirs, I kept all my paper records at home as well. Some are still here, but back then there were vast piles of them: newspaper cuttings, brochures, notes, records – and, above all, sketchbooks. The latter were mostly identical layout pads: superfine bank paper, 11¼in × 8¾in, with orange card covers. There were at least 50 of them, spanning four decades: more than 4,000 pages in all. If you knew what you were looking for – and could make sense of a scattergun approach that randomly juxtaposes revolutionary car designs, aircraft, chairs, toys, birds, finely calculated details with random doodles – you could retrace in their pages the ups, downs, dreams and digressions of my career as a designer.

All this left my home in early 2015, when I gave my entire paper archive to the Victoria & Albert Museum. They haven't yet shown a huge amount of enthusiasm for sharing it with the public – if you want to see the sketchbooks, you must visit their off-site archive in West Kensington. But they have at least catalogued them, and this allows you to see at a glance that the fifth book in the set, dating from late 1959 to early 1960, includes an 'award-winning Hotpoint washing machine'. Such guidance is crucial: if you did not know what you were looking at, you might not realise what all those knobs and dials were for, or recognise that among all those vague imaginings of kettles, fridges and cars can be found the essential details of the next big landmark in my career.

It might seem unexciting compared with many of the subsequent designs to which I have tethered my memories. It's just a big square block of top-loading washing machine, with a clever tray-like area on the top and a nice solid-looking block at the back for the controls. Nonetheless, it embodies a significant phase of my life, in which it played a pivotal role, so I make no apology for making it the focal point of this chapter.

By the standards of today's washing machines, it is primitive. Yet I am proud of it. It is an elegant improvement on what went before – and an example of how good design can improve even the most mundane product in terms of both feel and function. It also represents what might, had fate taken a different turn, have been the summit of my achievements as a designer.

I had got into washing-machine design by accident, by an indirect route. Shortly after my success with the Rascal, I wrote to Mrs Tomrley, who had previously advised me to spend four years at Ford before moving on, and asked her for her advice about my next move. I don't know how she went about it, but within weeks she had introduced me to a company that would change my life. David Ogle Associates was a design consultancy that had begun life four years earlier. Its founder, David Ogle, was a dashing figure, handsome, public-school-educated and seemingly incapable of doing anything without panache. He had won a DFC for his wartime heroics with the Fleet Air Arm, flying Supermarine Spitfires from aircraft carriers' decks in the Mediterranean. In peacetime he worked first for Murphy and then for Bush Radio, for whom he created the famous TR82 transistor radio. An MBE by the time he was 24, he had set up his own design consultancy, originally at home and then in a little office building in the Hertfordshire town of Stevenage, in 1954.

His dream was to design cars, and before long he would team up with car enthusiast, John Ogier, and a former saloon car racer, John Whitmore, in order to do so. Initially, however, his biggest clients were manufacturers of household goods. He talked Bush Radio into giving him a large contract. Allied Ironfounders, for whom he designed solid fuel heaters, were another big client. As charismatic as he was talented, Ogle seemed able to persuade almost anyone to give him a commission – for anything from graphics to office design. By late 1958, his client list was growing fast, giving him an urgent need for fresh design talent. Given his ambitions, he was particularly interested in people who knew their way around a car. Mrs Tomrley was aware of this, and David Ogle was happy to hire me on her recommendation. By the beginning of 1959, I was an Ogle employee.

The pace and variety made Ford seem sleepy by comparison. I worked on a cooker, a boat, a bicycle, a bath, an electric heater . . . it was hard to get bored, with so many things to think about. And, in contrast to what I was accustomed to, most of my designs were used. I would painstakingly prepare a finished, fully detailed drawing, and the moment it was completed it would be sent off to a model shop in London. That would be the last I would see of it: it was David Ogle who presented designs to the clients. So everything had to be absolutely right with them when they left my hands. This made it quite a high-pressure job.

I liked this. I also liked the range of challenges and the constant urgency. David Ogle was an exciting leader: daring, original, driven and demanding, but also inspiring. When he liked your work you felt a warm glow. But there was one big drawback. Ogle Design Associates was based in Stevenage, while I had a home in central London. I commuted daily by train; or, occasionally, in my car (a Mini, which David Ogle seemed rather taken by). It rarely took less than an hour each way, door to door. I never found a way of using this dead time constructively. It felt as though I was simply wasting a large chunk of every week.

Perhaps I should have considered moving to somewhere nearer. But the job didn't quite feel big enough or permanent enough to justify such a dramatic move. In any case, I was reluctant to leave London. My relationship with Nicole – mentioned in the previous chapter – had grown warmer and steadier by now. I had mixed feelings about this. Sometimes I thought about marriage, but the first thing that came into my head when I did so was my parents' disastrous relationship. I didn't want to end up as miserable as my father had clearly been. Nicole, however, had by then set her heart on marrying me. I was, in a way, quite eligible. I dressed well – something I had absorbed from my father – and, at 32, I was still relatively presentable to look at. I owned a house; I had a promising career, if my IBCAM award was anything to go by; I spoke several languages; and I think my Czechoslovak background seemed, in her eyes, sophisticated and glamorous.

We saw one another constantly. Each time we parted, she urged me to see her again soon. She had a confident, practical side that I felt might complement my dreamy creativity. On the other hand, I don't think I was head over heels in love. But my occasional coolness only seemed to encourage her. Then, abruptly, she ran out of patience. In the late summer of 1959, she announced that she was returning to Mauritius. Soon she was gone. My ambivalence gave way to longing. I booked some annual leave from Ogle and flew out to join her. We married on 5 September, in a colourful ceremony notable for the absence of a single relative or friend of the groom.

It was, it turned out, a rash decision. Even on our wedding day, I felt confused, torn between passion and a strong urge to run away. But that turned out to be the easy bit.

Back in the UK, my first challenge was telling my family what I had done. My mother and sister had returned from Czechoslovakia in 1949. They had had little luck in recovering their wealth but were at risk of persecution by an increasingly hardline Communist regime. Back in the UK, Bettina had become a nurse. She had lived in Doughty Street for a while, but she was now working in Kenya, where she would meet her future husband. Nicole and I stopped off to visit her there on our way back from Mauritius. My mother, meanwhile, had broken off all contact with *her* husband (my father), partly because she blamed him for all her troubles but mainly because he now had a new girlfriend – later, or perhaps already, his second wife. (This was despite the fact that 'divorces of necessity' such as my parents' had theoretically been annulled following the war.) From the early 1950s onwards, my parents communicated only through lawyers, and, as a result, my father, who had sold what remained of the family home and was living in Brno with friends, had more or less lost contact with his children. I wrote to him to inform him of my marriage, and he wrote back; but that was pretty much the only exchange I had with him in his later years. I bitterly regret our failure to communicate more.

I wrote to my brother Felix, too. He was temporarily back in England, where he was earning a living as a salesman, but he would soon move to the USA. My mother, however, was living and working in London. With no more money coming in from my father, she had managed to find employment at the international telephone exchange (in the Faraday Building in the City), making use of her skills as a linguist. It was a fairly menial job, but, never having done a day's work for the first five and a half decades of her life, I think she was proud to be earning her own living at last. I admired her for this, and as soon as I could I made one of the flats in my Doughty Street property available to her. But this new respect on my part did nothing to ease the awkwardness of our relationship; and nor, emphatically, did my marriage.

My mother was relatively relaxed about the news itself. That's one advantage of parents who take limited interest in their children. But she and Nicole failed to bond.

Looking back, I wish that my wife had helped me to become closer to my mother, urging me to be friendlier to her while I had the opportunity. In fact, she had the opposite effect, entrenching and encouraging my instinct to keep my distance. And I, to my regret, allowed her to do so. I mention this not because I enjoy washing my dirty linen in public but to illustrate the point that, for all my growing success as a designer, I remained inept at human relationships. I had just about learnt to maintain a façade of polite normality in the workplace, but when it came to anything more complex I was out of my depth. I was dimly aware that all was not as it should be, in my relationships with my parents, my siblings and, before long, my wife. But I had no idea whose fault it was – I just felt like a helpless bystander – and I certainly didn't know what to do about it. So I fell back on a strategy that would serve me well (although some would query the 'well') over the next 40 years of my working life. I thought as little as possible about the private side of my life and threw my energies and attention into work instead.

The only exception to this rule came at this very early stage in my marriage, when Nicole began to complain, with some justice, that my job in Stevenage was undermining our enjoyment of married life. She had a point. Unlike me, Nicole was sociable. She had many friends in London and liked to see them. (She was less keen on mine.) But my long daily commute to and from Stevenage left me neither the time nor the energy for parties or dinners or anything else. I barely even went to the theatre anymore.

In late 1959, therefore, with some reluctance, I wrote again to Mrs Tomrley, asking if she could point me in the direction of an interesting job slightly nearer to home. She waved her magic wand – or whatever it was that she did – and, once again, found a position for me. I became a designer at the Hotpoint Electrical Appliance Company, based at their Appearance Design Unit in Earl's Court.

The pay was better than at Ogle. Most other things were worse. I had no status. I was just a designer, even though

I had much more experience than my colleagues or my immediate boss, Oliver Hill, the design manager. Hill's cape and goatee beard helped him project an aura of being a guru – but his actual talents did not impress me. Even the unit's name was dispiriting: design is about more than mere appearance. But I wasn't in a position to argue about that.

Our brief was to design household appliances: fridges, cookers, washing machines and so on. The technical side of it was sometimes interesting, but once you had mastered that it was hard to get excited about much else. Ogle had felt like an adventure, and David Ogle had encouraged that feeling. Hotpoint felt more like well-paid drudgery. There was only a small team, the model shop was on-site, and Oliver Hill didn't seem to have the slightest interest in adventurous design.

My new job meant that I could spend a lot more time at home, or going to London parties at which, I was told, fashionable up-and-coming figures in the design world such as Mary Quant and Terence Conran could some-times be seen. I didn't see this as any kind of compensation for the fact that I was bored at work.

Luckily (although not deliberately) I soon provoked a crisis at Hotpoint. Mr Hill had got his design office to design a new washing machine. I didn't think much of it: it was just a conventional top-loading washing machine, ugly and complicated. It involved a big die-casting for the control panel at the back, which made it very expensive and very difficult to paint. It also had a great big heavy enamel top – another big expense. The fact that I even thought about the cost of manufacture tells you something about what I had absorbed from my experiences in Ford and, before, in the aeronautics industry. I always thought in terms of manufacture. Appearance is important, obviously, but good design marries aesthetics with function. You don't just come up with a look that you fancy and then subordinate the rest of the process to that. Good design makes virtues out of necessities.

In this case, however, the aesthetics were also all over the place. The hole through which you loaded the machine looked painfully small and in contrast to the soft shapes of the enamel top, the die-casting had very sharp edges. This juxtaposition offended me terribly, and I am sure that consumers would have felt the same. Nonetheless, Mr Hill had had a full-size model made and had sold the idea to management.

He then asked me to make some refinements to the control panel. I took the opportunity to tell him what I thought of the machine. It was going to be very expensive to make. Would he mind if I proposed an alternative? He told me that it was out of the question.

Not long afterwards, he went on holiday for a fortnight. While he was away, I drew an alternative design for the machine as I thought it should be. It was simpler and better-looking and provided the same functions much more elegantly. Instead of the massive die-casting, I used folded sheet metal: all you had to do was blank out the sheet metal and fold it together. This made it much cheaper, in terms of materials as well as manufacture. I put a bright trim around the edges of the top, to which I also added a covering panel like a big tray, in a quite durable material a bit like Formica, so that the space at the top of the machine suddenly looked useful, instead of just emphasising the smallness of the hole.

The other big improvement was that my machine was easy to paint and, for the same reasons, obviously easy to clean – and inviting to touch. Even then, I had worked out that these are desirable qualities in household appliances.

I had a full-size model made – they had a very good little model shop there – and when Mr Hill came back from holiday, there was my machine standing there. He was appalled, but before he could spirit it away, the engineering people saw it. They loved it. They could see at once that it would save them a great deal of money. And then the marketing people saw it, and they loved it too, because my design made it feel a lot more appealing to the customer. So they threw out my boss's design and, with a few minor changes, used mine instead.

You can imagine how Mr Hill felt about this. I should add that, until this point, I hadn't. I really hadn't given any thought to the consequences of my actions. Now, for the first time, I considered the broader picture, and I could see that my immediate future at Hotpoint did not look very promising.

I wrote to Mrs Tomrley again. Yet again, she found me a new position. I headed off for Philips, who had decided to start a studio to design products for their new white goods division. The studio was in Charing Cross Road, within walking distance of my home in Doughty Street, and I was to be its manager. It was the best-paid job that I had done so far, and it really wasn't very difficult. I had a secretary and two or three designers, and I struggled to find enough work for any of them to do. It would have been easier if it had just been me.

At the end of every day I would ask myself how much longer I could stand doing white goods; and then the next morning I would walk into work again, reflecting on the compensating comforts.

Philips were good employers. I think they realised that I was a bit better than the average designer, and they were full of praise when I invented a patent for a device for holding ice cubes inside a fridge. But their enthusiasm didn't compensate for my lack of fulfilment. I was quite pleased with one of my washing machines, but that was about the only thing that excited me.

Meanwhile, my Hotpoint washing machine won an award from the Council of Industrial Design. Oliver Hill collected it. I found the injustice more amusing than upsetting. What bothered me more was the sense of unused creativity within me.

Perhaps I should have counted my blessings and enjoyed the security. Instead, whenever I wasn't working on a particular product, I would fill my sketchbooks with all sorts of wild ideas: cars, chairs, toys – anything that seized my fancy. When I could, I entered competitions, just as I had at Ford. In one of them, the Timber Development Association's Office Furniture Competition, I won second prize. This didn't really make any difference to my situation, but it felt important to keep trying. When you have been a refugee and have had to make your way in a new country, you dare not relax.

This sense of insecurity intensified when news reached me of my father's death, aged 71. He had died in Brno, in February 1961, but the news travelled slowly. We had barely communicated in his later years, which makes me terribly sad when I think about it now. I loved my father and admired him enormously. We could have given a lot to one another, even if we had only corresponded, and I like to think that he would have been proud of what I have achieved. But because of the kind of family we were, neither of us made the first move. It seems ridiculous now. Back then, it seemed inevitable. I contemplated my loss with the same detached numbness with which I approached most forms of sadness.

Then I threw myself back into my work. At least, I tried to. If only I had had something more challenging to work on – something that might have made me feel that I was learning and growing. Instead, my professional development mainly took the form of a slight improvement in my ability to get my ideas across. At one point,

Philips bought a washing-machine company in France – Laden – and invited us and two French studios to submit designs for a new design for a machine. At the joint presentation in Paris, the other two studios brought along their sketches. I brought three beautiful 12in models. The management barely glanced at the details of the other designs before choosing mine.

If you want to make a difference in design, it is worth knowing how to communicate your ideas persuasively, and my time at Philips may have helped me to develop this skill. But developing as a designer was harder: to grow, you need challenges. I knew that I was doing good work for Hotpoint and Philips. I also knew that I had the capacity to do much more, and there is only so much that you can do with white goods.

My father, I reflected, had spent much of his life feeling unfulfilled, his creative and intellectual gifts unused. Perhaps, had we not been forced to flee in 1939, I too would now be working in the family business, no more enthusiastically than he had done. I had been spared that fate. All the more reason, I felt, not to settle for a similarly frustrated life in London.

But thinking such thoughts is easy. Actually finding the opportunities you dream of is altogether harder. I remained in my rut. In time, I would probably have adapted to it. But then, after I had been at Philips for about a year, there was yet another intervention from fate, as dramatic as it was unexpected.

8
TURNING UP THE VOLUME

I ALMOST made this a chapter about a telephone. But I no longer have the handset on which I received the phone call that changed my life; indeed, I barely remember what model it was. The telephone itself wasn't relevant. This radio, on the other hand, is a valued possession, which I cherish partly because it is an exciting embodiment of the remarkable adventure that I began in 1962.

It's a Bush TR130. I haven't listened to it for years, but it still works – or it would do if I gave it some batteries. Its uses are limited in the age of digital broadcasting, but I'd hate to live without it. I keep it in my front room, on a military chest which it shares with some wooden racing cars, a bowl of wooden fruit and an assortment of carved animals. The radio stands out. It looks like a device rather than an exhibit; something to be handled and used, not merely looked at.

It's actually a design classic: more than half a century old, despite its air of modernity. It was the bestselling radio of the late 1960s in the UK. It also represents a significant personal milestone, as my most visible early success in a new, longed-for role, as an independent industrial designer. If I hadn't got it right, that role might have been short-lived.

The circumstances in which this phase of my life began were strange and sad, the catalyst being the sudden death of David Ogle. In the two years since I had left him, David had been working towards the realisation of his big dream: designing cars. Ogle wasn't a manufacturer as such, but it had the capacity to design a car body, build it and mount it on a chassis ready to be driven away – which from David's point of view was all that really mattered.

Ogle's first car was launched while I was still there, in 1959. It was a high-priced variation of the Riley 1.5-litre saloon and had little impact: only eight were ever made. Much later, David designed a beautiful GT saloon body for the Daimler Dart SP250 sports car, but in between, he did create one design that is still remembered.

While I was churning out domestic appliances for Hotpoint and Philips, he continued to juggle the two sides of his business: the profitable David Ogle Associates, where I had worked, and a separate company called David Ogle Ltd, which designed cars at a loss. In 1961, David Ogle Ltd launched its most significant car to date: the SX1000, better known as the Ogle Mini. This was a sporty variation of the Mini, with a Mini chassis and a 1275cc Mini Cooper engine – but with the usual body-work replaced by a streamlined fibreglass version that looked more like a racing saloon. It was a lovely car.

There was something about David's design that particularly appealed to keen drivers. Longer and lower than a Mini Cooper, it seemed to hug the road. You felt as if you were sitting right on the centre of gravity – as if the car was an extension of you. In short, it was a joy to drive.

Sixty-six of these cars were made. Then disaster struck. In May 1962, driving an Ogle Mini to an event at Brands Hatch motor-racing circuit, David Ogle crashed and was killed. He is presumed to have been driving too fast – that was his habit. The fibreglass body did not improve his survival chances.

The news reached me on a Saturday. I remember how sorry I felt, for him and for his young family. He was only 40 and left a wife and four children. But that, it turned out, was not the only implication of the tragedy.

On the following Monday I received a telephone call from Ogle's senior director, John Ogier. He was struggling to come to terms with the loss not just of a friend but of the man around whom the two Ogle companies had been built. Ogier had recently appointed as his fellow director the saloon car racer John Whitmore, who was particularly anxious: he had just joined David Ogle Ltd and bought a third of it, largely on the strength of an anticipated contract with the British Motor Corporation – which pulled out as soon as news of David's death broke.

Ogier asked me to come down to Hertfordshire for a chat. I agreed to go that weekend. On the Saturday morning, I felt apprehensive – but was distracted when a passing bird excreted near the open window in our Doughty Street flat, by which I happened to be lying. The deposit landed on my forehead. This, said Nicole, was a sign of good luck.

It was hard to think in such terms so soon after David's unfortunate end. Yet the incident did bode well for my career. I drove down to Ogle's new headquarters – they had recently moved to Letchworth, about seven miles north of Stevenage – and was greeted by a clearly distressed John Ogier. He explained the situation and then made me a remarkable offer, inviting me to fill the gap that David had left. I never quite worked out the full chain of cause and effect, but I know that David had thought highly of me when I worked at Ogle; and I know that – as the car design side of the business demanded more and more of his time and vision – he had been thinking of sharing his workload with a new senior designer. I guess that he had already talked to John Ogier about hiring me; and that John preferred to trust David's judgement rather than anyone else's.

We talked, anyway, and John explained the situation. Then he offered me the posts of Chief Designer and Managing Director at David Ogle Associates. (I would have no formal connection with David Ogle Ltd – the car design business – at this stage.) The salary wasn't generous: just £500 more than I was getting at Philips. I didn't haggle but, on the contrary, accepted without hesitation.

This wasn't the kind of opportunity that came along every day; or, indeed, in every lifetime. If I didn't take it, I might easily spend the rest of my career doing vacuum cleaners and washing machines, probably as someone else's number two. At Ogle, I would be able to do almost anything, if I could find the clients. I might even get a chance to design motor cars eventually.

I started almost immediately. Within a week I was wondering if I had made a terrible mistake. The business was so deeply imprinted with David's personality and charisma that people seemed unable to imagine it without him. British Motor Corporation had already washed its hands of David Ogle Ltd. Then David Ogle Associates' biggest client, Bush Radio, gave six months' notice. David had worked for Bush from 1948 to 1954, and, as previously mentioned, had persuaded them to give him a hefty contract when he set up on his own. Losing that contract, which represented nearly half of our £25,000 annual turnover, was a potentially lethal blow.

A better manager might have panicked. I barely knew enough to appreciate what desperate straits we were in. I wasn't a complete novice at being in charge: I had managed the design unit at Philips. But I really didn't have much experience of it, and unfortunately I never had the opportunity of going on a course or mugging up on it. In any case, there wasn't time. There was only a tiny staff: one senior product designer and one senior graphic designer, each with two assistant designers, plus a secretary and a small model shop. Without major design input from me, the operation would have ground to a halt.

In addition, right from the start, I was running flat out trying to persuade our clients not to leave us. My powers of persuasion were limited, especially compared with David Ogle's. All I could offer were my talents as a designer. And so, with barely a thought for long-term strategy, I poured my energies into that.

The days passed in a whirl. So did the evenings: these were long days. There were existing projects to be overseen, new commissions to be set in motion, briefs to be absorbed, proposals to be made. My sketchbooks from the time are a jumble of disparate ideas: a car, baths, a twin-tub washing machine, an electric fire. I tried to attend to every detail, so that all we did reflected my design values. There were no management skills involved. I just worked flat out on design, and all the designers and model makers were somehow drawn along in the wake of my drive and creativity.

Remarkably, this proved to be just about enough. We brought several projects to fruition for Bush, while they were seeing out their six months' notice period. They were sufficiently pleased by what they saw to grant a stay of execution. Meanwhile, we tried to win other clients. Electrolux, who had a big factory nearby in Luton, were the most important addition. We designed a number of products for them, from vacuum cleaners to refrigerators. Luckily, their Swedish designer liked me and liked coming to see us. It would have been difficult for them to find another design studio of comparable sophistication so close to Luton.

I had also brought with me a three-year contract from Philips, which helped, and relatively soon we started designing for Plaxton, the luxury coach makers (although our first big project for them, for the Plaxton Panorama I, didn't see the light of day until 1964). Then there was Allied Ironfounders, an existing client who had to be kept on board. Their chairman, Bill Wilson-Bennetts, had been at Rugby with David. I found it difficult to establish a rapport to match their chummy relationship: like many of our contracts, this one had its roots in our founder's charisma. But we continued to provide them with occasional designs, and they must have been reasonably satisfied because when, soon afterwards, Wilson-Bennetts took over the running of a Scottish casting company called Carron, he asked me to design a bath for them. This was harder than it sounded: the product had to be different and obviously better than anything else on the market but also had to have exactly the same dimensions as all its rivals because of the replacement market. I worked away at it frantically – I remember doing four different proposals on one Saturday morning.

Wilson-Bennetts was delighted and gave the new bath – called the Swallow because of its elegant flowing lines – a special launch at The Dorchester hotel. An example of the cast-iron bath could be seen in the

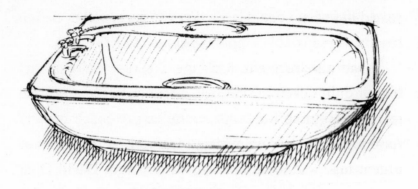

THE CARRON 'SWALLOW'
BATH.

fountain on the balcony. The Swallow bath went on to be a huge success, and over the next few years Carron kept asking for new versions of it – first in plastic, then in steel – just to keep up with demand.

To say that all this kept me busy would be an under-statement. Every day felt like a frantic last-gasp struggle to stave off disaster. The fact that the business survived was largely down to John Ogier, who did a fantastic job of holding things together after becoming chairman. One of the first things he did was bring in a proper accountant. David Ogle, who preferred the company of pretty young women to middle-aged bean-counters, had relied on his PA for that sort of thing. She was totally unqualified, and it showed in the mess that Ogier now had to sort out.

He asked me to buy him some time by keeping David Ogle Ltd – the separate company for car design – on the road. I did what I could, and foolishly neglected to charge for the work.

It was a thankless task. David Ogle Ltd was a shambles: it didn't even have a proper business plan. Morale in the workforce was poor, in contrast to David Ogle Associates, and labour disputes were common. My most urgent task was to complete a project that David Ogle had begun: the previously mentioned saloon body for the Daimler Dart SP250.

This car, which became the Ogle SX250, was a commission for the cosmetics tycoon Boris Forter, director of Helena Rubinstein. The idea was to use the chassis of the SP250 – a model, launched by Daimler in 1959, that had been widely criticised for its ugly bodywork and had failed to find many buyers. David had loved the idea of replacing that with a stylish fibreglass body, designed by Ogle, that would offer a big, upmarket alternative to the Ogle Mini. The initial plan was to make just six, but David had hoped that, if he got it right, Daimler would be so impressed that David Ogle Ltd would be rewarded with the big contract it so desperately needed.

David had almost finished a full-sized clay model when he died, but it wasn't complete. I had to create the back end and the interior, and I also ended up making some changes to the front, at Forter's request. A working prototype was required in less than six months, in time for the Motor Show at Earl's Court in October 1962. Somehow I succeeded in making this happen, and both

Forter and I were pleased with the results. I particularly liked the interior, with pale grey seats and carpets and a high, almost vertical walnut fascia.

Forter was happy enough to order a second SX250, for his mistress. But that was as far as it went. William Lyons – head of Daimler's parent company, Jaguar – expressed his enthusiasm for what we had done, but when it came to putting the model into production, he wouldn't be persuaded. And so, for a while, that project was forgotten. As we shall see in a later chapter, however, that was not the end of the story.

But it was the end of the road for David Ogle Ltd, which was wound down shortly afterwards. Both operations were then absorbed into a single company, Ogle Design, of which I was managing director and chief designer. I made sure that the best people from the transport operation brought their expertise over to the new company, and in due course there would be other Ogle car designs. In those early years, however, we had no time for grand ambitions. I was too busy with the more mundane challenge of trying to prevent our clients from drifting away.

The key aim was to secure the long-term loyalty of Bush Radio, who accounted for almost half of our business. This was easier said than done. Bush's bosses saw David Ogle as an old friend; their fortnightly meetings were as much for pleasure as for business. But they also saw him as a genius: designer of most of their most successful televisions and record players, and also creator of the legendary

TR82, the most iconic portable radio of the 1950s. What could I possibly offer that would compare with all that?

Trying not to be discouraged, I worked hard and patiently, going along to those meetings just as David had done and always bringing with me some beautiful models to illustrate whichever new design we had been working on.

I found it strange, but also stimulating, to work on products whose form bore little relation to their function. The guts of a radio have no predetermined form, and its functional requirements (speaker, dial, control switches) can be accommodated by any number of physical configurations. The old adage that 'form follows function' barely applies in this case. The challenge for the designer is to speak to the user in a symbolic language, finding physical forms to express the shapeless attractions of the product. It's all built out of nothing; and usually, other things being equal, the best design wins.

This was intimidating at first, but also exciting. I approached the work with enthusiasm, and I think Bush were impressed with the quality of my designs. They were even more impressed when I suggested some tweaks to another of David's radios – which had a problematic back and handle – which at a stroke made it much more saleable.

There was, however, another problem. Within weeks of my arrival at Ogle, the Rank Organisation – Bush's owners – had purchased Murphy Radio and merged the two companies into Rank Bush Murphy. This made sense from a business point of view. It was unfortunate for us.

Murphy had its own design studio – and it soon became clear that we had to compete with them.

Matters came to a head when Rank Bush Murphy decided that a radio I had originally designed for Bush should instead become a Murphy radio. Bush now needed a new model of their own, but it had to use the same chassis as the model that had just gone to Murphy. This was a highly restrictive constraint, but it didn't take long for me to work out how to deal with it. Then I sketched out a design, gave it to my colleagues to draw up, had a model made, and within a matter of weeks was able to present Bush with a portable radio that was unlike anything that had gone before.

David Ogle's TR82, which had been launched in 1959 and had proved an instant hit with the youth market, had been cheerfully full-bodied: plastic, durable and portable, with round corners, thick horizontal slats and a big circular dial on the front. My new model, which would eventually be launched as the TR130, felt more sophisticated. Its straighter sides and sharper corners gave it a slim, restrained appearance. Its elegant profile made it feel grown-up.

Powered by mains or battery, it was relatively compact – 235mm × 160mm × 73mm – but not at all flimsy. There was a fine metal grille for the speaker at the front, framed in chrome. A wide area of faux pigskin surrounded it: soft enough to make you want to pick it up. A small Bush logo in one corner acted as a focal point. A leather strap at the

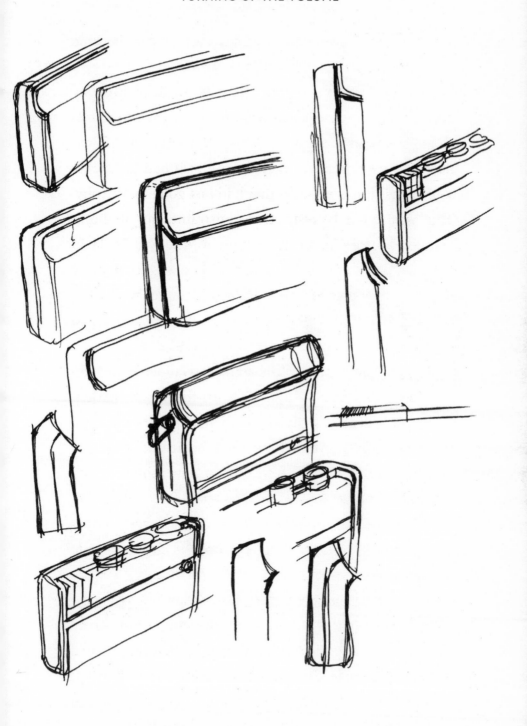

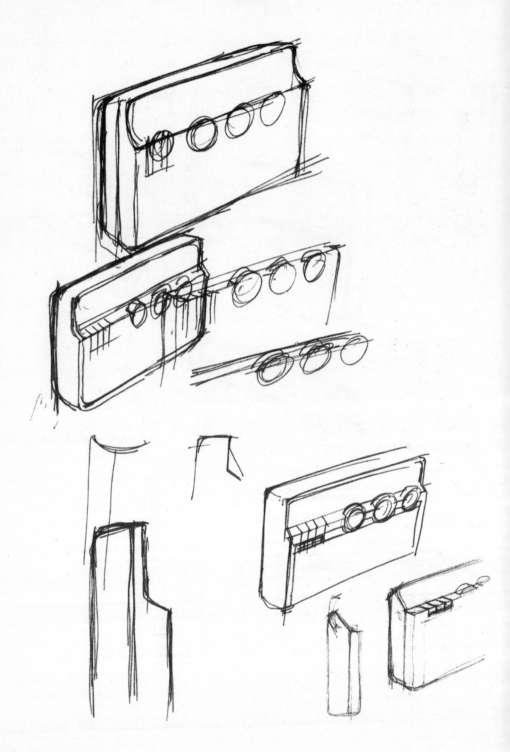

top added to the tactile appeal. As with a good sculpture, I believe that the best industrial design creates objects that you want to touch as well as look at. I could imagine people looking at this radio and wanting to pick it up – almost like a designer handbag – and wanting to use it. Every detail, from the texture to the weight (2.1kg), had been calculated to give it the most pleasing feel.

Best of all, where the TR82 had had a sunken row of controls along the top, which made it look a bit like a toaster, the TR130 had a nice solid chrome die-cast top, with controls at either end and the tuning panel protected not by the usual flat glass but by a thick, curved lens. All this was slightly raised – you could even grip it by the top, if you chose – and the combined effect was to make it feel reassuringly substantial.

It was the best piece of work I had done at Ogle so far. But it turned out that the design was the easy part of the challenge. As soon as it got beyond the initial presentation, the designer at Murphy – who saw us as competition – tried to torpedo it. It nearly didn't see the light of day at all, but our contact at Bush dug his heels in and insisted that my radio should be made for them. Even so, it didn't actually reach the shops until 1966 – a considerable time after we started work on it. I had almost forgotten it by then. The initial crisis at Ogle had passed, we were less dependent on Bush than we had been, and my mind was full of other challenges. Yet the Bush TR130 proved an almost instant success and went on to become the bestselling radio of the second half of the decade. It was the first big hit of my career at Ogle.

These days, most surviving examples of the TR130 are in attics or museums. I like to keep mine in full view – somewhere where I can see it daily, if I choose. It is a trophy: a reminder of one of the more vital battles of my early career – and of the fact that, despite daunting odds, that battle ended in victory.

Also, although I say it myself, it is a piece of design that's too good to be forgotten.

9

FINDING MY WAY

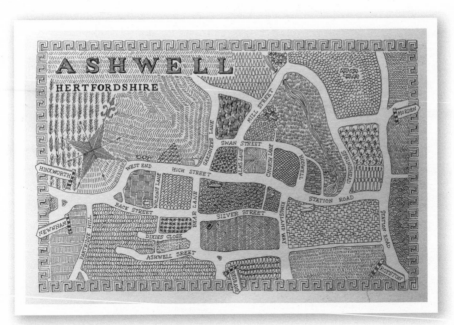

I LIKE maps. They appeal to my instinct to think of the world in terms of shapes and spatial relations. Some people will go to an unfamiliar place and be struck primarily by its colours, smells or sounds. For me, everything starts with form.

I made this map of the ancient Hertfordshire village of Ashwell after taking over at Ogle, as a Christmas card. I had developed the habit of drawing and printing my own greetings cards rather than buying someone else's. I still have the habit, but most of the cards are lost – beyond a few rough designs in my sketchbook. But I have kept this card, which usually lives on a shelf above what I loosely call my desk. (The worktop is too cluttered for any work to be feasible.) I sent it out for Christmas 1963. It has since be turned into a tea towel and as cards for sale, with proceeds going to charity, at Ashwell's museum. Today it serves as a sentimental memento – because this, for more than 30 years, was where we lived.

Ashwell is in north Hertfordshire, about 45 miles from central London and 20 miles from Cambridge. More importantly for me, it is less than eight miles from where my office was in Letchworth. We moved there within a year of my taking up the job at Ogle, which was demanding enough already without a daily commute to and from London. Compared with Chipstead, which had been a typical Surrey stockbroker village, this felt like the darkest depths of the countryside. There were around 1,500 inhabitants, in a compact settlement whose houses – mostly cottages – seemed to reflect every possible architectural style, from Tudor onwards. There were no electric trains from London – the station is over two miles away – no fast roads and few commuters. Most people worked in agriculture. The countryside was unusually green and lush, partly thanks to a major chalk spring at one end of the village (one of the sources of the river Cam), and there were farms all around. We lived at the opposite end of the high street, on a lane called West End, in a cottage – opposite a pig farm – that we had bought on the recommendation of Lewis and Eliza-beth Pepper, my landlords in Chipstead a decade earlier. They lived in Ashwell now and, having heard that I was working in the area, they alerted us to the fact that a property that might be suitable was on the market.

I am not sure that Nicole considered it very suitable. It was a tiny timbered cottage about 300 years old, rather rickety, with lots of low beams and non-parallel walls, while her ambitions were for something much grander. On the other hand, it was a step in the right direction – her best hope of a grand house lay in my having a success-ful career, and the location was ideal from that point of view. As for me, the cottage seemed nice enough for my purposes (which were mainly eating, sleeping and changing my clothes). It was tiny and primitive compared with the grandeur of my childhood in Brno, but I had long forgotten those luxuries. My points of comparison now were my years as a refugee in France or in digs in Luton, which had quite undone the effects of any childhood pampering. Many years later, my youngest daughter told me how fascinating she had always found it that, whenever I washed my face in hot water, I would pause, visibly relishing the sensation. I realised that this was because the sensation of hot water felt – and still feels – like a luxury, of the kind that I had once thought I would never enjoy again.

Other forms of joy were becoming harder to find. Our marriage was still functional, and indeed there would soon be children. But what closeness there had been between us was already fraying. I thought back to those moments of panic and doubt immediately before our wedding and realised that my instincts had been right: I had never been in love with her and never would be. The best relationships probably have stronger foundations than that.

I spent most of my time at work. Nicole, initially, spent much of her time at local auction houses, finding furniture for our rather bare cottage. She had a good eye, but her taste was for heavy, dark, Victorian pieces; I preferred lighter, more modern styles. But home was

Nicole's realm, not mine. My only contribution, over time, was a series of objects and appliances that Ogle had designed: we had a Bush radio, an Electrolux vacuum cleaner, an Electrolux fridge, a Carron bath. At its peak, Ogle designed many products a British family could need – clothes and food were the big exceptions – and the Karen family got to try out many of them. These weren't just perks. Designers need to use the products they create. Otherwise, how do you sense their limitations? Looking at a product tells you only about appearances. But when you live with it, week in, week out, you find yourself musing about how it could be better: not just better to look at, but fundamentally *better* – more enjoyable to use, more desirable to live with; better at fulfilling its purpose. And that, of course, is the essential first step towards coming up with a better design.

I even drove an Ogle Mini, for a while. I loved that car. It must have been one of the last ones Ogle produced. Far from being deterred by David Ogle's tragic demise, I drove dementedly fast. I had always thought of myself as a skilled driver, and the Ogle Mini cried out to be driven fast around corners. I wince when I remember it, although in my defence the roads on my route to work were much emptier then than they are today. There was one particular series of steep bends, just outside Stotfold, that challenged my skills to the limits. I loved testing myself and was always wondering if I could take the bends a little faster. One day, predictably, I lost it completely, and the car ended up on its roof. Amazingly, I was undamaged, apart from some glass in my mouth. But that was the end of the car. Thereafter I drove more sensible models – for example, a Cortina estate; but it was a long time before I began to drive more sensibly.

The material rewards of my job were in other respects limited. David Ogle had paid himself spectacularly well. I lacked his sense of entitlement and, indeed, have never been very good at looking after myself financially. I just went to work, poured out every last drop of my creative juices in pursuit of successful designs, and was paid whatever John Ogier felt it was appropriate to pay me. I was very aware of my limitations as a manager, and I was happy to report to the board once a month and benefit from John's greater experience.

I also made two good appointments. One was Valerie Murray, a local woman, relatively young but infinitely patient, who became my PA. A bit later, I also hired the Peppers' son, Christopher, who as a teenager had been a valued and enthusiastic member of the Chipstead Players but who was now almost 30, married, and working in a senior sales role for a newspaper company in Kenya. I lured him back to become Ogle's director in charge of administration and finance. We interviewed other candidates for the post, but with Christopher I knew that I could count absolutely on his loyalty and good judgement.

So it proved. Those two appointments – both made in what with hindsight seems a rather casual manner – proved crucial for everything I subsequently achieved at Ogle. Valerie and Christopher stayed with the company for the rest of their working lives, and I always knew that, between them, they would cover my back. They did all the tiresome tasks that I was no good at, never let me down, and saved me from all sorts of mistakes that I might otherwise have made.

Over time, Ogle became an expression of their personalities as well as mine, and it would be partly thanks to them that, over the coming decades, the company expanded significantly. I just did my best to win new business through great design. Christopher and Valerie's calm, practical and clear-headed approach – backed by John Ogier's steady hand as chairman – ensured that growth was smooth. My focus was always on creative challenges, not administrative or financial ones.

For the first three years, my chief product designer was an American called Carl Olsen, who had been recruited by David Ogle just before his accident. I think Carl felt that he would have been a more appropriate choice than me as David's replacement. Nonetheless, we worked fruitfully together until Carl decided to set up on his own. Meanwhile – fortunately – there was one administrative task to which I did devote considerable time and attention: the recruitment of designers. Mrs Tomrley retired soon after my return to Ogle, so I could not use her as a talent scout (although I did persuade her to visit our Letchworth site before her retirement). But talent still had to be found, recruited and nurtured. Otherwise, Ogle could never achieve what I wanted it to achieve. So I began to make time to visit art schools and scout for new talent, just as Terence Beckett had recruited me from Central for Ford. I never regretted it. Over time, I realised that raw young talent often had more to offer us than experienced designers did. The latter tended to be set in tried-and-tested ways. I wanted people who would think outside the box.

As for the nurturing, you'll have gathered by now that my people skills are limited. Yet my work-focused approach did seem to strike a chord with many of the people who worked at Ogle. I tried to give promising designers a chance to develop, channelling their talents strictly – just as mine had been channelled at Ford and by David Ogle. I gave them free rein when I could, but only when I was satisfied that they were on the right track. I also learnt to appreciate the particular strengths of different designers and to match people to appropriate tasks. And I found that my ability to speak the language of design compensated for my lack of broader management skills. Good designers can tell when a boss knows what he is talking about.

As the Sixties began to swing, Ogle developed a rather inspiring atmosphere. There was a sense of shared creative standards and values, and people were very motivated. I loved being at work, and part of that was due to the pleasure of being surrounded by people who could turn my ideas into reality. (I particularly adored the model makers, who were so creative in the way they meshed their work with our design aspirations.) I suppose my pleasure and my passion must have communicated themselves, and the result was a workplace with a buzz to it.

These were exciting times in the world of design, and, to the irritation of some established design practices in London, Ogle was starting to be talked about. Ours was a useful name to have on your CV. A rural backwater like Letchworth couldn't match the excitements of the capital, where most leading consultancies were based. As far as design was concerned, however, it was the happening place. Ogle became a magnet for talent, and the more this continued, the stronger the magnetism became. Some designers used us only as a temporary stepping stone to more lucrative employment elsewhere, but many found themselves staying much longer than they had originally planned.

Ashwell, too, turned out to be a long-term choice. We spent 12 years in that cottage, where all four of our children were born, and then about 20 more in a larger Victorian house at the other end of the village. I never really put down roots in the community in the way that I had at Chipstead, though. I was too busy with my work to get involved. But I did develop a deep familiarity with the contours of the village's lanes – especially after we bought a dog, a boxer called Peter. I named him after a boxer we had had in Brno, but he wasn't as clever as that earlier Peter. He had a lovely temperament, though. I used to take him for walks before and after work, and together we absorbed the subtle logic of Ashwell's layout. I was very fond of Peter. We both enjoyed boxing matches, in which he would jump up and try to push me with his nose. But I always knew that he would never do anything to hurt me. Looking back, I realise that, even then, I found it easier to have a relaxed, friendly relationship with my dog than with my wife. It wasn't a miserable marriage – yet. But the warning signs were there. We muddled along, but without joy. It felt tolerable largely because, until our children came along, I didn't look for any other kind of satisfaction outside Ogle. Home was for practical necessities, and I deferred uncomplainingly to Nicole on practical matters. It was easier than arguing. But happiness was a different matter. The only fulfilment I got came from my work. That's a terrible thing to say, but it's true.

I was usually the first to arrive at Ogle, although the model shop tended to start early as well. I was usually the last to leave. I liked the quiet time at the end of the day, when everyone else had gone, and I often lingered for an extra half-hour, just to enjoy the peace and, often, to see what ideas popped into my head. Even when a brief was relatively mundane, I wanted us to fulfil it with a design that really sang. I hated the idea of missing a trick because it hadn't occurred to us – and you could always find inspiration if you thought hard enough. I was particularly proud of one project we did for Electrolux. It was just an ordinary cylinder vacuum cleaner, on castors, but in an inspired moment I added a pair of big wheels at the back, creating a sense of power, like a racing car. Electrolux loved it, and so did I. I wanted every design we produced to have that kind of panache.

I became fairly obsessive. In my earliest months at Ogle I often used to go off to the pub at lunchtime with the other guys. But after a while I concluded that it was better to walk up to a café where I could quickly get a sandwich or beans on toast and then get back to work as soon as possible. Getting my work right was what motivated me, not having a good time in the pub.

And that, I suppose, is the story of my map of Ashwell. Even when I came back from Ogle and my work for the day was supposedly done, I didn't really feel relaxed or at home. I don't think I knew how to relax, or how to have the kind of intimate relationship in which it is possible to feel at home. So I just carried on creating: that was how I found my fulfilment, even in my leisure time. I was always drawing, and I always took a sketchbook home with me from work – partly because, if an idea came to me, I wanted to be able to get it down on paper straight away, before it melted away again. But I found something safe and comforting about the mere act of drawing, irrespective of the usefulness of the results.

My village map is a product of that restless impulse. When I look at it today, I am grateful that I made it. It helps me to call up impressions of a village to which, while I lived there, I paid too little attention. The quality of the work pleases me, too. I have rendered the lines of the village with surprising accuracy, considering that it was done from memory. But I also like the suggestive way in which it evokes a sense of the world beyond the map's boundaries. That's one of the things I love about maps – or at least about the kinds of map that I like to draw. Mine tend to include signposts, or pictures of landmarks, or nuggets of helpful information, such as distances. They thus give an accurate account of the way in which a particular corner of the world is arranged. But ideally they should also evoke the world they depict in more nuanced ways as well. They should be geographical as well as topographical, conveying a sense of place and, consciously or unconsciously, the underlying forces that have made that place what it is. In a sense, they tell stories: if you went from here to there, this is where you would go and this is what you would see. The most creative maps can evoke such imagined journeys as vividly as the printed word.

But perhaps the most revealing aspect of this particular map is the fact that, plainly, a lot of work has gone into it. All that detail, meticulously drawn, is gratuitous. I have included it because, creatively, I wanted the design to be just as it should be. That, in a way, makes it a snapshot of my life at the time: the creation of a man who came home from a long day's work and, instead of unwinding in more conventional or companionable ways, spent many more painstaking hours with his sketchbook, trying to create an image that pleased him – and trying to recreate in two dimensions the village in which he lived.

10

IN THE FAST LANE

THERE ARE many bookshelves in my home, as you've seen. Barely half are filled with books. The rest are dotted with objects that please me: models, toys, artworks. One shelf, halfway down a wall in my front room, has a pair of brightly painted birds at one end, and a big wooden racing car at the other, whose wooden driver wears a bright red-and-orange fez. In the middle is another car, smaller and without a visible driver. It is painted green – British racing green – with plain wood for the windows. It is only about 160mm long and 60mm high, yet it represents one of my biggest achievements.

David Plagerson, the craftsman who carved it for me (from a single block of wood), usually carves Noah's Ark animals. Yet despite his lack of automotive expertise, he captured the essence of the Reliant Scimitar GTE. Its form is unmistakable. That is why I am so proud of it.

This was my first big car project. Its seeds were sown around the time I took charge at Ogle, but it bore its most exciting fruit six years later, which is why I have saved it for a chapter of its own. Even now, more than 50 years after that, it still excites me.

Looking afresh at its long, confident lines, I feel a glow of pride that not all of my old work evokes. This design has stood the test of time. Back in 1968, when the Reliant Scimitar GTE was launched, much of the buzz related to the way it changed the rules. No one had imagined a vehicle that was both an estate car and a sports car, and the motoring press couldn't decide if it approved or not. Today it is easier to see that, in addition to being mould-breaking, the Scimitar GTE is in itself a satisfying piece of design. Its form is well resolved; its coherence makes it pleasant to look at and to use. Owners of Scimitar GTEs tend, as a result, to cherish them. Even when Reliant eventually ceased production, in 1986, an attempt was made a few years later (by Middlebridge) to revive the model. I suppose you would call it a classic.

Its origins, however, were as random as its ultimate design was carefully considered. The story began in 1962, when, as previously mentioned, Boris Forter commissioned an Ogle-designed body to go on a Daimler SP250 chassis. David Ogle began the project; I completed it after his death. The resulting car, the Ogle SX250, appeared at the 1962 Motor Show in Earl's Court. David Ogle had hoped that Daimler would then put the SX250 into production. They decided to pass. Yet the model did cause a stir, and one of the people most impressed by it was Ray Wiggin, then assistant general manager of Reliant Motors but shortly to become its managing director.

Reliant were best known for their cheap and cheerful three-wheeled Reliant Regals. In those days, they had broader ambitions. In 1961, they had even launched a sports car, the Sabre, but this had proved a disappointment. It performed respectably on the rally circuit but flopped commercially – a failure some blamed on its unattractive fibreglass body. So when Ray Wiggin saw what Ogle had done with the SX250 – replacing Daimler's unattractive SP250 body with a beautiful fibreglass shell of its own – he saw an opportunity. What if he were to apply a similar process, or perhaps a similar body, to the Sabre?

Wiggin discussed the idea with John Ogier, and the two men struck up what would be a fruitful relationship. What Wiggin had in mind for the Sabre was not far removed from the body we had done for Daimler, so we remodelled the body to adapt it to Reliant's way of manufacture to fit the Sabre platform. The resulting vehicle, the Reliant Scimitar GT SE4 Coupé, was launched at the 1964 Motor Show.

It was Ogle's first piece of commissioned work for a car designer, and it was well received. Reliant were pleased, and our relationship with them became long term. We would do many other pieces of work for them over the years – from a little three-wheeled truck called the TW9 (or the 'Ant') to a family car called the Anadol for the Turkish market. There was also the Rebel, the Kitten, the Regal – and, much later, the famous Robin. But the Scimitar was what made the relationship special.

Sales of the GT Coupé were modest, but its elegance was widely recognised. Despite being the product of two different design brains, it had a pleasing unity. I think David Ogle may have shared my sense that a car is like a sculpture, although unlike me he may not have thought explicitly in such terms. To me, everything is about form. Each line, inside and out, needs a purpose; and all the different lines must harmonise. I am a great admirer of Henry Moore, and in the 1960s, when I became more aware of the great sculptor's work, I may have absorbed some of his influence.

With cars, of course, there are additional concerns. Moore didn't have to worry about aerodynamics, or legal requirements, or the need to take into account the fact that cars are made mostly from reflective materials. Nonetheless, I longed to design a car with the same kind of visceral aesthetic appeal as a Moore sculpture. I think the Scimitar went some way in that direction, at this stage. But it was a start.

Minor refinements of the Scimitar were released in 1966 and 1967, but the variation that mattered was another Motor Show one-off, commissioned in 1965. Triplex, a company that made safety glass for cars, asked Ogle to create a special version of the Scimitar to show off their latest products. The result was the Scimitar Triplex concept car, referred to as the GTS, or Glass Top Special.

The GTS kept the Scimitar's wheelbase (i.e. the modified Sabre wheelbase) and the Scimitar's body. But we replaced the 'greenhouse' above the waistline with an estate-type passenger cell, whose extensive glazing showed off Triplex's different kinds of glass. The object of the exercise was to display state-of-the-art materials – laminated safety glass, heated glass for the rear window, special heat-absorbing glass for the roof – and state-of-the-art methods for attaching the glass to the rest of the car. I couldn't help noticing, however, that what really grabbed people's attention at the Motor Show was that it became, in effect, a hybrid of sports car and estate car. To some extent, this shape had been determined by the need to show off the materials; within that constraint, however, we had tried to create a form that we could be proud of, and on the whole I think we succeeded. As I said earlier, good design makes a virtue of necessity.

Motoring enthusiasts who were impressed by the GTS included the oil tycoon Nubar Gulbenkian, who wanted to buy it on the spot. Triplex foolishly failed to take him up on the offer – they could have named their price, and they could always have asked us to make another one. Instead, they sold the car to the Duke of Edinburgh, who had also expressed enthusiasm. He used it for a while as his personal vehicle, which delighted us. (Triplex had arranged for it to have the registration 660 GLE and had subtly shifted the '0' towards the letters on the number plates.) Then, after a couple of years, he decided that it was making him too conspicuous and gave it back.

Meanwhile, the model had also impressed someone more important: Ray Wiggin. He pondered for a year or so. Then he asked me to submit designs for a sporting semi-estate version of the Scimitar, not unlike the GTS but in normal materials, for the general market. The key objective was to create more luggage space, and much more room for passengers at the back. Like all coupés, the Scimitar GT was so cramped at the back that it was barely worth having the rear seats, and Reliant thought this was holding back sales. Hence Ray Wiggin's commission, to which he had clearly given a lot of thought. The new model would have a three-litre Ford V6 engine and a new, longer chassis, with wider outriggers, created by Reliant's chief engineer, John Crosthwaite. The body needed to be both stylish and practical, and not too expensive to produce. The scope for economies of scale was limited – Reliant weren't planning to produce more than around 40 of these cars a week – so for some parts (headlamps, tail lamps, bumpers, instruments) we had to use off-the-shelf items rather than tooling them specially. But the finished car still had to look exciting and sporty: like the Scimitar GT, but better.

This was the kind of big, serious design challenge I had been longing for. It wasn't easy, and we had only a few months in which to do it. But we had the practical capacity we needed. We had kept the best people from David Ogle Ltd when that was wound down, and thanks to our previous work for Reliant we had learnt how to make the most of their expertise. By 1967, our model shop was a well-equipped department that could even, in effect, create prototypes of cars. It would soon be accepting commissions from outside clients, in addition to working with Ogle's designs. For the time being, however, they had more urgent work to do.

We put a Scimitar body shell under our 'bridge' (a pre-computer age system for making accurate measurements in three dimensions) and proceeded to produce two half-models, with the right-hand half showing a relatively conservative approach. A talented Australian designer, Bryon Fitzpatrick, was in charge of this while I was on holiday. Our attempt on the right-hand half involved extending the Scimitar's 'greenhouse' backwards – in effect, lifting the ceiling at the back – which resulted in a shorter, smaller, more vertical boot. The effect was not like the Ford Escort Mk 3. It answered the brief to some extent, but it didn't thrill me. Meanwhile, I had arranged to go on holiday. This was a rare occurrence (as Nicole often reminded me), and although I felt uncomfortable going away at such a critical juncture, it would have been very troublesome to cancel it. So I left this part of the project in Bryon's hands and went off for a few days to revisit my wartime haunts in Nice.

I spent those days thinking: not about childhood traumas but about the Scimitar project. Something was missing. The design that Bryon was working on would look nice enough, but this was a once-in-a-lifetime opportunity. Where was our once-in-a-lifetime solution?

I returned to Letchworth, and by the time I got there the answer was clear in my mind. It was like a vision: we would give the left-hand side an estate car body. For this to work, we needed a touch that had never been tried before: a 'waistline' that rose all the way to the back. Every car has a waistline: the line that divides the body from the greenhouse above it. In existing cars, this line was always flat, with perhaps a slight droop at the back. In my vision, the waistline would be rising, from front to back – and immediately it would feel like a sports car. I've always had a thing about power being generated from the rear. That's why my Electrolux vacuum cleaner had mimicked the big back wheels of the racing cars I loved in my childhood. Now, finally, I could apply my foible to a car that would really benefit from it. The waistline of this new model would go up and up, all the way to the back.

No one had ever thought of doing this, yet the advantages were dramatic. At a stroke, it made the car look exciting and powerful, giving it a pouncing, nose-down look. There was loads of headroom and luggage space at the back, and a great big back window, which was actually the hatch for loading. But it also had a sleek profile, while the aerodynamics were superb, with low drag, lift and lots of cross wind stability.

The design seemed too revolutionary to some colleagues. Yet I knew that it had to be done. In the end, I worked directly with our model maker, Norman Teece, who was better than anyone else at taking direction. I even got my own hands dirty a few times, shaping the clay myself. There was a lot of resistance – from some very talented people – to what I was trying to do.

The funny thing is that, these days, it is almost impossible to think of a car that doesn't have a rising waistline. All cars are designed that way. The only exception I can think of is the Rolls-Royce, and perhaps a Mercedes model or two. Yet back then this simple adjustment, which anyone could have thought of, was unthinkable. Perhaps that's a characteristic of good design: it leaves other designers kicking themselves for not having thought of it first.

But the rising waistline wasn't the only startling feature of my design. The overall form was highly distinctive. The fashion at the time was for rectangular cars, usually pulled out at the corners in the American style and possibly featuring fins, to make them look bigger. For my GTE, the corners were rounded off, and the sides wrapped around into the back, giving it a much more organic, sculptural feel. This allowed us to build in more 'tumble home' at the back – the effect when an object grows narrower as it approaches the top.

Inside, the two back seats could be folded down either individually or together, so the car could be a two-, three- or four-seater, while the total amount of potential luggage space was enormous. There was no boot, in the traditional sense. Instead, the GTE featured a large glass window that acted as the hatch, with the lights and registration plate on a fixed transom panel beneath, and luggage space within. The glass extended a long way downwards, which made parking easier, and had a distinctive, very flat shape. I loved the way it closed off the rest of the form – yet it was in fact another off-the-shelf item, chosen partly to keep costs down.

There was a fuel tank under the loading area at the back. The spare wheel was at the front, behind the radiator. Steel tubes at key points strengthened the shell. This was not just a sleek, streamlined car. As soon as you drove it you sensed its luxurious solidity.

The reimagined body was also very performance-friendly. The GTE never went in a wind tunnel while we were creating it, but it didn't need to. It was entirely predictable that, thanks to the long roof, airflow could settle down after being disturbed at the top of the windscreen; and that this would reduce drag. The shape was also stable. The long estate configuration allowed the engine to thrust through a centre of gravity that was well in front of the centre of pressure (through which drag acts). The result was a 'horse-pulling-a-cart' effect: if strong crosswinds ever threw the car off line, it would naturally correct itself. (This was in marked contrast to the VW Beetle.) As for the front, it was subject to minimal lift at high speeds (in marked contrast to the Ford Capri). Subsequent tests revealed that, despite that larger body, the Scimitar GTE was faster than the Capri, even if both cars were given the same engine.

Some of these technical advantages would not emerge until sometime later, but my aeronautical studies had probably given me a fairly good instinct for such matters. At this stage, meanwhile, what mattered most was that it should look and feel like a performance car. As a last-minute flourish, I added a little upward 'kick' at the back end of the roof. I'm not sure how much practical difference this made, but it helped complete the form sculpturally. It felt right aerodynamically, and, like the rising waistline, enhanced the car's sporty look.

Apart from that, it was just a matter of making the other details as pleasing as possible. The layout for the dashboard was based on the Ogle Mini, with an L-shaped arrangement of dials in front of the driver and miscellaneous controls and air vents mounted on the centre console. It looked as if it had all been designed especially for the GTE. In fact, most of the elements were sourced from existing lines.

Overall, it was a very well-resolved package, and when we presented our two-halved clay model to Ray Wiggin I was confident that we had found a triumphant solution to the problem we had been given. Of course, that did not guarantee that Reliant would choose the right – that is, the left – half; generally, they were very conservative about design. There were some nail-biting moments while we waited for Ray, who had been delayed at the Motor Show. But when he did arrive, he made up his mind in an instant. My design was given the green light, and the pre-production process began.

A running prototype left Ogle three months later, and the Scimitar GTE was launched seven months after that, in August 1968, with a relatively high price tag of £1,998. It was the world's first Gran Turismo Estate, and the reception ranged from the delighted to the baffled. Ian Morton, the influential motoring correspondent of the *Evening Standard*, called it 'one of the most handsome and significant bodylines to come out of Britain for some time', while *Motor* magazine declared that 'happiness is Ogle-shaped'.

Design magazine called it 'Britain's first sports-wagon' – an unsuccessful coinage that was intended as praise. But *Car* magazine was ambivalent – 'We are not unstinting in our feelings about the styling' – while *Autocar* published an editorial explaining that half its staff loved the car but the other half couldn't stand it.

The car-buying public was more decisive: Reliant soon had orders worth more than £1 million. The only limit on sales was how fast they could produce them. It was a triumph of marketing as well as design. In terms of comfort and space for luggage and passengers, the Scimitar GTE was a huge improvement on its predecessor. Yet it was also astonishingly elegant. Estate cars had hitherto been associated with practicality rather than style. They were used by travelling salesmen, or families with children and dogs. The Scimitar GTE had the capacity of an estate and the sleek looks of a sports car. A press advertising campaign used the slogan 'Scimitar offers the impossible', under a picture showing a thoroughbred racehorse in front of a cart loaded with luggage. It was a perfect summary of its unique appeal.

The model proved so successful that, in 1970, Reliant ceased production of the original coupé version. That same year, the Guild of Motoring Writers named it 'Britain's Most Beautiful Body' at a beauty pageant at their annual dinner. Around the same time, news broke that Princess Anne had been given a Scimitar GTE by her parents as a joint birthday and Christmas present. This, wrote the motoring journalist Christopher Wilkins, 'shows her to be a thoroughly fashionable young woman'. Two years later, as a further boost, the princess was caught speeding in it on the M1. (She was let off with a written warning but was fined £40 for a similar offence, in another Scimitar GTE, in 1977.)

As for Ogle, we never looked back. The Scimitar GTE took our reputation to a new level, as designers whose work was commercial as well as marketable. New commissions became easier to come by, while a steady stream of further work ensued from Reliant. We were involved in a major facelift for the three-wheeled Regal, and its successor, the Robin. It was hard to get hugely excited about such projects, which were largely a question of keeping the vehicles within tight weight limits (355.6kg and 450kg respectively) so that they could be taxed at lower rates. But I was quite proud of the Robin, which in addition to having room for four adults boasted one revolutionary detail. Until then, every car had a rain gutter, which for convenience of construction went right around the roof. This was conspicuous and, often, ugly (on the Mini, for example). Fibreglass exacerbated the problem, because the thickness of the panels to be joined there could not be controlled with hand lay-up. For the Robin, therefore, I decided to hide the gutter under the door frame. This was revolutionary: so much so that Reliant's body engineers eventually toned my proposal down. But it was such a simple and obvious improvement that there is barely

Right: This is my grandfather, Arthur von Ferraris, and me. I loved visiting his atelier in Vienna which was Egyptian themed and a great inspiration to me.

Below: One of the only photos I have of my parents, Margaret and Paul, together.

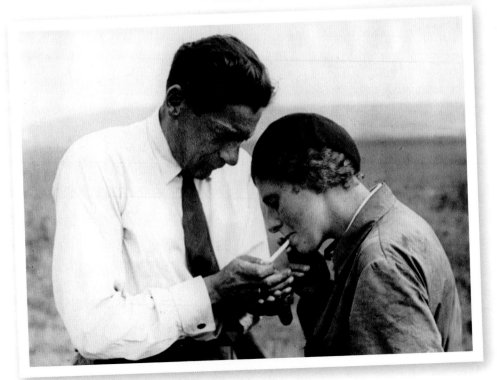

Above: My childhood home in Brno, Czechoslovakia.

Right: My older brother, Felix, younger sister, Bettina, and me playing on the Hispano-Suiza. This is the very car that we fled in from Brno.

Left: I think I was about 10 years old here. We went to the Alps at Easter and Christmas to ski.

Below: Felix in a Bugatti we shared. From the age of 2, I could recognise 12 different makes of car.

A lot of paperwork when it came to designing, which often meant a very untidy desk...

Only 2,270 Bond Bugs were built. The enthusiasm for it never faltered, there are Bug owners round the world and there is a lively Bug Club organising regular events.

The Ogle team in the 1980s.

The Transport Design department at Ogle.

Receiving the Prince Philip Designer's Prize in 2002.

I received an Honorary Doctorate (Doctor of Technology) at Loughborough University in 2001. Left to right: my daughters, Eugenie and Josephine, my son, Max and my sister Bettina.

At the anti-Brexit march – in vain.

With six of my grandchildren. Left to right: Roob, Theo, Zachery, Arlo, Louis and Maia. Maia and Zachery now have a sister called Aalia.

Eugenie and Josephine, and my son, Nicolas, with me at Buckingham Palace where I received an OBE in 2019. My other son, Max, is based in Zambia and was unable to attend. A very special day for us all.

a car manufacturer in the world that has not imitated it – although I doubt that many designers would admit to having been inspired or influenced by such an unglamorous model as the Reliant Robin.

In fact, thanks to Ogle, Reliant was by then known for its upmarket models as well as its cheap and cheerful ones. The Scimitar GTE was typically driven by professional people, who had money to spare but considered Jaguar and Mercedes too stuffy. Much of our subsequent work for them aimed to consolidate this newly sophisticated reputation. An SE5a version of the Scimitar GTE, with assorted minor enhancements, was released in 1972; in 1975 there was an SE6, which was longer and larger, followed by an SE6b (with a bigger engine) in 1979, and a Scimitar GTC convertible (SE8) in 1980. There were also lesser updates: for example, Scimitar GTEs produced from 1969 onwards came with a rear windscreen wiper – a complete novelty that was subsequently copied by the entire industry. And I have fond memories of a special deluxe edition of the GTE that I designed for Lady Hodge, wife of Reliant's chairman, in 1968. I had great fun with that and went to town with special golden glass and ridiculously lovely fabric for the interior. I understand that it is still on the road today, although the Hodge family no longer owns it.

But no amount of refinement or luxury, or celebrity endorsement, could compare with the satisfaction of bringing that first Scimitar GTE into the world. I was able to lease a succession of them on favourable terms – the one I liked best was brown – and it would be many years before I felt any urge to try another car. To drive around in a car that you have designed, of which you feel proud, is a privilege granted to few, and I always felt very fortunate when I was at the wheel of my GTE. I never wholly shook off my tendency to drive too fast, but I treated my Scimitar GTEs with a lot more care than I had my Ogle Mini. With the Mini, you were always trying to compensate for its feeble engine; with the Scimitar, there was a sense of contained power. It really was a performance car, and for all the brilliance of the Ogle Mini's handling, the Scimitar GTE's was better. I am proud to say that I never turned one over.

But I do sometimes pick up that painted wooden model GTE from my bookshelf and turn it over in my hand, savouring its form. A successful career in a creative field can bring many rewards: acclaim, respect, opportunity, even wealth. But none remotely compares with the deep joy of looking back on a piece of work you once did and realising that you got it right. Even now, it looks fresh and new. I wouldn't change a thing about it.

11

BATTLE OF THE BIKES

DESPITE MY enthusiasm for driving, I have never been much of a cyclist. I have already mentioned my embarrassing two-wheeled experiences in the street outside our home in Brno. My other main childhood memory of cycling was even more traumatic. I was riding one of those old-fashioned bikes that don't have brakes: instead, the pedals are linked directly to the back wheel and you slow down by slowing the pedals. This worked fine for me until I tried a fast descent down one of Brno's bigger hills – and realised that my little legs lacked the strength to counteract my momentum. I ended up going flat out straight into the path of a car, missing a fatal collision by inches. I never told anyone: I felt too shaken up, and somehow ashamed of myself as well. But I never felt much love for bicycles after that.

It is ironic, therefore, that I am often introduced these days as 'the man who designed the Chopper bike'. When visitors to my home catch sight of the shiny red Chopper in my front room, leaning on its stand in an out-of-the-way corner, they tend to rush to it delightedly. Yet of all the objects through which I am reassembling my memories, this is probably the one that the greatest number of readers will recognise. It was one of the defining products of the 1970s (even though it was launched in the 1960s); and it represents a significant episode in my life.

The core concept originated elsewhere, in America. That's one reason why I'm lukewarm about what followed. My favourite ideas come from nowhere. In this case, a US bicycle manufacturer called Schwinn had launched a very successful model called the Sting-Ray, which scandalised parents but delighted young teenagers by mimicking the style of the 'chopper' motorcycles then favoured by West Coast bikers. The Sting-Ray had a long, curvy frame, a long banana-shaped seat and high 'ape-bar' handlebars. After a slow start, it became a bestseller, and Raleigh, the British bicycle manufacturer, decided that it needed a product to compete with it. Raleigh's internal designers did some work on it, but their first attempt, the Rodeo, was a flop. In early 1966, therefore, their marketing director, Peter Seals, called in Ogle.

This was our first ever contact with Raleigh. No one approached them from our end: they were drawn by our reputation. The Scimitar GTE had yet to be unveiled, but even the original Scimitar GT had made waves, and we had many other satisfied customers. Now we were seeing the rewards. But a design consultancy is only as good as its most recent project, and the challenge with which Raleigh presented us was an interesting one.

Peter Seals came to Letchworth to explain. He was very clear. Raleigh wanted a design that communicated roughness and toughness; a product that would challenge the Sting-Ray head-on; a chunky, robust machine that would appeal to rebellious young teenagers – but would also seem substantial enough for parents to want to pay for it. They wanted a product that was like the Sting-Ray, but also quite different; unique, but instantly accessible in its appeal.

The key elements of my solution to this problem had sketched themselves in my mind before we had finished the meeting. I kept this to myself, because there were many loose ends to tie up, but I knew that I had found the heart of the matter. What we needed was a bike whose back wheel was bigger than its front wheel.

I have talked already about my fascination with the idea of power coming from the back, and the idea of big back wheels which generate that power. I have mentioned the big-wheeled vacuum cleaner I designed for Electrolux, and the use of the rising waistline in the Scimitar to create a sense of powerful rear thrust. But now my favourite foible had found its perfect place. This was a project for which the big back wheel could be not just a flourish but the beginning: the conceptual core around which everything else could be built. Immediately after my meeting with Peter Seals, I retreated to my office and started sketching.

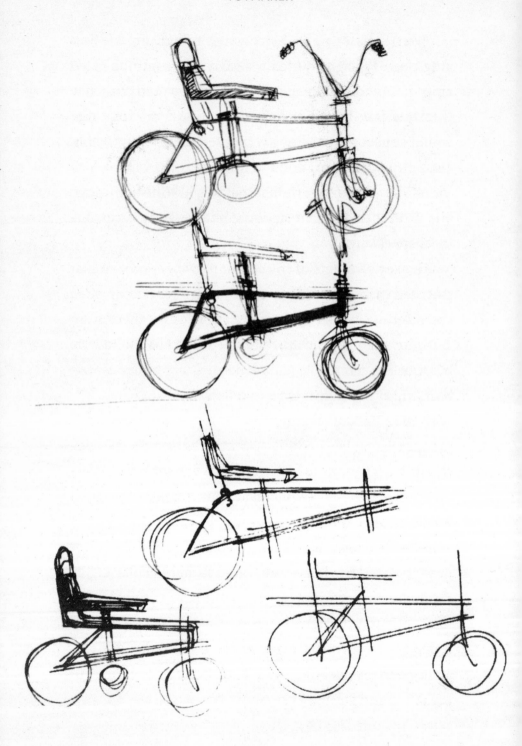

When I was ready, I shared my vision with Jimmy English, one of our most gifted designers and, more importantly, the perfect man for this particular job. Some design shops like to get lots of designers involved in important projects of this kind, so as to get the widest possible range of options. I preferred to work out the direction in which I wanted us to go, and then assign the project to the person or people best suited to take us there. Jimmy's advantages included the fact that he was a great motorbike enthusiast. He used to ride these huge American motorbikes with drop handlebars, even though he himself was quite small. He was very talented but very intuitive and somewhat impulsive. He had been a model maker at Ford but then somehow ended up working on a building site, from which I rescued him for Ogle.

I knew that he would 'get' what I was trying to do. And because he could draw very well and loved and under-stood form, I felt confident that my vision would not suffer in his hands. We worked on the project together until he had come up with three viable renderings of the same basic idea. He also made a crucial contribution by writing the word 'Chopper' onto one of his designs. Then we presented these concepts to Raleigh – who, to my amazement, rejected them.

Actually, it wasn't as simple as that, or – with hind-sight – so surprising. There were some in the company who liked our approach, including Peter Seals, but those responsible for the technical side of things – in other words, engineering and manufacturing – rejected it. They seemed to feel that it would be a problem having to stock two different kinds of wheel for the same bicycle. I suspect that Raleigh's technical director, Alan Oakley, felt predisposed to dislike our design, and I think it was he who emphasised the production difficulties. If I had been in his position I, too, might have felt offended by the involvement of an external design consultancy.

Whatever the explanation, word came back to us that our design was unacceptable. Peter Seals was apologetic – he liked the idea; but, he explained, the big back wheel had to go. I thought for a moment and then took a big risk. I was sorry, I said, but the bigger back wheel had to stay. It was the best I could do. We could not and would not do a design that did not incorporate it.

It was all very polite, but it would have looked very bad, internally and externally, if the commission had ended early because we refused to do what the client asked. Yet I really meant it. I found it impossible to imagine an alternative solution that achieved Raleigh's objectives better than this design did. Wheels of different sizes were the whole point.

Eventually, Peter Seals decided that the idea was worth fighting for – a crucial turning point. He went back and twisted the necessary arms, and the concept was accepted. Not for the first time in my career, I had cause to be grateful for the courage of an executive who was prepared to stick his neck out for one of my designs. Sometimes I wonder how many other good designs have sunk without trace for want of an executive with similar strength of character.

Once the basic concept had Raleigh's blessing, I got a larger team involved to produce proper technical drawings and, later, prototypes of some of the parts.

Of course, it wasn't just a question of a big back wheel. The Chopper had other distinctive features, all growing from that starting point. In contrast to the Sting-Ray, whose frame was curvy and over-elaborate, I gave the Chopper a much tidier frame, with straight lines and an arrowhead shape.

Those were the basics. Everything else was embellishment – but the embellishments were crucial. The alloy wheels – 20in (51cm) at the back and 16in (41cm) at the front – had chunky tyres with car-style valves. The three-speed gears were changed not with a lever on the handlebar but with a lovely car-style gearstick mounted to the frame. There was a curved, high-backed, padded seat, with a big reflector on the back and an unnecessary metal hoop on top that echoed the 'sissy bars' on some kinds of motorbike. The seat was one of the parts for which we built a prototype. It was even fitted to a Raleigh Rodeo, to see what it would look and feel like on a real bike.

Beneath the seat there were springs – which didn't actually do anything – and on the rear wheel there was what looked like a disc brake, which, similarly, was purely decorative. We also raised the mudguards right off the wheels, to imply that there was racing suspension and that it needed that kind of clearance to cope with it. Again, this was pure fantasy, but children loved it. With a kick-stand that allowed you to park it as if it were a stationary motorcycle, it looked and felt like a proper, dangerous, noisy, high-performance adult machine. I knew it was a winner.

The Chopper was launched in the US and UK in September 1969. In between, the cult film *Easy Rider* – in which Dennis Hopper and Peter Fonda cruise across the US on chopper motorbikes – was released. Our design seemed to have caught the spirit of the times, and, sure enough, the bike was a huge success on both sides of the Atlantic. The basic version cost £32, with a huge range of colour options that included 'Infra Red', 'Flamboyant Green' and 'Fizzy Lemon'. It wasn't actually a very good bike, in terms of getting from A to B: it was far too heavy to be fast. As one commentator said, however, it was 'more fashion accessory than means of transport', and it became one of the defining embodiments of 1970s youth culture. Raleigh saw its fortunes turned around – previously, the company had been struggling. And it was all thanks to an Ogle design that, once again, appeared to defy the rules of common sense.

That should have been the end of the story, as far as I was concerned. Sadly, it wasn't, because most people have heard a very different narrative.

The first hint that something might be amiss came when the Chopper was launched in the UK. I wasn't invited. Perhaps I should have been concerned, but it was a phenomenally busy period. We were still working on the Scimitar GTE and, as we shall see, several other important projects were also at a critical stage. Sometime later, however, I was alerted to the fact that Oakley was claiming the design as his own. Ogle was never mentioned.

On a basic level, that was fine. Raleigh had bought the design. They owned it. They were under no obligation to credit Ogle every time. As the Chopper's success grew, however, so did the injustice. The design had proved a sensation, and it needed a story to go with it. Someone had the stupid idea of giving that story to the technical director, without any mention of Ogle. That got up my nose, especially when Oakley embraced the fiction with enthusiasm. It would have been one thing to have suggested, correctly, that the full design had evolved over time, and that while it was evolving there had been many meetings and discussions in which representatives of both Ogle and Raleigh were involved. Nor would I quarrel with the assertion that the marketing initiative – the idea of producing a rival to the Schwinn – came from Peter Seals, or that Oakley and his team very ably carried out all the downstream development once we had made our contribution. But Oakley went further. In interview after interview, he claimed the Chopper as entirely his own work, and each time he told the story it got better. He claimed he had been inspired by drag-racing cars with big wheels at the back; he had sketched the design on the back of an envelope; he had done so on a flight over the US in March 1967. With each retelling, the fibs became more specific. And there were many retellings.

I first became really bothered by this in 1998, when Raleigh celebrated the Chopper's thirtieth anniversary and Oakley and his envelope featured heavily in the media coverage. I tried to interest Raleigh in my side of the story, with little success, although the Chopper Owners' Club did publish an article about Ogle's contribution in their magazine, *The Hot One*. I also wrote to Oakley himself, who initially promised to answer me but never did. Instead, he went on telling his version, until eventually – as a former Raleigh employee once told me in private – he had 'repeated the story so often, he probably believes it to be true'.

Yet it isn't my word against his. I have all the documentation of our involvement, including the earliest sketches and concept drawings that we made, and records of more than 20 meetings with Raleigh between January 1966 and November 1967. I also have supporting statements, in writing, from several former employees. But the very fact that Raleigh came to us in the first place reveals the truth:

if Oakley had designed the Chopper, they could have made the prototype themselves.

I feel petty mentioning this. It wasn't the first time, or the last, that someone tried to take credit for my work. Generally I shrug it off as a kind of tribute: no one would want to claim credit if I had created lots of ugly products. Yet the brazenness of Oakley's claim was particularly annoying. Not only was it Ogle's design, but Oakley had initially argued against it.

My patience finally snapped in 2004, when Raleigh launched a lightweight aluminium version called the Chopper Mk 3. Oakley's version of events was being repeated everywhere, even on the BBC. I began to make a fuss: not just on my own behalf but for all the other people who had been involved in Ogle's work on the Chopper, notably Jimmy English. They had all been working for me. It seemed wrong to let them be denied their place in design history.

Eventually, I managed to get the record set straight in the places that matter most, such as the BBC and the Design Council, where Ogle is officially listed as the Chopper's creator. Yet Oakley was still claiming the credit when he died in 2012, and several of his obituaries repeated the claim.

The controversy has drained some of the joy from my memories of the Chopper. I also recognise that the thinking behind it was not entirely original: it would never have happened had Schwinn not identified a hitherto unimagined gap in the market. Yet it's hard to ignore the pleasure that the Chopper's admirers still take from it.

The one in my home belonged, originally, to Nicolas, our eldest son. Later, our other children shared it. It was pretty battered by the time they had all left home, so I spent a few hundred pounds having it refurbished by the Chopper Owners' Club before I moved here. My grandson Theo has ridden it a few times since then, but I always try to keep it clean and shiny, because I've lost count of the number of visitors who have asked to be photographed with me and it.

I suppose that part of its magic comes from the fact that, in its own peculiar way, it was a very pure kind of design. Its key features didn't arise from function: the basic concept of a bicycle is almost beyond improvement, functionally. Instead, it was all about perception. The design is a purely aesthetic attempt to influence the way the user feels about the product.

Every bicycle is an example of brilliant functional design, simply because it's a bicycle. The Chopper persuaded a whole generation that it was better than other bicycles – purely through the symbolic language of visual design. In fact, functionally, it was worse than most bicycles: too heavy for speed and awkward to handle. Yet young people on both sides of the Atlantic responded to it, because it spoke to them in a language they understood. *Total Bike* magazine called it 'a triumph of form over function', and they were right. But that triumph was less superficial than it sounds. Unlike many people creating products for children and teenagers, I respected my young customers. Because of that, I respected what they wanted from a bike; and I think that many Chopper enthusiasts sensed this.

Nothing on the Chopper grew from inner necessity, apart from such fixed functional basics as having pedals, chain, wheels and so on. Yet none of my embellishments was gratuitous: they were all called for by the mood of the target audience. Without those gimmicks, such as the fake disc brake and the functionless springs, it would not have hit that sweet spot in terms of public image.

Even the design's weaknesses turned out to be an attraction. It was the little luggage rack at the back that created the temptation to carry a passenger. Yielding to that temptation created a hard-to-resist risk of unintended wheelies. These drawbacks only added to the Chopper's rebel credibility.

A Mk 2 edition was launched in 1972, with more robustly fixed handlebars, a T-bar gear shifter in place of the original knob, and a frame less likely to break under the strain of an extra passenger. (It also came with a warning pointing out that it was an offence against the 1960 Road Traffic Act to carry a passenger on a bicycle that was not made or adapted for that purpose.) In 1977, Raleigh built a gold-plated version to celebrate the making of the millionth Chopper. By the time the last true Chopper was built, in 1980, more than 1.5 million had been made. The Mk 3 version released in 2004 was lighter and safer, but the design was somewhat emasculated by health and safety improvements and in any case had been totally eclipsed by then by the next must-have bike, the BMX. Anyone who was still tempted by a Chopper was more likely to look for a well-preserved original.

I suppose that, as a product designer, that's one thing you always aim for: to embody the spirit of the times. That's why my Chopper design succeeded in the 1970s; and, for the same reason, it was unlikely to thrive in a different era. Yet its power to evoke the mood of that particular moment remains undimmed. If you were alive in the late 1960s or the 1970s, you either had one or wanted one, and you have only to look at a Chopper bike for your memories of that period to come flooding back. And that, if nothing else, seems like a good reason to have devoted a chapter to it.

12

BABY STEPS

The Formula One baby-walker that I
designed for my first child Nicolas.

I WISH I knew where to find my Formula One baby-walker, but I've lost track of it. I tend to lend out objects, just as some people lend out books. I don't always remember whom I've lent them to; and, like many people who lend out books, I don't always get them back. (If anyone reading this has the baby-walker, I would be grateful if you could return it, please.) But I've got some fairly good photographs of it – if I could only find them in my slide collection – and of course there are my sketches for it too, in one of those books in the V&A archive.

But there's no need to worry about any of that. I can still visualise it in every detail. That's one of the odd things about my memory. Major events of a personal nature swirl around vaguely in a pool of mingled impressions, rarely attached to specific dates or places. But objects that have featured in my life I can recall exactly – especially those I designed myself.

If I drew the baby-walker now, I doubt it would differ much from the version in my sketchbook. It was a bit like a wheeled trolley, about 500mm high, with a leg at each corner. The legs were tapered steel tubes, taken from an office chair. The front legs had castors at the end of them but the back legs had fixed wheels. This made it easy to steer. The flat top had rounded corners at the front and squarer ones at the back. A big central hole for the driver, just behind the halfway point, echoed that shape. A leather bucket seat within this hole could support some or all of the user's weight as required; but in order to move around the user would 'walk', either upright or paddling from a sitting position.

In the finished version, the flat top would be painted and accessorised to look like a racing car, with accessories including horn, steering wheel, gearstick and fuel cap; but that came later. In my sketchbook there are only outlines, evolving from shapes that look like buggies or trolleys to the final, pleasingly resolved racing car.

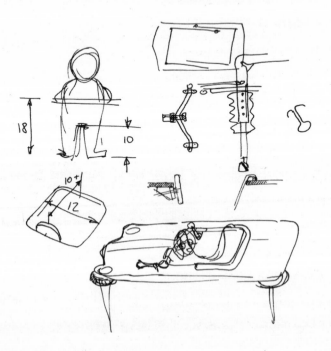

All these scribbles are jumbled in among commercially important sketches for Ogle's clients, including a bath for Carron, a radio for Bush and some versions of the Chopper bike for Raleigh. There is also a page of toy animals (sheep, cow), a strange figure that looks like a table footballer, a baby's high chair with built-on drawing board, and a page headed 'Karen family housing needs', under which I have failed to write anything. So you may not be surprised to learn that, just as I was preoccupied with bringing some of Ogle's most memorable designs into the world, we had also begun a family.

Our first child, Nicolas, was born in 1965. Josephine followed in 1967. I didn't attend either birth; nor did I that of Max, our third, who was born in 1968. In each case, Nicole gave birth at home, in the cottage. She didn't like hospitals, and she knew a friendly Polish doctor who lived nearby and was happy to oversee matters at home. There was also a local nurse, Nurse Armitage, with whom she felt very comfortable; and we had a succession of Danish au pairs. I don't think she gave much thought to the question of whether or not I was there, for the births or afterwards. I tried to make sure that I wasn't.

Instead, as with other aspects of domestic life from which I kept a safe distance, I worked. My responsibilities at Ogle justified any number of absences. I don't think I consciously used the office as a refuge; or, usually, as an explicit excuse. It was just an emotional comfort zone, to which I naturally retreated. And although there were many important work-related reasons why my presence was required at Ogle for most of each day, I realise now that there may have been other reasons as well.

Yet I was not an entirely bad father. When Eugenie, our fourth and last child, was born in 1970, I even attended the birth – on Nicole's insistence. I was in a meeting at Ogle when the news reached me, but I made it home in the nick of time.

At subsequent stages of the children's development my record was slightly less pathetic. I was quite competent at changing nappies and giving baths – when I was there. And once the children were old enough for games and stories, I was in my element – unless I was at the office instead. I wouldn't win any prizes for my parenting, but I enjoyed my children's company, and their play was a subject that genuinely enthused and intrigued me. Eventually, this enthusiasm would have a significant impact on my work, as thoughts about toys and games began to form themselves in my mind and my sketchbook. But the design at the heart of this chapter ended up in someone else's home.

At some point in late 1966 or early 1967, we noticed that Nicolas seemed to be slow in learning to walk. Eventually we sought expert help, from several quarters. The advice we received was confusing, contradictory and barely helpful. The only official diagnosis we were ever given, some years later, was that Nicolas suffered from dyslexia, whereas common sense suggested that, if he had a problem of that nature, it was dyspraxia – that is, difficulty with physical coordination. (I suspect that it was both.) That expert also claimed that Nicole and I were to blame for any difficulties he had, because we often spoke French rather than English at home, hoping that Nicolas would learn both languages. This, we were told, confused him. So from then on we restricted ourselves to English, which I now greatly regret.

But that was later. What Nicolas needed as a non-toddling toddler was practical help. Rather than wait for it, I decided to build him a device that would make walking easier for him and, ideally, more fun. The result was something unique: a wheeled baby-walker which is also a car.

The physical design was all geared towards helping Nicolas to walk. Within the constraints of that function, however, it was as realistic as I could make it. There was a green stripe running along the centre of the top deck, just like a real racing car, with a race number ('1') superimposed. There was a gear shift and a steering wheel and a hooter, and a lovely leather seat at the back of the bit where you stood. There was even a fuel filler cap at the back. It was an object of beauty and, I presume, still is. I just wish I knew what happened to it.

I created it in much the same way that I would have created something for an Ogle client. Once I had a sketch that satisfied me, I drew up a proper plan, then had a model made. The guys in Ogle's model shop were delighted to help. And Nicolas was delighted to use it. Suddenly he could walk around and chase the dog and do all sorts of things that he hadn't been able to do before. So he was happier (although the dog wasn't); and, in due course, his balance improved and he was able to walk unaided.

It wasn't the end of his troubles. He continued to struggle with the ordinary challenges of childhood. Once, when he was a bit older, I took him to play on the slide in the village recreation ground. He climbed to the top, paused – and then suddenly fell backwards to the ground, breaking his hip. But the baby-walker did at least provide him with a precious positive experience: a chance to enjoy some of the pleasures of free, confident, safe move-ment. Knowing that such pleasures existed must have been a valuable motivation during his difficult years of development.

Later, one or two of our other children liked to play with the baby-walker too. Perhaps they had acquired a taste for elegant vehicles when they were babies, when I sometimes used to drive them around Hertfordshire lanes on Sundays in my Scimitar GTE to encourage them to go to sleep. More plausibly, they enjoyed playing with an object that had been designed with a child's needs in mind. (I should add that Josephine, who was such a natural athlete that she was climbing in and out of her playpen before Nicole had finished building it for her, never bothered with the baby-walker.)

When I ask my children about their earliest memories, the baby-walker gets an occasional mention. A more constant theme is that I was mostly away. I can't deny this. In addition to being at Ogle, I seemed to spend inordinate amounts of time travelling, visiting clients in various distant corners of the UK or, sometimes, beyond. Sometimes it felt like a privilege to do so. I enjoyed my occasional trips to Sweden, to see Electrolux's design chief, Hugo Lindström, with whom I had a very friendly relationship and who always looked after me well. Then there were my visits to Plaxton, a UK client who made luxury coaches. We designed a number of their models, and I made frequent trips to their factory in Scarborough to discuss designs. It was a three-and-a-half-hour drive each way, yet it always seemed worthwhile. Their managing director was an enthusiast. He had no experience of industrial design, but he understood what we were trying to do. He encouraged us to let our hair down: to push our ideas as far as they would go, even if he subsequently reined them back in. I in turn tried to make my presentations as exciting as possible. I used to bring models with me, or unroll giant plans on the floor and get down on my hands and knees to explain the key details. We did some great work for Plaxton – the

Panorama 1 and the Panorama Elite were particularly admired, and we eventually helped them to overtake their great rival, Duple. I'm sure this was partly because his enthusiasm stimulated us.

Other clients were less rewarding. I made regular visits to a company called Canon in Wolverhampton, who made cookers. It was run by a man who had inherited the business from his father. He had no discernible talents of his own but delighted in reminding everyone, me included, that he was the boss. Sometimes it seemed that the only thing he enjoyed was pouring cold water on other people's ideas; I have never had such a dispiriting client. On my long, late, homeward drives I would usually be fuming, wondering if I could afford to sack the client out of sheer personal frustration. In fact, the unhappy relationship dragged on for what felt like ages, but it was of little benefit to either party. It was, however, yet another call on my time.

Perhaps in some ways it was just as well that I was away so much. Our little cottage was becoming very crowded: hence that unstarted list of the family's housing needs, which I think dated from when Nicole was pregnant with Max. Yet I did enjoy the moments I was able to share with the children. I loved encouraging them to draw or colour things; I even let them do so in my own Ogle sketchbook. As for bedtime stories, those were precious moments. I can still remember lying next to Nicolas as I read to him, only to realise some time later that I had fallen asleep before he had.

No doubt I repeated some of the mistakes my parents had made in my upbringing, but I was determined that they should at least get a chance to use their creative instincts. I think I was a good playmate for them – when I was there – and I enjoyed imagining toys that they might like and then making them, or having them made. The Ogle model shop was very obliging in this last respect. I remember once Nicole told me, on a Sunday, that she had invited some children round for Tuesday afternoon. I had recently seen a lovely horse-shaped climbing frame in a Scandinavian publication, so I went to the office on Monday morning, sketched it, and gave it to the model shop. By Tuesday afternoon it was ready for the children, beautifully finished with a tail of plaited rope.

I also got their help when, at some point, I came up with another vehicle-cum-walker, more like a bike than a car, with a castor at the front and two wheels at the back. Max liked to use this when we walked together to the village shops. It allowed him to go faster than Nicole could walk, which gave him great satisfaction. I also made a boat, which you could sit in and rock, and as you rocked it moved forward. It wasn't so effective as a method of getting about, but it seemed to give a lot of pleasure.

People often comment that my children were lucky to have a father who made them such lovely things. But that's just one way of looking at it. A more negative spin would be that I was more in tune with a child's way of thinking than with that of a responsible parent. That, I think, is how Nicole saw it. In terms of family dynamics, the children and I represented the forces of chaos, while she had to represent the forces of order alone. She was a very controlling person, and our joking and messing about at mealtimes used to infuriate her. Once, we were all laughing so much that she threw her soup bowl into the air, soup and all, in rage.

I suppose a better husband, or a better parent, might have seen this as a cue to modify his behaviour. I just saw it as confirmation that Nicole didn't have a sense of humour and, increasingly, would not tolerate insubordination from those around her. If I ever disagreed with her, she would raise her voice; and I, to avoid a shouting match, would give in. This kept the peace but did not make our relationship happier. I retreated into my work and diverted my paternal instincts – and my childish instincts – into imagining toys.

Back then, in the late 1960s, design organisations never touched toys. They left them to the specialist toymakers. Yet the tide was turning: in December 1967 the Design Centre held a small 'Under Fives' exhibition showing innovative designs for toys and nursery furniture – including Nicolas's baby-walker. And I felt sure that there was scope for Ogle to add toy design to its portfolio. I knew that we had the talent, and I was bubbling with ideas. I think it was in 1967 that we made our first toy car. It was a wooden racing car, based on the Lotus 49, with big back wheels and rubber tyres, and transfers that gave it the look of a real car. Part of the beauty of this toy lay in its fidelity to the original: I remembered from my childhood how much I had valued the accuracy of toys such as my Water Line ships, or my beautiful wooden Lysander. But this racing car was also a pleasing design from a technical point of view. The curved outer parts of the body were made as a single turned piece, which was cut in half lengthways so that the middle could be inserted. I don't think many of the big toy manufacturers could have created such an aesthetically pleasing object. Yet children do appreciate toys that are beautifully formed – or so I believed.

In fact, we didn't have much luck with this particular product, which we called the Boystoys racing car. One potential stockist turned it down with the observation that it 'looked like the kind of toy a Hampstead architect might go to bed with'. I replied, 'Why deprive them of that pleasure?' He agreed to stock it. Generally, however, it was a bit of a struggle to manufacture and market it; but we did get help from one unexpected quarter: my mother. I had recently bought her a home in Ashwell. She was no longer working and had little to keep her in London. So now, from her little cottage in the high street, she helped to assemble and package our Boystoys cars. This was extremely helpful: Ogle wasn't really set up for that kind of repeat production. But I think she enjoyed it, too. We made the cars in three colours, and I was quite proud of the packaging, but our marketing was amateurish. We wrote to a few retailers and hoped for the best, or occasionally someone would drive up to London to offer them around. The response was very disappointing. We did eventually sell a reasonable number in Denmark; but the commercial return never really justified all the effort that went into it.

On the other hand, it did give us credibility as a toy designer, and I was sure that it was only a matter of time before this kind of work became part of Ogle's portfolio. I felt confident that I understood toys and children as well as design. Over the coming decade I would make countless playthings for my own children: not just the usual theatrical props (I made many swords) but unique creations which filled them with delight, such as a lovely little wooden desk that I made for Eugenie, with little holes for her yoghurt-pot pen-holders. If someone was asked to make something for a school project, I was delighted to help – sometimes too delighted. Once Josephine's class were given the task of each making a musical instrument. I made her a beautiful pink banjo, with the body made from a biscuit tin and the finger-board in the form of four fingers and a thumb. I was terribly proud of it, but poor Josephine came bottom of the class, because it was obvious that she couldn't possibly have made it herself.

That's the kind of father I was. The truth was, I liked making playthings because I still liked playing myself: I often used to unwind in the evenings by assembling little plastic Airfix models of aircraft. Who could be better qualified to explore new toy ideas with a child's perspective in mind?

Our work on the Chopper brought with it other commissions from Raleigh. Peter Seals was pleased with the work we had done for them and now hoped to get into the market for baby goods. We did designs for prams, pushchairs and swings, and even a toy or two, although none of them got beyond the prototype stage.

We also got some small commissions from ESA, the educational supply company. They were gadgets rather than toys: there was a mini-microscope, for example, or a balance to help you understand equations by you putting different weights on different sides. But they were at least designed for children.

These were just baby steps: the kind of slow, shuffling progress that Nicolas used to make when he first tried using my racing-car baby-walker. Baby steps are better than nothing and, as Nicolas soon proved, can lead on to more exciting things. But what we needed where toy-making was concerned was a giant leap: a game-changing breakthrough.

13

GAME CHANGER

My daughter, Eugenie, playing with
the Marble Run.

WE DIDN'T make a huge amount of money from Marble Run. That was the main flaw in the project. None of us anticipated the scale of its success; and, as a result, neither Christopher Pepper (who agreed the contract) nor I (who signed it off) gave sufficient thought to the need for a long-term global rights deal.

That small detail apart, it was a triumph. I think I may be more proud of this product than of any car I've designed. But there was one other flaw: because it was so successful, I don't have one – or not an original, anyway. You'll have seen the partially assembled version on the table by my front window, partially assembled and ready for visitors young or old to continue the construction process. Many do so, but it's a later edition, and I sometimes think it lacks the pure, brilliant simplicity of the original. We had an original one at home when it first came out, but that's in the V&A now. My daughter Josephine bought another one on eBay – I always look at it enviously when I visit – but they are unobtainable through normal channels. Usually, therefore, when I want to enjoy it, I have to rely on my memory.

Luckily, that's not a problem. My Marble Run means so much to me that I can call every detail of it to mind without reference to a physical example. It is one of my most perfectly resolved designs. What I love about it is that it came from nothing – or almost nothing. It met a hitherto unidentified need; it was beautifully executed; and, as a result, it was spectacularly successful.

Like many of the best ideas, it began with an everyday observation. My sister had given our children a traditional wooden marble run toy – I think it was in early 1969, although it may have been at Christmas 1968. It was a simple wooden device, a bit like an empty picture frame, with three sloping sticks of wood zig-zagging across the space within it, each with a track through which a marble could roll. You dropped a marble in the top and watched it roll down: zig, zag, zig, clatter . . . That was all.

I often watched my children playing with it, and I was struck by the enormous amount of pleasure they seemed to take in it – more than such a tame design really merited. The observation got me thinking. There was clearly something mesmerising about the moving marbles and the clatter they made as they zig-zagged their way down. Yet there was nothing interesting about the route they followed, and nor was there any creative input: you just released the marble and watched. I began to think about how the toy might be improved. Could a more imaginative development of the core concept create a better experience? If so, how? Such questions are the essence of design.

I mulled it over. Every now and then, I would make an exploratory drawing, to free my mind to consider the next step. But these were busy times: the Scimitar GTE and the Chopper, both more or less completed by then, had been just two among many important projects vying for my attention. There were more commissions from Raleigh, for their Dreamtime range of prams and push-chairs; from Carron, whose Concorde bath was launched around the same time as the supersonic passenger jet after which we named it; and from Reliant, for a big project that I will describe in the next chapter. So rolling marbles were not high on my list of priorities. Yet the questions I had posed about my children's marble run continued to fascinate me; and at home, at least, my thoughts kept drifting back to them.

Wouldn't it be better, I asked myself, if the marble zigged and zagged in a more interesting way? What if you could vary the route? What if there was some element of challenge and reward?

Then, suddenly, the answer came to me. What would really transform the game would be to let children build the run themselves. They could build it in different ways, depending on how ambitious or impatient they were feeling. They could still enjoy the sounds and the sights of the marbles rolling down the run, but that would be only part of a much richer satisfaction.

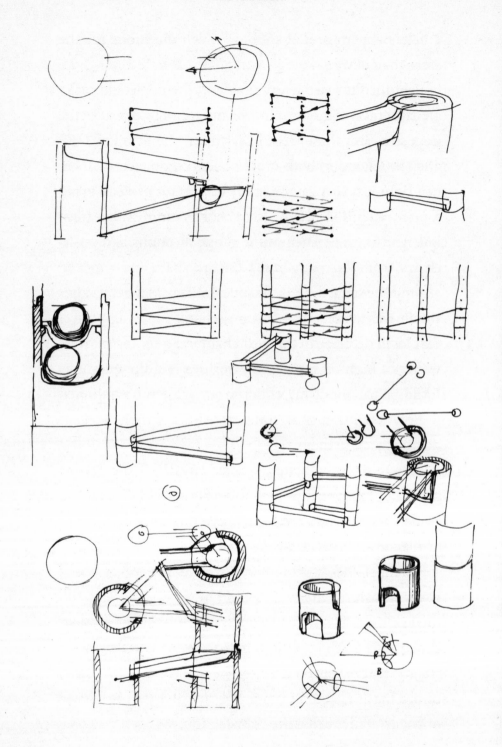

I knew at once that this was a winning idea. I also knew that it would only work if the whole thing was thought through to the tiniest detail. Instead of designing one structure that would work as an entertaining toy, I needed to design something that created a huge range of possibilities, any one of which would be satisfactory in its own right. The toy needed to be rewarding for children of many ages and many different degrees of sophistication. And at every level, in each possible configuration, it needed to work.

In a sense, it was as ambitious as anything I had attempted. At least with a car you only have to design one configuration at a time. But for that very reason I was confident that, if I got it right, my Marble Run would be a brilliant toy.

Now that the challenge was clear in my head, I progressed surprisingly quickly. For a few frantic days – I suppose by now it was late 1969 or early 1970 – I developed my earlier sketches into precisely calculated 3D plans. I decided that I could create the game I wanted with just three kinds of part: bridges (straight sections of gutter-like channel), which could be linked at different angles; spacers (short cylinders), for adding height; and hoppers (in which marbles could collect), which were mainly for the start and finish but could also be used in between. I also imagined other components, such as curved bridges, but it seemed best to keep things simple at this stage. The game we finally made would include just 22 pieces: ten bridges, eight spacers and four hoppers. Players could construct from them any kind of structure they wanted, weaving and winding in three dimensions like mad plumbing systems. And then they could watch the 'runs' they had envisioned being turned into reality by rolling marbles – a set of which would also be included in the game. Players still got the pleasure of watching the marbles roll and hearing that satisfying clunk as they reached the bottom. But the pleasure was deepened by the knowledge that the structure was their own creation. And because you could build a new structure each time, there was no limit to the number of times you could enjoy playing it.

By the spring of 1970 my design was ready to be shared with Ogle's model shop. Looking back at my sketch today, I am fascinated by its quality. Every last detail is already fully thought through. I'm not sure that there's a single feature of the finished product that isn't already in this design. It was all there, in my head.

Stranger still, this very complex concept resolved itself at one of the busiest periods of my entire career. That tells you something about my state of my mind. This was my purplest patch: a phase of my life from the late 1960s to the early 1970s when I overflowed with creativity. Everything was at an optimal point: my age, my energy, my experience, my team at Ogle, and the range of opportunities our previous successes had opened up for us. Ideas kept occurring to me. The only thing limiting the flow was the finite number of hours in each day.

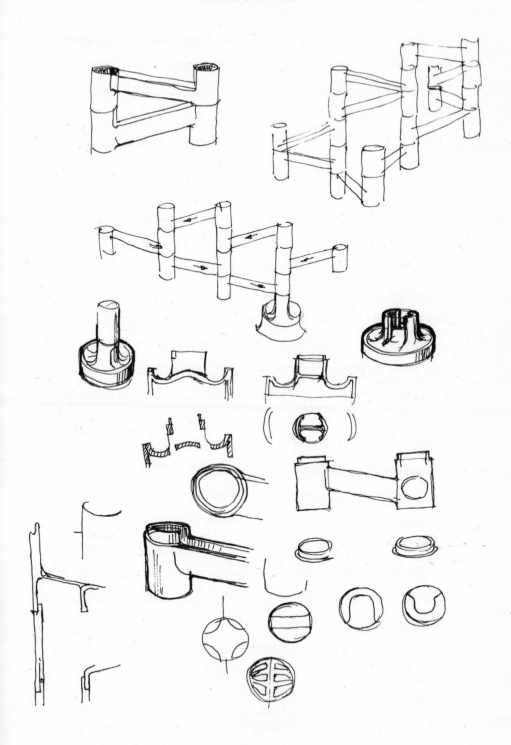

Like many people who work obsessively to become the best in a creative (or sporting) field, I found that the harder I worked, the luckier I became. The stroke of good fortune with my Marble Run was the fact that, when I got our model shop to realise my design in three dimensions, that wasn't the end of the story. The model makers made a gorgeous prototype, with beautiful details and all the right colours. We tested it and it all worked perfectly.

Then, at around the same time, I was approached by one of the directors of Lines Brothers, the famous toy manufacturer. The company was struggling and would soon call in the receivers, so one of the directors, David Lewis, was looking for new sources of income. He asked if we had any products that he could market on our behalf. I asked him to see what he could do with our Marble Run – and soon afterwards he sold it to Kiddicraft, who marketed it with huge success as Builda Helta Skelta.

I think our royalty, for this and any other toys he sold on our behalf, was set at 5 per cent – in the UK. This seemed fairly generous: before long the Marble Run was earning Ogle up to £5,000 a year – a significant sum in those days. Yet if I had stopped to think more carefully about the future, or about how successful the Marble Run might ultimately become, I would have insisted on a harder bargain and a tighter contract. But we didn't really consider the possibility of wider sales – or, crucially, that Kiddicraft might one day be taken over, as it was in 1977, by Hestair. I was just delighted that one of my toy designs

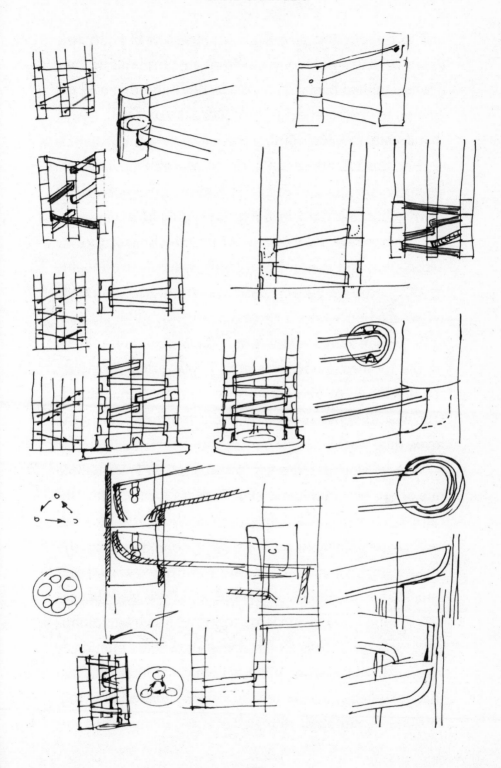

was to be sold and properly marketed. David Ogle had dreamed of using his company to create cars; I shared that dream and had begun to realise it. But I also dreamed of using it to create products for children to play with. Now that dream, too, was coming true.

My direct involvement with the Marble Run stopped as soon as we sold the design, but thereafter we worked on many other children's products, for Kiddicraft and others. For example: we did work for Airfix, which made model aeroplanes, and then for Meccano (which Airfix bought in 1971). The simplified plastic version of Meccano that we worked on wasn't a success, but I was quite pleased with the new range of steel toys – the Mogul range – that we did for them a few years later. We launched Mogul at the Brighton Toy Fair with a special promotional model that was 13 times the size of the actual toys; the press loved this.

As our work for the toy industry grew, I persuaded one of our best designers, John Pape, to focus on toys to the exclusion of all else. He grumbled about this, because he was very talented and was capable of doing many other things as well. His real enthusiasm was cars. But he knuckled down and did as I asked, and I was glad that he did. We did a lot of good work together. Much later, John left to work as a designer for one of the big toy manufacturers. He did well for himself financially but I suspect that he sometimes regretted the fact that, instead of trying to create beautiful playthings that could be cherished for a lifetime, he was designing mass-produced plastic toys that would be thrown away after just a few weeks of use.

At Ogle, meanwhile, we continued quite successfully without him. Growing commitments in other areas, notably heavy goods vehicles, diverted our focus from toy-making, but I continued to explore new ideas for toys and other products for children. My sketchbooks from the 1970s include drawings of rockets, rattles, rocking horses, rocking boats, box puzzles, a cot, a slide, toy animals, cars; and hard-to-describe creations such as the toy that I called a 'Wobbly'. Many never left my sketchbooks; a few were sold as products. Some got as far as our home but no further: for example, the rocking boat mentioned in the previous chapter; and also a beautiful cot that I had made for our third child, Max. This cot was an elegant wooden creation, mostly in a mild orange colour, with lovely lines and soft corners. A string of cubes hung from it, spelling out the word 'MAX'. Max still has the cot, and his own children have slept in it, too.

Having children – and grandchildren – has always been a big motivation for me when designing toys. There are few things more exciting than creating a plaything with a particular child in mind, imagining how they will react to it, then watching them actually do so and learning from their feedback. Yet I think I would still have wanted to make toys even if I had never had children. There is something about creating objects for play that is purer than most kinds of design. There are none of the functional constraints imposed by a car or an aeroplane or a washing machine. You are simply trying to give physical form to an idea: the idea of an act of play, from make-believe to experimentation to competition. And because children have few preconceptions, they are more likely to approach unfamiliar propositions with an open mind. In this sense, they are ideal 'clients'.

In practice, unfortunately, it is hard to design toys commercially without first marketing them to adults, whose minds are rarely as open as a child's. I found this repeatedly during Ogle's peak toy-making years, and I still find it today (because even now I sometimes come up with new ideas and suggest them to people). For example, I once tried to talk Airfix into doing toys with more obvious appeal for girls – or, rather, for children of either gender who weren't interested in military hardware. I even mocked up models of some royal jewellery that I'd seen at the Tower of London. But they couldn't make that leap of imagination; and nor could Matchbox, when I made a similar proposal to them. Matchbox were great at the one thing they did well, which was die-casting. Everything else was guesswork and luck, which is why the business eventually ran into trouble.

Of course, resistance to new ideas isn't confined to the toy industry. But for some reason I find such narrow-mindedness more frustrating when it relates to toys. Children play to explore the world. Why should their horizons be limited just because some marketing executives have decided that there is nothing else worth exploring?

Even today, in retirement, I'm constantly making a nuisance of myself with the toy industry. One of my bugbears is that many of the toys my grandchildren play with don't seem to have been made with actual play in mind. A toy car might be beautifully die-cast on top, but the working mechanisms beneath are typically made of the flimsiest plastic. They're constantly breaking, which is so frustrating for the child, and even I sometimes struggle to repair them. I've contacted several big toymakers since I retired, offering ideas and advice, but as far as they're concerned I'm just a random member of the public. They don't remember the days when Ogle was Britain's most talked-about design consultancy, and some of them don't even remember the Marble Run.

This seems a major oversight on their part. Marble Run has a lasting quality – a classic quality – that very few toys have. Even when Hestair Kiddicraft, as the company became following its takeover, started bringing out updated and expanded editions, the core concept remained the same – even in the version with 60 pieces. The toy was what you made it. How you used it was unique to you, and you could carry on doing things with it for as long as you liked. This made it a classic. It had depth and integrity; and, in contrast to some designs, it wasn't trying to imitate anything. In the half a century since its creation, I have heard from countless adults who played with my Marble Run as children and kept it for their own children. In some cases, the toy is already being enjoyed by a third generation. How many toys can boast that kind of classic status?

One of its secrets, I think, is the fact that – like other successful products I have designed for children, including the Chopper – it respects the user. Millions of children around the world have enjoyed playing with the Marble Run. What more can one hope for? Many toys today often seem to be designed with the adults who will pay for them in mind rather than the children who will play with them. It's all about profit and packaging – no one is thinking about how much lasting satisfaction the child will get from it. Even the Marble Run has been messed around with in recent years.

From the toy industry's point of view, that's normal; perhaps even desirable. If children have had enough of one toy, they can discard it and hope that someone buys them something else. For the toy maker who makes things with love, that's a failure. The best toys aren't necessarily those that make the biggest profits (although Kiddicraft and Hestair did extremely well from Marble Run, as did Ogle, for a while). They're the ones that are also used with love – the kind of thing you'd select if you were woken in the night and told to choose one favourite toy to take with you before fleeing for your life with your family.

I like to think that, for many people, the Marble Run has been that kind of toy. It is a gift that keeps on giving. And that means far more to me than the fact that we should have negotiated a more lucrative contract.

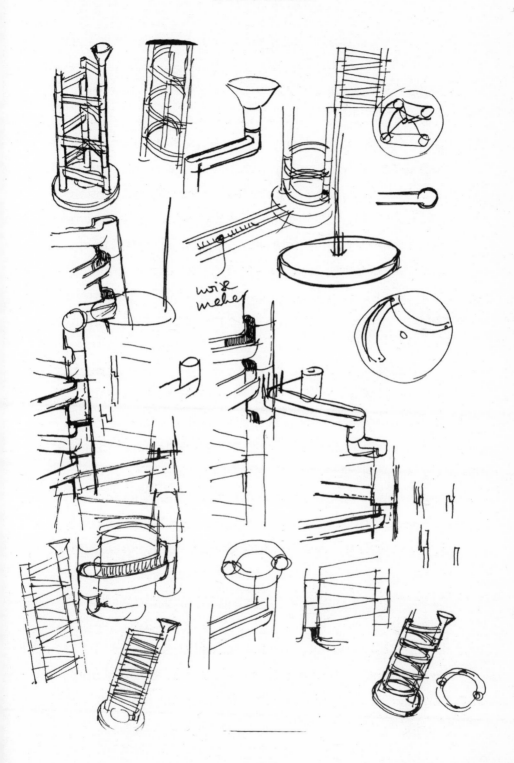

14

TANGERINE DREAM

THE LOW table in my front room is actually a display cabinet. Its glass top covers a whole car park of model cars. There are nearly 40 of them. Most are die-cast, but some are clay models made by me. Few are bigger than a matchbox. All are based on actual cars with a special place in my life – which usually means that I designed them. In most cases, each design features just once – but there are three Bond Bugs. That's a fair reflection of what it means to me.

It's always the Bugs that claim your attention. That's partly because two of them are orange (the third is pewter); but it's mainly because of their distinctive form. The wedge-shaped car is instantly recognisable, even in miniature, and its deceptively simple form repays close attention.

I love it. Look more closely at those two orange Bugs (which are worth about £200 each), and you'll notice how the paint has been rubbed away in places by repeated handling. Much of the wear and tear has been inflicted by enthusiastic visitors, who like to open the canopies by pressing the button at the back, but much has been inflicted by me. I never tire of handling them. Commercially, the

Bond Bug was a commercial flop, but it came from my heart, and I think of it as one of my biggest achievements.

It was the fruit of a dream-like episode, right in the middle of a creative purple patch, when I was, in effect, commissioned to design the car I had always wanted to make. Most car designers dream of creating a high-performance sports car. My dream was to make a fun vehicle that I could imagine driving as a child. Most designers never get a chance to make their dream a reality. I did. I realised what a privilege this was and relished every moment.

I was given the commission in 1969. The vision with which I fulfilled it was years older than that. Ever since my first attempts at car design, I had wanted to create a sporty, two-seater, three-wheeler that applied top-of-the-range design values to a minimalist vehicle. Even my humble Vimp was inspired by this vision; so, more loosely, was my (four-wheeled) Rascal that won the IBCAM prize in 1958. Then the vision evolved: my sporty two-seater was also a three-wheeler. Go back through my sketchbooks for the 1960s and you'll find very few in which there isn't at least a sketch or two in which that basic concept can be discerned – usually in the form of a three-wheeler. Many are little more than doodles when I was supposed to be working on something else; some had a more specific purpose. Between them they meant that, when my big chance came, I was ready.

The crucial development came in February 1969 when Reliant took over Bond Cars Ltd, makers of a series of three-wheeled Minicars and Reliant's chief rival in the microcar market. A few months later, Ray Wiggin told Ogle that Reliant needed a new product with which they could make their mark on Bond. They didn't want it to be expensive to manufacture, just stylish enough to find itself a place in more fashionable dealership networks than Reliant could usually reach: in short, a microcar with real panache. The challenge was design heaven – or my idea of design heaven, anyway – because the obvious answer was precisely that sporty three-wheeler that I had been nurturing in my heart for years.

In fact, I had been doing more than nurturing the concept. I had been trying quite hard to turn it into reality – ever since we started working for Reliant in 1963. I had been floating my idea for six years by then and I had made drawings of four different versions. I had had a couple of one-eighth-scale models made. Reliant had rejected all of these: they considered my thinking too crazy for the no-frills market they were aiming at. But when they bought Bond they asked us to build a prototype.

Their acquisition of Bond put the whole idea in a different light. Reliant badly needed a new model for Bond and my vision of a three-wheeled sports car suddenly began to feel like an idea whose time had come.

Reliant gave us the go-ahead to make a three-wheel two-seater and provided a chassis. My aim was to create a body that was a model of simplicity, cheap and easy to produce, with a character that caught the free spirit of late 1960s counter-culture.

The earlier designs from which I started were all quite different from one another, but they did share certain key details: a three-wheeled chassis; a simple body, using the smallest possible number of fibreglass shells; a strong roll cage; and a chopped-off back that exposed the back axle and suspension.

The joy of these forms came from simplicity. Reliant's usual method of fibreglass body construction required complicated moulds which needed to be endlessly bolted and unbolted during manufacture. My proposed shapes not only minimised the number of moulds required but allowed the shells to be made without undercuts. The main body shell extended all the way from front to back and included the floor, seats and roll bar that could be lifted straight out of a mould. The canopy had an inner and outer shell. The only other shell was the 'skirt' for the lower body and the engine cover. Reliant had never done anything as simple and elegant.

Simplicity – and thus affordability – was the theme throughout. Wherever possible, we would use existing Reliant components, such as an all-alloy 701cc engine, which came from the Regal. The chassis was designed by John Crosthwaite. It was a shortened version of the

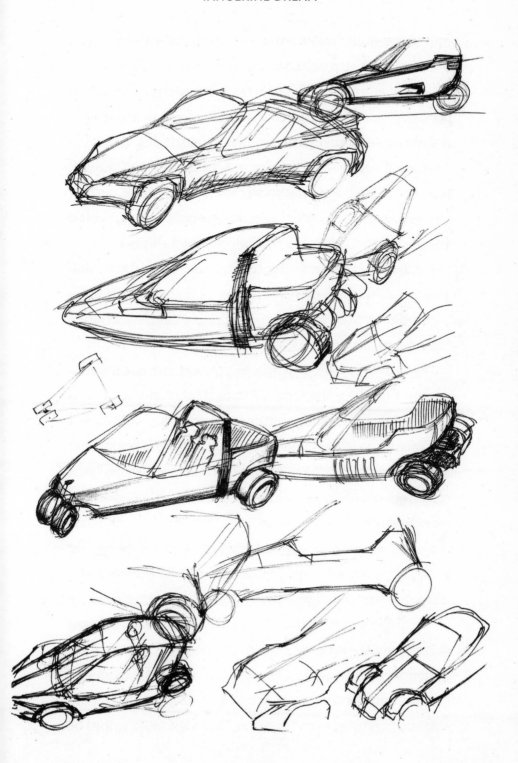

one that would later be used in the Reliant Robin, with one wheel at the front and two at the back. (Many people feel safer with the wheels the other way round, but this configuration was a given.) The chassis was fitted with a revised rear suspension set-up, which improved its cornering ability – fairly essential if we wanted to present our new model as being 'sporty'.

I was convinced that, starting from this base, I could create a car that perfectly fitted the bill for the Bond project. It is hard to exaggerate the warm surge of gratitude that a designer feels at such moments. Brilliant design ideas count for nothing without the executive courage to make them happen.

Now it was down to me to convert my dream into reality. Using the chassis as a starting point, we developed the 'package' by mocking it up in wood. We worked out the relationship between all the mechanical components and the driver and the passenger. For the prototype, I had already decided on a basic wedge shape, with a sharply cut rear. I wanted to expose the 'guts' at the back – the rear axle and suspension – and decided to paint them bright red to accentuate the effect. But the cut-off rear was also desirable for aerodynamic reasons, helping the car to run straight in a crosswind. A long tail would have been better from the point of view of drag, but that would have added weight and cost. The chassis had a low centre of gravity, and the fibreglass body I had in mind for it, with soft roof and side screens, would keep it low; it would be near the rear, too, thanks to the relatively backward positioning of the driver and passenger. All this would make it very stable when cornering. Small (10in) wheels, widely spaced at the rear, added to the stability.

It took no time to work out the remaining details, which was just as well, because the work had to be fitted into a working day that was already overflowing. In addition to developing the Chopper and the Marble Run, we were doing big projects for Plaxton (the Panorama Elite coach), Bush (the TR162 radio) and Electrolux (assorted domestic appliances). In contrast to my years as a young stress-tester in Luton, I never became ill. I barely even seemed to get tired: the work consumed me. The more challenges we faced, the happier I felt.

Nicole may have felt differently. By early 1970, when the bulk of my work on the Bond commission was done, we had three children under the age of three. They were cared for almost exclusively by Nicole (sometimes helped by an au pair); and she was also pregnant with our fourth child, Eugenie. I take no pride in this imbalance, although such divisions of responsibility were not unusual in those days. Yet I don't think it was as disastrous as it sounds. Nicole was far more practical than me, except where things like DIY and household appliances were concerned, and she always liked things to be done in the way that she wanted. She was a brilliant cook, took great care to ensure that the children were always beautifully dressed, and had a strong sense of what the inside of our house should look like. Any attempt by me to contribute in such areas would have been seen as unwelcome interference, and she obviously felt undermined by my preference for playing with the children rather than coping with other duties. Much of the time, therefore, she was glad to have me out of the way: the cottage felt crowded enough without me. Yet my constant absences cannot have helped our relationship, and Nicole sometimes made it clear, quite forcibly, that she was not content.

In my sketchbooks, designs for cars, coaches and radios are punctuated by occasional tentative plans for extending our cottage at the back. The very fact that such matters were intruding on my thoughts at such an exciting time for my work tells you something about the urgency of the problem. Even I conceded that we needed to do something to relieve the pressure on Nicole. But there were always other things on my mind that seemed more pressing (although I did at one point find time to build a shelter for our car). So Nicole struggled on and our marriage began to wither, while Ogle thrived.

If I did contribute anything to our family at this time – beyond my salary and a useful range of objects that Ogle had designed – it was the spirit of exuberant creativity that was simultaneously powering my work. I did not want my children to miss out on stimulation in the same ways that I had done. So when I did play with them, or read to them or draw pictures with them, or when I changed nappies or bathed them, I was at least intently involved: curious about their responses and seeing the world through their eyes. I wish I had found more time for fatherhood. Now that I am a grandfather, I realise that I could have been a very good father. Instead, all I can say is that I am, I think, a very good grandfather.

For work, on the other hand, I was always able to find as much time as was necessary – and, as a result, I feel satisfied that I became the best designer I could be. This was especially true for the Bond Bug, for which I left nothing to chance: this opportunity was too good to miss.

By the end of 1968 we had built the prototype. I called it 'Rascal', in fond memory of my award-winning design from my Ford days. (Others later referred to it as the 'Rogue'.) When Reliant saw it, they liked what they saw but suggested some modifications. We were asked to get rid of the retractable headlamps, which were replaced by fixed, rectangular ones; and we replaced the open luggage compartment at the back with a closable, lockable one. The NACA air intake, which owed much to my aircraft days, enhanced the sporty appearance. The body was widened at the front and the roof slightly raised to increase passenger comfort. And, crucially, we replaced the soft top and side screens with a single solid canopy, comprising both windscreen and roof and slots for soft, detachable sides. The canopy was hinged at the front: to get in and out, you lifted it, assisted by a pneumatic gas strut that held it open. It was a bit like my original Rascal a decade or so earlier, but felt much more like the cockpit of an aeroplane. A steel tube reinforced the roll bar, which was part of the main body. The detachable sides provided an easy escape route if the driver happened to roll the car over. I was very conscious of the need for this: when I rolled my Ogle Mini, I was only just able to get out through the one door that was still working.

All these adjustments made the moulding a little more complicated, but not enough to undermine the overall concept. Some designers felt strongly that we needed a curved windscreen, and I was nearly persuaded but I stuck with my flat one, which was much cheaper as well as looking more distinctive. A second prototype was made, and everyone seemed happy. We made a few final tweaks, of which the most significant was the addition of a boot. I preferred the dramatic, cut-away rear end – but it was hard to argue with Reliant's logic. The boot made the car look less like a racing car but also less wildly impractical.

Colours were discussed in a meeting at Reliant and I proposed that all should be the same colour. I was much happier when I got the go-ahead for my choice of colour: a bright, cheeky, tangerine orange colour that caught the car's character perfectly. I was determined that every car should be the same colour, and we all agreed that my original choice of green wasn't right. In addition to being distinctive, this particular shade of orange retained its brightness when dirty – important for a tiny car that needed to make itself visible.

Reliant then came up with the perfect name: the Bug. Initially, they tried to put this on the front in the form of a plastic badge, but I managed to stop them. Instead, we designed bold decals – then barely used on cars but common on trucks and in the aviation industry – and developed special Bug lettering for the sides and front. The decals added to the sense that you were looking not at a car but at the front end of an aircraft; but the graphic, by Mike Walker, also hinted at the ethos of an album cover – perfectly capturing the free, youthful spirit of the psychedelic age into which it was about to be released.

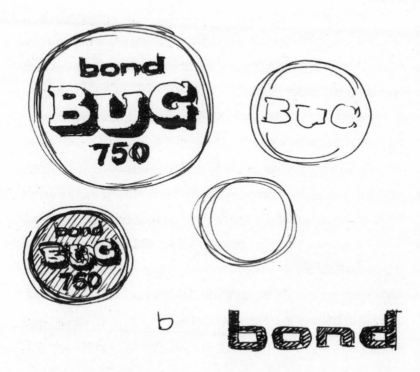

In fact, the design was striking enough even without the lettering, and at Ogle there was palpable excitement about it. When the prototype went off for its first outing to be photographed, it was accompanied by a whole team of our people, all wanting to have a go at driving it. I left them to it. I think that by this point I was starting to feel that I had achieved what I had set out to achieve.

A few key motoring journalists were lent Bugs to test-drive before the launch – with all the branding taped over to keep the vehicles' identity secret. They were repeatedly pestered and gawped at by curious passers-by when they stopped at traffic lights. We began to realise quite how remarkable a car we had created. This was design with the 'Wow!' factor.

The Bug was launched in June 1970, in the grounds of Woburn Abbey in Bedfordshire. Journalists were invited to test-drive a whole fleet of identical orange Bugs, which we lined up in front of the stately home as if they were a formation of Red Arrows. Several hacks got carried away by the fun atmosphere. One, *TAB* magazine's Stuart Marshall, turned his over. It rolled back onto its wheels and he was unharmed. (It turned out that the Bugs that were rolled over had a tendency to right themselves.)

The subsequent write-ups were enthusiastic. *Motor* magazine called it 'fast, safe and above all fun'. The 'fast' was open to question, but the design had done its work. The journalists had enjoyed their day out, and their reviews reflected this. The initial public response was similarly enthusiastic. The Bug's obvious practical limitations didn't bother people. It looked like a supercar, even if it didn't drive like one. Not since the first Minis had a car on British roads turned so many heads.

It continued to do so long after its launch, making headlines and winning hearts. I wince when I look today at an early advertising campaign that claimed: 'There's never been a car like this for pulling the birds . . .' – but I suspect that some Bug owners thought in such terms. They loved their car, and they felt that it expressed their personalities in ways that pleased them – just like a Lamborghini, at a tiny fraction of the price. One enthusiast described it as 'like your own private aircraft' – which couldn't have been further from the truth in terms of performance, but which caught well the sense of adventure that many people felt when they sat in one.

Three versions of the Bond Bug went on sale: the 700, the 700E and the 700ES super-Bug. Prices ranged from £548 to £629. The £548 version, with a fixed canopy and no doors, didn't attract much interest. The £579 version had a heater and a canopy that actually opened. Most buyers preferred to spend £629 on a version with opening top, detachable side screens (which could be stowed in the expanded boot), a leather-covered 'Formula 1' steering wheel, twin horns and a high-compression engine that delivered marginally more power than the other models (31bhp compared with 29bhp). If you were going to buy into the dream, you might as well go for the full Bond Bug experience.

Sadly, for all the initial excitement it generated, the Bug didn't persuade enough people to shell out what were still relatively substantial sums of money. Production – divided between Reliant's factory in Tamworth and Bond's in Preston – was slow and hampered by quality problems and industrial disputes. As a result, the spectacular success of the launch was undermined by the fact that, at that point, there were only 350 Bugs available to buy. By the time more came on stream, the summer was over and the Bug's sunny charms felt easier to resist. It was not a total disaster, commercially, but it was certainly a disappointment; I don't think dealers really appreciated what it was that they were selling. Reliant terminated production in 1974, by which time only 2,268 had been made.

In terms of sales, the Reliant Robin, on which I worked before and after its launch in 1973, was a much more successful product. But the Robin was never memorable in design terms. The Bond Bug was a celebration of the joy of three-wheeled design relative to the more conventional wheel-at-each-corner approach. ('For those too young to be square' was how one early sales slogan expressed this.) The Reliant Robin merely took the economic logic of the three-wheeled microcar to its ultimate conclusion. It didn't fill you with excitement each time you took the wheel. We remember it as the butt of jokes, not an object of desire.

The Bug, by contrast, never stopped generating a buzz. The comedian Bob Monkhouse (who drove one) presented one as a star prize on his TV game show, *The Golden Shot*.

Jersey Ice Cream used one as a publicity vehicle; Fine Fare supermarkets held a 'How-many-bottles-of-cider-can-you-fit-in-a-Bug?' competition; Rothmans cigarettes commissioned a six-strong fleet of white ones; a Hong Kong manufacturer started selling models of it, and Corgi later produced a 1:43 die-cast version. Later still (as we shall see in a later chapter), the 'Landspeeder' that Luke Skywalker drove in *Star Wars* would use a Bond Bug chassis, with angled mirrors beneath to make it look as though it was floating without wheels. The market may not have embraced the Bug, but it certainly struck a chord culturally.

Perhaps that's one reason why I'm so fond of the Bond Bug. The people who bought it somehow intuitively absorbed what I had put into it. They weren't just satisfied with it, they loved it. Of those 2,268 models, more than half were still registered, decades later, with the Bug Club (of which I am proud to be an honorary member). Through the club, owners have been traced in 17 different countries, on four continents – all pleased enough with their purchase to be enthusiasts.

We never actually owned a Bond Bug, although Ogle did and I did sometimes drive it. I was happy with my Reliant Scimitar GTE, and the Bug was neither a performance car nor a family one. It wasn't even especially comfortable for a single driver: I remember driving it 90 miles to Norwich for a television programme and arriving with my bottom a bit numb.

Yet for all its limitations, and for all its failings as a commercial proposition, I think of the Bug as a resounding success: the opposite, if you like, of the Chopper, which was a commercial triumph but had taken its lead from another. The Bond Bug was a classic: a timeless creation that reconciled dream with reality, embodying in three dimensions a cheerful, optimistic, free-thinking outlook on life – qualities that it still projects today.

There aren't many products of which you can say that. And it is certainly not often that you can get away with creating something that still turns heads after 50 years.

15

FIFTIETH
PERCENTILE MAN

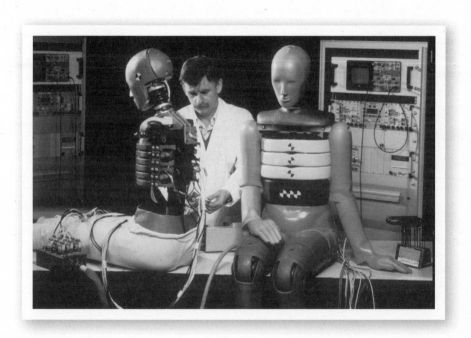

THERE ARE no crash test dummies in my house today. Most people wouldn't feel the need to point this out. I do. There was a time in the 1970s when the Occupant Protection Assessment Test (OPAT) Dummy was one of the products most closely associated with Ogle, and at one point in that period we briefly had one at home.

It left years ago: a development I do not regret. When you're 94 and live alone, you find yourself being visited by many strangers: carers, nurses, children, concerned neighbours. There are already quite enough strange objects here for them to get their heads around. If they saw me sharing my home with a disconcertingly realistic replica human as well, the strangeness might make them uncomfortable.

But the role of crash test dummies in my life was significant – even though my creative contribution to their development was limited. Indeed, they became so emblematic of Ogle's work, and so central to our fortunes, that I can hardly leave them out of my story.

They came into my life by a stroke of luck – although as usual it was the kind of luck that you have to make for yourself. I went to a seminar at the headquarters of the Motor Industry Research Association (MIRA) in Nuneaton. It think it must have been in late 1966. It was hard to find time for such things, but I felt that it was important to keep abreast of developments in the industries we served, and this one more than justified the effort. Its theme was motor industry safety standards, and its specific focus was on the dummies used in vehicle safety testing. In those days – I learnt – the dummies used in such testing (developed in the US by Alderson Research Laboratories or Sierra Engineering) were so different from real human beings that relatively little could be learnt from them. Could a satisfactory alternative be developed? In the course of the discussion it emerged that Ford and General Motors, both of whom had representatives at the seminar, were each separately funding the development of their own crash test dummy. It struck me that there was an opportunity here. At some point, an independent body would need to endorse a standard dummy for the whole industry, and someone would need to design and make it. Neither Ford nor General Motors would want to rely on the other's dummy, and nor would most other manufacturers. What if Ogle were to develop a standard international dummy?

I did some exploring and found that others had had the same thought. Indeed, Ford and General Motors were already beginning the process of merging their research programmes, under the supervision of The National Bureau of Standards in Washington DC. I almost gave up. But the idea intrigued me, and I wondered if there might be scope for pursuing a parallel project in Europe, or at least in the UK.

It was a fascinating field. Researchers had been attempting to develop reliable dummies in the US since the late 1940s, much of it in a military or aviation context, but the dummies produced so far lacked 'bio-fidelity'. In all sorts of important ways, they were unlike real humans: their weight was distributed in different ways, their joints moved differently. For accurate testing it was better to use a real human corpse, as US motor manufacturers some-times did. But there were obvious drawbacks, ethical and practical, to that kind of research. Hence the urgent need for a more sophisticated artificial dummy: one that was designed with experimentation in mind, but that resem-bled a human being more closely than anything that had gone before.

It felt like the sort of challenge that could bring out the best in Ogle. We already had what was arguably the UK's best model shop, and a lot of the necessary technical data was already in the public domain. I asked Anthony Smallhorn to take charge of the project. Anthony was a doctor's son and had already carried out a project to develop the specification for an emergency ambulance. He seemed like the right person for the job. But he then left the company to work independently, and so I handed responsibility to one of our bright engineers, Peter Warner, to see how far he could take the idea.

The model shop made various experiments with materials and techniques. It was starting to look quite promising. Then, in 1968, MIRA published a report expressing dissatisfaction with the standard crash test dummies that were starting to come into use in the US. It observed a marked and consistent discrepancy between the 'injuries' received by the dummies in tests and the actual injuries suffered by real-life crash victims, and it did not want the resulting safety standards to regulate British manufacturers. Instead, it would prefer to develop its own, British programme.

For a moment this sounded like the death knell for Ogle's dummy programme: how could we compete with a research body which had the resources of the entire British motor industry behind it? Then I realised that there was a more positive way of looking at it. Why did we have to compete?

Somehow, we were able to persuade MIRA to collaborate with Ogle, and over the next couple of years Peter Warner developed a strong relationship with them. Eventually, in 1970, MIRA and Ogle signed a joint contract with the UK's Transport and Road Research Laboratory (TRRL) to produce test dummies for use in its Vehicle Occupant Test Programmes. Given all the other big projects we were doing that year, investing resources in such a speculative venture was quite a gamble. Yet something told me that the investment would pay off. Peter was joined by another of our brightest people, an engineer-turned-designer called

Roger Mills, and for the rest of the year our dummies team worked diligently and discreetly to build a testing mannequin more sophisticated than anything that had gone before.

In early 1971, M50/71 came into the world. The name indicated that, in size and weight, the dummy represented the 50th percentile adult male in 1971. It weighed 165lb, with the weight distributed in the same way as in a real human. Its basic phosphor bronze and aluminium frame was fitted with polyurethane 'muscles' and 'fat' and enclosed in a blue PVC 'skin'. The colour was chosen to make it easy to film in crash simulations. Its joints could bend in exactly the same way as human joints; it had a humanlike clavicle and floating scapula; its ribcage mimicked a human ribcage in shape and in the way it collapsed under violent frontal impact. It could fold its arms, sit in a chair with legs crossed or uncrossed, stand, sit on the ground in the lotus position and even, crucially, shrug its shoulders – an essential attribute for tests involving lap–shoulder safety belts. The shoulders were among several parts that we patented. The dummy was also equipped with sensors at various key points, to measure deceleration, load and impact. And despite the violence to which it was subjected, the M50/71 dummy offered remarkably good 'repeatability'. You could dust it down, reset it, repair or replace any damaged parts and put it through test after test.

It proved an almost instant success. I don't mean that it became a bestseller: it didn't. I think we sold about 15 in the first 16 months, for £2,250 each, to motor manufacturers around the world. But the effect on Ogle's image was dramatic. News of the dummies spread quickly beyond the specialised world of car safety-testing, thanks to something that we had barely noticed: M50/71 wasn't just sophisticated; it had a haunting beauty to it. Even though it was little more than an artificial skeleton, it had a very human bearing, perhaps because weight distribution and joint movements so exactly replicated those of a human being. Sometimes it looked almost alive. Even its blank face seemed somehow benign. Journalists were fascinated by this. In the words of the celebrated architectural critic Reyner Banham, 'It can do such neat and human things that it can only be read as friendly.'

Banham's article was particularly influential. Published in *New Society* magazine in January 1972, it argued that the dummy embodied design in its ideal sense: 'humane, moral, British, functional and beautiful'. On the one hand, he argued, they satisfied 'a real human need'; on the other, he speculated that 'by producing something exquisitely adapted to its function' Ogle might have 'satisfied one of the Platonic canons of beauty'. With hindsight, this article could be seen as a landmark in the British public's relationship with design. This may have been the first piece of modern journalism – the first since John Ruskin and William Morris – to treat industrial design as an art form in its own right, and to write about it in the airy terms favoured by art critics. Banham compared our dummies to the sculptures of Jacob Epstein, George Segal and Marino Marini; to the paintings of Richard Hamilton; to the writings of Isaac Asimov. He wondered whether London's Tate or New York's Museum of Modern Art would be first to acquire one as an exhibit. Crucially, he emphasised Ogle's role in the project, praising our initiative in undertaking such public-spirited work without government grants and suggesting that I had built the company up into 'something very like the ideal picture of an industrial design office: a free-ranging combination of inventiveness, craftsmanship and vision that can turn its hand to anything'.

I would never have dared to brag about my company in such terms, yet Banham's words did come close to encapsulating my aspirations for Ogle. We weren't just a place that produced clever car designs, or bicycle designs, or toy designs. We were Designers, with a capital D.

We were also firmly established, from this point on, as the go-to company for dummy-making. In August 1973, TRRL awarded us a £21,000 contract (a big sum in those days) to develop a new anthropometric dummy that could be used as a standard testing device for all new cars. Our original M50/71 dummy was considered too sophisticated for this – it required very precise care to be set up properly for tests. The new one would be capable of being used by any manufacturer in the world, and would, we hoped, become an international standard for regulatory testing.

The OPAT dummy was launched in 1974 and made headlines all over the world. Unlike the M50/71, it resembled a mannequin, not a skeleton, which allowed much more realistic replication of the movements of a human driver or passenger in a crash situation. (This was particularly important in relation to seat belts.) As a result, it appeared even more humanlike than its predecessor. Photographers and editors were quick to see its visual potential: several newspapers published pictures showing dummies posed in seeming interaction with attractive young women. Other poses included: waiting to cross the road; sitting, clothed and seemingly alert, at the steering wheel; riding a motorbike; sitting in an office chair; strapped into a MIRA testing unit; or perched on Ogle's reception desk. Groups of dummies proved particularly photogenic: side by side on a bench, for example; or sitting in a crowd like a latter-day Terracotta Army. As the word spread, the orders and enquiries poured in, both from Europe (on both sides of the Iron Curtain) and from Asia.

In fact, later that year, the OPAT dummy lost out to the US-made Hybrid II as the international standard dummy for regulatory testing, which was disappointing commercially. But OPAT was so good that many manufacturers decided to use it anyway, for their own research. For regulatory compliance, the most important quality in a dummy is repeatability: you need a simple model that will always behave in exactly the same way in a small number of specifically defined situations. For research, on the other hand, versatility and sophistication are what matter. A manufacturer might want to test any number of different things – impact from different angles, for example – and for that the Hybrid II was too basic. And so it was that, although it never produced the lucrative global monopoly I had hoped for, our dummies operation nonetheless more than paid its way. Rolls-Royce, Saab and BL all bought dummies from us, and commissioned new ones.

At the same time, the sheer gorgeousness of the OPAT dummy added lustre to Ogle's image as pioneers of pure design. We became increasingly expert in the biomechanics of the human body – for a long time there was a real skeleton in the model shop, borrowed from the Lister Hospital in Hitchin – and in the materials most appropriate to the purpose. Some of the plastics involved were not very pleasant to work with, which led to an opportunity to put Geoff Platten, who had recently joined Ogle as model maker, to take charge of this. Geoff was prepared to deal with the unpopular job of 'cooking' the materials for the dummies. A lot of the soft-tissue work involved polyurethane and was smelly and messy. Geoff made the field his own and, when Peter and Roger moved on to fresh challenges, ended up running our entire dummies operation.

I remember at a board meeting, I was once asked why we persevered with the dummy work, when this was only marginally profitable. I argued that it may not be very profitable but it wasn't losing money either and it was good for Ogle. Dummies of one kind or another would eventually account for almost a quarter of our business. The success of the OPAT dummy spawned more and more spin-off projects: two child dummies (a six-year-old and a ten-year-old, with aluminium rather than steel bones to make them lighter); a pedestrian dummy (to assess impacts from vehicles); even a female dummy. I say 'even' because, in the long term, the female half of the population has been shamefully under-represented in dummies used for safety-testing. Yet Ogle were working on one as early as 1974. I know this because there was a miners' strike at the time, and we were allowed electricity for only three days a week. We employed a local 19-year-old, Sheila Cherry, as a model, and the resulting dummy was generally referred to as 'Miss Bianca'. The default name for the adult male dummy was 'Henry'. (When the afternoon tea trolley was taken around Ogle, there was usually an extra mug for Henry; I don't know if Miss Bianca ever got one, too.)

Later still, we made dummies for maritime research (testing life jackets), for aircraft (testing ejector seats) and for the fire service ('Ogleman' slumped over firemen's shoulders exactly as an unconscious human would). These were often bigger challenges than they sound. One of the ejector seat dummies, for example, required accurately articulated hands, to mimic the way in which pilots grip the controls.

A separate challenging project was to develop a dummy that would float in the water like an unconscious person. This was to develop effective life jackets. It had to have the correct weight, centre of gravity and centre of buoyancy for every part of the body.

We even did a little baby dummy ('Baby Ogle'), with the same enigmatically benign blue face as all the other dummies. I took him home and was surprised to see how much Josephine and Eugenie enjoyed having him. They carried him around and put clothes on him. They also annoyed Nicole by putting him in a Moses basket that she had been keeping plants in. The plants were casually discarded, and the resulting maternal displeasure prompted me to make a wooden cot for him instead.

He didn't stay with us for long – perhaps not even long enough to use my cot. But I don't think any of us forgot him, and, indeed, I shouldn't think anyone at Ogle forgot the crash test dummies. It's no exaggeration to say that they transformed the company. By the time Geoff Platten was running the operation, in the late 1970s, product and transport design accounted for barely half of our revenue. The rest came either from the model shop (roughly one third) or the crash test dummies. Geoff Platten led a team of five technicians and three design engineers who worked exclusively on dummies, and although the increasingly technical nature of the work slowed down profits, it seemed healthy to let them get on with what they did without unnecessary interference from me.

By the late 1980s they had taken crash test dummies to levels of sophistication that had been unimaginable when we started. Among other things, Ogle spent eight years collaborating with various European companies – notably the Dutch firm TNO and the French firm SEREME – to create the Euro Side Impact Dummy ('Euro SID'). The Dutch did the abdomen, the French did the pelvis and neck. Ogle's key contributions were the ribcage and, crucially, the thorax, which had hitherto been considered an insoluble problem. This was important, cutting-edge work, which had to be absolutely right: when Euro SID was launched, in 1987, each one cost £35,000, and the dummy in due course became a standard testing device, used by anyone who wanted to import a car into Europe. Eventually, it all became so specialised and technical that we joined forces with TNO, in 1997, to form a new, separate company, Ogle/TNO Safety Products.

None of this made much difference to me in terms of my day-to-day work. My involvement in the dummies had been minimal for a long time and, indeed, had never been that great in the first place. Yet it wouldn't make sense to try to tell my story without them. M50/71, the OPAT dummy and their successors were wonderful ambassadors for the company I had created, and for the ideas and standards we stood for. Their sophistication and charm cemented our reputation as a centre of rare excellence, increasing the quantity and range of commissions that came our way but also, perhaps more importantly, acting as a magnet for talent. More than ever, the best young designers wanted to work for us. Some, admittedly, used us as a kind of finishing school before moving on to better-paid jobs (for example, designing cars in West Germany); but others stayed for decades. The combined effect was to cement our reputation as a company at the cutting edge of design.

With hindsight, I think I underrated the dummies' importance. I wish I had made more of a song and dance about what we achieved with them. Anyone who wanted to import a car to Europe, from Japan or America or anywhere, had to put it through tests using our dummies. That was quite a big thing to grow from one casual thought I had had at a lecture.

And the fact that you have only to say the words 'crash test dummy' for the same visual image – an Ogle design – to appear in the listener's mind's eye is, again, not an achievement to be sneezed at. Our dummies never made it to the Tate or MoMA, but they did feature in exhibitions at the Design Centre (1979) and the Science Museum (1980). They had a lasting practical and cultural impact, and they also must have saved an awful lot of lives over the years. It would be strange if I didn't take pride in them.

16

BIG BUSINESS

EVEN I wouldn't keep a full-sized lorry at home, although there must be a dozen toy ones scattered around. But we did have a full-sized model of a Dennis RS fire-engine cab in our garden for a while. It offended several of our neighbours. They felt that such a big, bright red object was disturbing the rural peace. I tried to placate them by painting it various shades of green; we even added camouflage. But it still caused grumbling. After a few years we got rid of it – which was easier said than done.

We were in a much bigger house by then: still in Ashwell, but away from the village centre in a secluded lane called Springhead. We left the little cottage in 1975. We had four boisterous children, aged between four and ten, and it couldn't cope. Luckily, we could afford somewhere bigger. Ogle, unlike most of the British economy, was thriving. The new house, Ringstead, was big, draughty and grand: a six-bedroom Victorian manor house with a huge garden. The architecture was handsome, in a slightly ramshackle way, but it wasn't very comfortable. It did give us abundant space, though, especially outdoors, where the children and their friends could play; and where I, when the opportunity arose in 1978, could park a full-sized fire-engine cab for them to play in.

This probably seemed less strange to the Karen family than it did to everyone else in the village. The children were used to playing with things that I had designed and made. They knew all about the extraordinary range of objects that came out of Ogle's model shop, and using them – or getting inside them – was seen as one of the perks of having me as a father. Nor was there anything remarkable about the fact that I had installed a cab at home. The family knew that what got made at Ogle didn't always stay at Ogle. I had been bringing things home from work for years.

If there was any surprise in the Karen household about the sudden appearance of a fire-engine cab in our garden, it probably related to the fact that I was working on such a utilitarian, lorry-like vehicle at all. Most people underestimate the significance of large commercial vehicles in my work, and I don't think my family were any different. There's a preconception that 'design' relates mostly to the refined, luxury aspects of life, not to big, crude vehicles like trucks and lorries. I think this is misguided, and indeed snobbish. Big commercial vehicles are as susceptible to good and bad design as anything else. Given the amount of time their drivers spend in them, and their vital importance to countless aspects of modern life, their design quality is something that really matters. I didn't bring many examples of my commercial vehicle work home: it wasn't very practical, or useful. But to me, my design work on such vehicles was some of the most important I ever did.

We did our first truck work at Ogle back in the late 1960s, when we somehow got the chance to redesign the front end of a dumper truck for Aveling-Barford. I loved doing that. We improved the ergonomics and the look of it and improved visibility for the driver. But our most important contribution was to change the radiator. The old version was very ornate, like a motor car's. But Aveling-Barford weren't capable of pressing thin sheet metal, which meant that they had to get it made, expensively, elsewhere. So I redesigned the front so that you could make the whole lot out of thick steel, which not only looked better but greatly simplified the manufacturing process. We made a full-size model, 12ft high, which ended up at Aveling-Barford, and from that came a lucky break. One of their suppliers saw the model and fell in love with it. His name was Merrick Taylor, and he was managing director of Motor Panels, a Coventry-based company that made cabs for trucks. They were a biggish firm, but their cabs weren't very nice, and seeing our model opened Taylor's eyes to what was missing. If he wanted Motor Panels to succeed – and he was determined that they should overtake their great rivals, GKN – he needed to get a designer involved.

It took a while for the relationship to develop, but in the early 1970s we worked together extensively on a new

Transcontinental lorry cab. This was unveiled at the 1972 Motor Show, as was a separate project – for a sleeper truck cab – that we had done for Seddon Atkinson. Then, in August 1973, we signed a long-term co-operation agreement with Motor Panels, under which Ogle would work with them exclusively on styling projects for commercial vehicle cabs.

From then on we did a lot of work for Motor Panels, all through the 1970s and beyond. We had show cabs at the 1973 and 1974 Motor Shows as well: the last one was called the MPO – with the 'O' standing for Ogle. But the most important project we did together did not bear fruit until the end of the decade – although it began much earlier. British Leyland's Truck & Bus division had been struggling for years with its lorries, as lack of investment allowed foreign competitors to eat into its market. Its best lorry, the Marathon, was a laughing stock: drivers joked that it got its name because it could run for only 26 miles before breaking down. Then a new chief executive, Michael Edwardes, secured massive public investment – the government was Leyland's biggest shareholder – for the most ambitious lorry development programme the UK had ever seen, for a new range of trucks called the T45.

So much was riding on the new vehicle – which Leyland claimed would be 'not simply a new truck, but a whole new way of life' – that a competition was held for the manufacture and design of its cab. I joined forces with

Merrick Taylor to bid for the work. First Motor Panels presented their detailed proposals for the manufacture. This was difficult without any kind of agreed design; nonetheless, they were provisionally awarded the job, in December 1974. Then proposals for the cab's body shape and interior design were considered. This was Ogle's contribution – but we were working in the dark. Nonetheless, we and Motor Panels were clearly a successful team, and they were impressed by the depth of our early-stage thinking. We were awarded the contract – against stiff competition from John Beck, Lionel Sherrow and the Austin Morris design department – and we began work in earnest in the spring of 1975.

We then had around nine months – a much shorter time span than you would usually expect – in which to convert our concept into prototype-ready plans. I should have felt stressed. It was a huge, high-profile challenge: one that could make or break our reputation. Yet I felt strangely calm. If a world-beating design was needed, who was better suited to the task than Ogle?

The brief was demanding. The cab needed to be versatile enough to work on six different sizes of truck, from the top-of-the-range Roadtrain (whose name was generally used as shorthand for the entire T45 range) to smaller variations such as the Cruiser, the Freighter and the Constructor. This required various different configurations, but there were only 120 parts in all, and 40 were common to all the models – hence the cab's code name, the C40. The cab had to be equally suitable for use in the UK and overseas. Also specified were good built-in safety, environmental friendliness, a 'non-aggressive' appearance and 'acceptable' production costs. And – although this was never explicitly stated – it needed enough panache to help justify that vast public investment.

Accomplishing all our goals by the end of the year felt like an improbable target, especially with Leyland rigorously interrogating every detail as we went along. Yet it turned out to be one of those projects where everything falls into place. Leyland's team was headed by an outstanding young engineer, Keith Hemmings, who never compromised good design in favour of engineering convenience. They knew what they were doing and made decisions quickly, so even though they sometimes seemed obsessively demanding, the weekly design reviews never became fraught or frustrating. It felt as though we were all part of a team. I shared their desire for perfection, and we were happy to debate each detail until we were all satisfied.

We built a full-size model in expanded foam in the first few weeks. Detail design then started and by December 1975, our model shop had produced a fully detailed interior and exterior model that showed exactly what the production cab was intended to look like. A few changes were made before it went into production. We then followed up with models of every cab in the range.

The key to the design was that it looked at things from the driver's point of view, in a non-patronising way. Lorry drivers spend countless hours in their cabs, after all; so it seemed only reasonable to try to make the experience as pleasant as possible for them. Most cab designs took insufficient account of this. Drivers were just workmen who were expected to make the best of whatever tools their bosses threw at them. But I wanted the interior of my cab to be like a Porsche.

So, to take just one small example, I didn't want the usual black PVC on the seats. I wanted something that drivers might enjoy sitting on. I felt so strongly about this that I dashed into London and went to Savile Row, where I found a fabric that I liked the look of: a cloth called 'West of England'. I took away a sample and had it translated into moquette, which is a beautiful material – and at a stroke the cab became a place where someone might want to spend their working day.

It was the same with other details. There was a lovely leather gaiter for the gear shift, and a parking brake lever, integrated into the dashboard, that was shaped like a spade handle. Nothing was there by accident. Every detail had been exhaustively considered and discussed – even such questions as whether the shutlines (the lines on doors and bonnets) should be 3mm or 5mm.

The design quality was superbly flexible. The 40 parts that were common to all the different variations of the cab could be produced in relatively high volumes, which justified the expense of tooling and resulted in exceptionally high standards of fit and finish. The basic cab construction was all steel but could in future be replaced, if desired, by aluminium.

Some things were there to improve the driver experience: the unusually accessible controls, for example. Other advantages were more commercial. Parts that wore out or went wrong could be replaced with unprecedented ease: you could replace the entire pedal unit in 20 minutes. For a large fleet, over time, that could result in huge savings.

I was particularly proud of the flush external door handles, which I was able to combine, visually, with the side air vents. But it wasn't just about detail. The overall shape of the cab was unlike anything else on the market. Most trucks on the roads then looked square and brutalist. The C40's rounder corners, which we were able to achieve by using slightly curved glass for the windscreen, reduced its perceived width and gave it a softer, less aggressive feel. It was unusually aerodynamic, as we knew from repeated testing in a wind tunnel (not our own, sadly), but its profile also looked somehow friendly. A black panel immediately below the windscreen was cleverly shaped and placed to make the area of glass seem larger than it really was. This emphasised the presence of the driver within, framing him; and that, in turn, seemed to humanise the vehicle. A soft upward rear curve at the bottom of the side windows continued

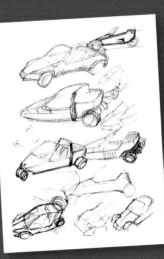
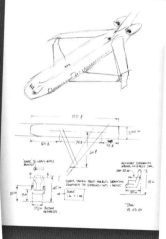

THE TOM KAREN ARCHIVE

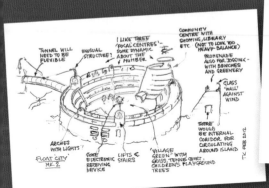
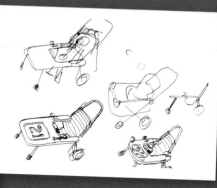

Left: Early learning educational fruit stacking game. Teaching children about colours, forms and numbers.

Right: The posting box uses food items instead of geometric shapes. Children are smart and find it easier to slip the banana through one of the bigger openings.

Above: These 36 triangular blocks can be assembled to make endless different patterns.

Right: Three different pictures or a combination of them can be created by manipulating the red knobs.

Left: Pressing the pilot's head releases the Big Fat Peace Bomb which spreads a mist of love and goodwill to end all conflict.

Right: Otto the blue dog snaps at the ball and wags his tail by cranking the handle.

Left: A helicopter which has two pilots and can carry cargo. This was made for my grandson, Arlo.

I don't like throwing things away. I see potential in turning items of no apparent value into something pleasing, and I have always liked using my hands to make stuff. Here are a few items I've made from unwanted materials.

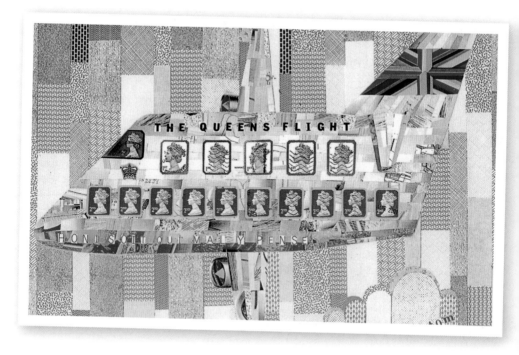

Above: The Queen's Flight is made with stamps and newspaper clippings and the sky background is made from the insides of envelopes.

Below left: Henry the bird is made from cardboard, newspapers and coat wire hangers.

Below right: This ship is made from flattened tin cans.

Above: Kinetic toys are wonderful and I really enjoy making these. You pull the string and their arms and legs start moving!

Below: This is a hedgehog and bird made out of driftwood. The nails on the hedgehog were all found on a beach.

One of two Range Rover based Popemobiles built at Ogle.

The Jet Stream J41 model under construction.

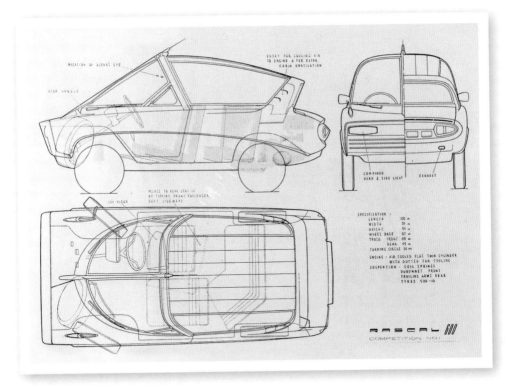

The Institute of British Carriage and Automobile Manufacturers (IBCAM) ran a prestigious annual car design competition. In 1958, I won the competition with my design of the Rascal. At the time I was working at Ford and it was three years after starting my career in industrial design.

Above left: I love dogs and had made some in clay before creating one laser cut from a thick sheet of steel and folding it to give him three dimensions. Named Rusty, after being left to rust outdoors.

Above right: A bronze bird on marble.

Below: 'Ladies in Waiting' was made after observing how ladies have to queue in public places. This was featured at the RA Summer Exhibition in 2010.

the non-aggressive theme, without the driver losing any useful vision.

Another thing that pleased me was the unity between the C40's interior and its exterior. This was unusual. Most companies used a different team for each, sometimes even working in different physical locations, but that didn't work for me. I wanted the same design values to apply throughout. The C40 looked as though one person had designed the whole thing right through, down to the tiniest detail.

Some themes recur throughout the cab, notably a kind of sausage shape that you get inside and out. This started off as the shape of the ventilation grilles by the door handles but is echoed on the front air intake, the pedals, on the air cleaner inlet stack, on the steps, on the dashboard controls, on the fitted rubber mats. You might not notice this consciously, but you absorb the sense of unity. As a result, everything feels more *right*. To me, that sense of rightness is the essence of good design.

The journey from our design work to the appearance of actual C40 cabs on the road took years. Leyland's testing of the T45 was the most extensive ever conducted, involving more than 500 detail tests, 265 major rig tests, 80 test vehicles and 1.5 million miles of driving by prototypes. Just finalising the paint specification took time. Yet Ogle's design remained unchanged. Production began at the end of 1979, and the T45 Roadtrain was launched in March 1980, five years after we had made our first sketches.

We had of course had plenty to keep us busy in the meantime. We still had big contracts with Bush, Electrolux, Reliant and Plaxtons. (Sales of the Plaxtons' coaches had doubled since we started doing their interiors.) Our baby's pushchair for Cindico, which appeared the same year, was widely admired. Our crash test dummies were going from strength to strength. So were our motorcycles: from 1973 we designed several classics for BSA/Triumph, including the BSA Rocket 3 and the Triumph Trident T150. These don't feature in this book because I had almost nothing to do with them. I just gave the work to Jimmy English and that was it.

We also did an influential electric taxi for Lucas, exhibited at the 1975 Motor Show, while the previous year we won both a Design Council Award and a Queen's Award for Industry for a knitting machine we did for Camber, the work of Stuart Mason, one of our exceptional designers. And then of course there were those Mogul toy trucks that we developed for Meccano at around the same time. When the T45 was finally unveiled in February 1980, on a cold night in Birmingham, I could hardly wait to see how the world would react. Forty gleaming T45 Roadtrains were parked outside the NEC, each with its C40 cab facing proudly outwards. It was rather like the fleet of Bond Bugs we had presented at Woburn Abbey a decade earlier, but without the sunshine – and with a lot more riding on them. Media interest was intense, but the reaction was universally positive. It was almost as though, in those troubled economic times, there was a longing for a British success story. Our cab went down particularly well. The C40 was praised for its sleekness, for its aerodynamics, for its non-threatening appearance; for the driver comfort and ease of mechanical access it offered; and for its high levels of built-in strength and safety. Overall, it seemed to justify hopes that the long-awaited launch would prove that the British were still capable of producing world-beating new products.

The C40 cab received a Design Council Award for its 'thoroughly practical design', and the T45 was later voted International Truck of the Year. The success of the project helped British Leyland to increase its share of the heavy truck market: they went from seventh to second place within a year. But what mattered more to me was the sure knowledge that it was a piece of work of which I could be immensely proud. It was the best-looking cab on the road, deeply thought through in every detail and setting new standards for ergonomics and aesthetics. In the world of commercial vehicles, it became an icon.

Our high-profile success for British Leyland led to other work with big commercial vehicles. We restyled the front end of the new Freight Rover Sherpa (launched in June 1982); we did a facelift for the relaunch of the Atkinson big 'A' for Seddon Atkinson; we designed the Shelvoke municipal cab. We did at least one other job for Leyland: the experimental TX450 truck, in 1985; and the Roadtrain's successor, the Roadrunner, which won its own design award in 1986. In the long term, I think Ogle probably did more work on commercial vehicles than we ever did on cars.

One of my favourites – in fact, it may be the lorry of which I am most proud – never actually made it into production. After we had done our work for Leyland, Motor Panels decided that they wanted to do a light-weight aluminium show cab, which they could use at Motor Shows to demonstrate what they could do. They asked Ogle to design it for them, and I gave them the Hemitech. They gave me a free hand with the design, and so I was able to introduce all kinds of fresh ideas. There were so many nice touches. You could raise the roof – it was a sleeper cab – and the instrumentation was beautifully arranged. I put the main displays some distance from the driver, very high up, to minimise the eye movement and refocusing required. These days, that would seem normal but back then it was unheard of.

It was a very futuristic vehicle, which caused a big stir at the 1980 Frankfurt Motor Show. In Frankfurt there were trucks from all the big manufacturers: Mercedes, Iveco, Scania, MAN, Volvo, DAF, Renault. But when the main German magazine for commercial vehicles came out, it was our cab that they put on their front page. They said it was the best cab in the show – and I think they were right.

What saddens me is that, even now, most people don't care about trucks. I look back on the Hemitech proudly as a magical piece of design. But for most people a truck is just a truck. They are wrong: not just because without trucks the supermarket shelves would be empty, but because trucks are utilitarian vehicles and, as a result, their design needs to be precisely adapted to their function – far more so than for most cars. Even boring trucks are boring for a reason. The fire engine in our garden was a good example.

Commissioned by Hestair Dennis and launched in 1978, it was above all a municipal vehicle. It needed to move quickly but safely through built-up areas – but not to speed up and down motorways for hundreds of miles. Its key features were those you would expect: the functional equipment (ladder, hose, siren, etc.) that allows firefighters to do their work. We designed a steel cab in which they could sit comfortably while fully kitted out, with unglamorous but essential details such as quick-release seat belts. Aerodynamics and long-distance driver comfort didn't come into it: the priorities were roominess, safety and ease of access. By Ogle's standards, the design was basic. It wasn't even the most interesting fire engine we had done. We did a Crew Safety Vehicle (CSV) cab for HCB Angus in 1976, whose safety standards were so rigorous that it could be used in fire stations all over the world.

The main thing the Dennis cab had to recommend it was that it was made of easily pressed steel, and that there was plenty of room inside. In looks, it was startlingly square. The RS stood for 'rigid steel', and it would have been hard to imagine a more rigid-looking fire engine. At least one commentator found it hard to believe that the boxy Dennis RS came from the same design stable as the curvaceous C40. Yet the design worked: it was suited to its purpose. The Dennis RS was sold all over the world, and in some fire brigades it is still in use today. This shows how important it is for a designer to be flexible. You cannot just impose the same aesthetic on everyone. Each challenge must be approached on its merits.

I installed the full-size cab model in our garden partly because I could. It was only made of wood, but it looked pretty convincing. Dennis didn't want it, and it seemed a shame to destroy it. I would have preferred the HCB Angus, had that been an option; or, for that matter, the Hemitech. But I admit that, from a child's point of view, a bright red fire-engine cab was probably more fun.

It was a shame that the village didn't appreciate it. It seemed a harmless enough idea, especially after we toned down the colour. (I remember having a lovely day camouflaging it with the children.) But perhaps it seemed different from other perspectives. I couldn't really tell. I had done my best to put down roots in the village, but even after a decade and a half, I was still largely an outsider. I used to walk around the village with my dog at the beginning and end of every day, but I rarely stopped to chat, and otherwise I was barely there. So I probably still seemed like an incomer – and it may not have helped that, in many eyes, I was also a foreigner.

But even I could grasp that, in a small English village, you can't afford to put too many noses out of joint. I wasn't too bothered by what my neighbours said about me, but Nicole and the children spent their lives almost entirely in the village. We didn't want the Karens to become pariahs. So I asked some of the guys from Ogle to come round and demolish it, and the good people of Ashwell – who I suspect felt uncomfortable at the very thought of big vehicle cabs, let alone the thought that one of their neighbours designed them for a living – could once again sleep easily in their beds.

17

SELLING THE DREAM

OUR ASHWELL neighbours might have minded less if we had kept my Aston Martin Sotheby Special outside our house, instead of the fire-engine cab. It would only have been the show car – the real thing cost more than many villagers' houses – but it was a pretty convincing show car. Then again, it might have seemed ostentatious to keep it parked in our drive; and I wouldn't have felt comfortable with letting the children run wild in it.

It was a rare and special car: so much so that the only two fully working models ever made have vanished from general view. I am told that both are still theoretically on the road, but it is half a century since I last saw them. Uniquely among my significant car designs, I don't even have a miniature model in my home, but there are many drawings of it in my sketchbooks, and I have a few photographs, too.

It always brings me pleasure when I see these because, for all its current invisibility, this was an influential and rather beautiful design. It also represents an important strand of my work that might otherwise be forgotten: the bespoke indulgences. Every now and then, a client would come along for whom cost was not a constraint, and I would design, at their request, a special edition vehicle. Sometimes the object would be to showcase a particular approach, as we did with the 'Glass Top Special' based on the Reliant Scimitar for Triplex in 1965. On other occasions, it was simply a question of indulging the whim of a super-rich individual, as with the special de luxe Reliant Scimitar GTE we did for Lady Hodge in 1968.

I had mixed feelings about such projects. Generally, the pleasure I get from design is related to a sense of improving life for everyone. Whether it's a toy or a car or a radio, a lorry cab, a pushchair or a piece of furniture, the satisfaction comes from knowing that through sheer creative thinking you have found a way of improving the world. You have found a way of doing things *better*. But when you make something that no one is ever going to use, or that at best may be used by one or two people, that satisfaction is largely missing. There are, however, compensating pleasures: chiefly the fact that you have both the resources and the licence to develop your ideas beyond the usual limits. If you take full advantage of this, you become a better designer, exploring strange new possibilities which you can explore again more confidently in years to come. In other words, you develop. Perhaps aficionados who see such designs develop too, becoming more receptive to your future work. Meanwhile, you can at least have some fun thinking the impractical.

The Aston Martin Sotheby Special epitomised this. It was commissioned in early 1971 by W.D. & H.O. Wills (part of the Imperial Tobacco group), who wanted a car to promote their new premium brand of cigarette, Sotheby's. Using creativity to promote smoking products was acceptable in those days; indeed, in the advertising industry it was considered the ultimate creative challenge. It never occurred to me to question the ethics of taking part in such an exercise, although I would today. Instead, I felt a mixture of excitement and fear at a challenge for which there could be no excuses for not producing something I was proud of. My brief was simply to create the supercar of my dreams.

It would have been hard not to enjoy such a commission, even if it felt rather indulgent. I played around with some concepts – my main sketches for it share a sketchbook with my Marble Run drawings – and ended up with a design that felt both luxurious and thought-provoking.

It was based on the Aston Martin DBS V8 chassis and engine unit. With a 5,340cc engine and a five-speed ZF manual gearbox, it could theoretically generate up to 320bhp, with a predicted top speed of 162mph. In fact, the show car that we initially produced was incapable of moving at all under its own power, because there was no time to put an engine in it. So the performance figures could not be tested; but that was unimportant. There were other things about this Aston Martin that mattered more.

The body, which was my contribution, was made of fibreglass rather than metal. This should have improved its power-to-weight ratio, although the gain was offset by the extra weight of other features. Above the waistline, the car was almost all glass – lightweight Perspex in the show car with heat reflecting, green tinted safety glass and gold lines printed across the roof. The lines opened up at the back for rearward visibility. The effect of this was to make it easy to look out of the car but hard to look in. The intensity of light coming through was also reduced. The roof was supported by Reynolds 531 steel tubes. The all-round transparency created a thrilling sense of lightness.

The back of the car was finished with a satin stainless-teel panel with 22 holes cut into it. These were partly for the rear lights and indicators but mainly for the brake lights. The idea was to reflect, with unprecedented accuracy, the variable realities of braking. The harder you braked, the more lights would light up – instantly conveying vital information to the driver behind. Progressive braking lights are quite common now, but in 1972 they were unheard of, and the big panel of lights looked like part of a spaceship – an effect with which I was entirely happy.

Other innovations included pop-in door handles and a pair of pneumatically operated panels to cover the headlamps. (These dropped down when you turned the lights on.) There was a head-up display in the windscreen for warning lights, which the driver could see without looking down to the main instrumentation panel on the dashboard. A single passenger in the back could sit diagonally with their knees over the tunnel.

But what really mattered was not the gimmicks but the thing I had drawn and refined countless times in my sketchbook, and then honed further with Ogle's designers and model makers: the form. The 'Black Streak', as it was provisionally known, was a car that seemed to glow with power and confidence. It was elegant, aerodynamic, stable and solid, yet visibly light relative to its power. For speed aficionados, it was a car that cried out to be driven – fast.

In fact, the show car that went to the Montreal Motor Show in 1972 was never even registered for road use; nor was it black. Instead, it was dark blue, with a gold coachline: the colours of the Sotheby's brand. Even so, it caused quite a stir. *Motor* magazine put it on their front cover. And I was even more pleased with the reaction a couple of months later, when the car appeared at the Geneva Motor Show. The celebrated Italian designer Giorgetto Giugiaro was there as well, showing his Maserati Boomerang. He came over to the Ogle stand and studied our car for a long time. He later sent me a book about his organisation.

The show car then retired to the back of a workshop at Ogle, where it was partially stripped for parts and, a few years later, sold off by Christopher Pepper to a private collector. The engine had been added by then. Meanwhile, what was supposed to be a single 'real' version of the car went into production in our models and prototypes department. Finished in May 1972, this road-going version (reg: GHU120K) used proper safety glass above the waistline rather than lightweight Perspex. It was initially painted in blue-and-gold Sotheby's colours and spent about a year being driven around the country for promotional purposes. But Sotheby's cigarettes never caught on, so Imperial Tobacco eventually repainted it in the white-and-red colours of their more established Embassy brand. The Embassy motor-racing team (including F1 champion Graham Hill) drove it around for some time, after which it was sold off.

But that's not quite the end of the story. A super-rich motor-racing enthusiast – an oil tycoon's widow from the Newport Pagnell area – saw a photo from the Motor Show and decided that she wanted one of her own. She made enquiries, was told that such cars could not be bought, tracked down Ogle, and asked us to make her one. We told her that it would be unfeasibly expensive compared with a usual Aston Martin price tag. She insisted that she didn't care: she wanted it at any price. And so, in 1973, we ended up making a third version of the Special, this one with an automatic gearbox and with

Weber carburettors instead of the original fuel injection system. Keith Jacklin, our wonderful bodybuilder, did most of it. It was maroon in colour, with a gold coach-line, and the badging on the back said 'Ogle' rather than 'Sotheby Special'.

I heard later that she didn't drive it much, partly because it seemed inappropriate during the mid-1970s economic crisis but also because, despite having dabbled with motor-racing herself when she was younger, she struggled with aspects of the high-performance design. With no bumpers and limited rear visibility, it didn't lend itself to easy parking – it wasn't intended as a town run-about. So she left it to her chauffeur to do most of the driving and, a few years later, sold it – reportedly for £35,000. Repainted bright red, it is now thought to be in a private collection overseas.

And that was that. Was it worth all the effort and invention? With a few fleeting exceptions – an appearance at an Aston Martin centenary celebration in 2013, for example – our Ogle Aston Martin has been to all intents and purposes invisible for the past 45 years. That is frustrating, given the time and thought I put into the design, and considering how much it pleased me at the time. But that's the trouble with special commissions: you throw your best ideas at them, and then they disappear.

It was the same with all the other one-offs and specials I created during my 37 years in charge of Ogle: '10–20

Glassback' version of the Austin Princess that we built for Triplex's owner, Pilkington Glass, in 1978; the 'Laser Metro' (a tarted-up version of the Austin Metro) for the 1980 Motor Show; or the 'Ogle Astra' we did with Avon Coachwork in 1983. Each caused a stir at the time, helping to build the Ogle brand, but no one remembers them today.

But each of them helped me to grow as a designer, and the Aston Martin Sotheby Special, especially, felt like a significant landmark in my creative development. It was also a slightly more enduring achievement than my other one-offs. Enthusiasts still track the whereabouts of the three vehicles that were built, and for their owners they have proved a good investment. In October 2015 I saw the original show car sold at auction at the Imperial War Museum in Duxford. It was, said the auctioneers, in 'barn find' condition – having spent most of the previous 40 years in a succession of barns in Bedfordshire and Hertfordshire. Nonetheless, it fetched an eye-watering £88,140. Aston Martin was reported to be 'happy to help' with any restoration that was required.

It would be wonderful, if at some point before I die, I could see that Aston Martin Special – or either of the other two – being driven on a British road. It's not very likely to happen. But, if it did, it would be a dream car come true.

18

TOTAL DESIGN

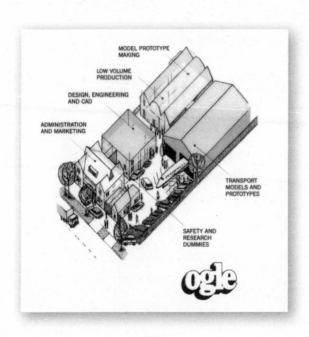

MODEL PROTOTYPE
MAKING

LOW VOLUME
PRODUCTION

DESIGN, ENGINEERING
AND CAD

ADMINISTRATION
AND MARKETING

TRANSPORT
MODELS AND
PROTOTYPES

SAFETY AND
RESEARCH
DUMMIES

ogle

I CAN'T remember who drew this sketch, but I have always had a soft spot for it. It's just a perspective plan of my old workplace, the Ogle site in Letchworth's Garden City.

It shows what Ogle's site looked like from 1980 onwards. We printed many cards from it, and I've kept this one. It usually lives on a shelf above my desk, where it has a way of catching your eye as you walk past. I am always glad when that happens to me. It reminds me of a crucial underlying theme of my story: Ogle's remarkable success as a design business.

When I took over the company, in 1962, the Ogle companies had been on their Letchworth site for about 18 months. David Ogle Associates had an annual turnover of around £25,000 and a staff of around ten. By 1980, Ogle Design Ltd now including the transport company David Ogle Limited had a staff of 80 and clients all over the world. And the size of our site had doubled.

The headquarters I inherited from David Ogle was a drab, unprepossessing building, with white pebbledash walls; a low, black tiled roof; a hard-to-find main entrance; a scrap of land for parking; and a couple of trees to separate us from traffic there then was on Birds Hill. But the site grew with the business. In 1973 we bought a patch of adjacent land, expanding our site to two acres and making room for two new offices and workshops. The main building was quickly restyled. I got a big central entrance made, with a weatherboard roof doubling as a porch with an enormous Ogle logo attached to it. You couldn't really miss the place. We repainted the exterior of all our buildings to a plummy brown, which was then my idea of the company colour. Pale brown carpets complemented the theme inside.

Then, in 1980, we opened a big 4,500-square-foot extension to our model-making facilities. This was a big and slightly scary investment, but it took the business to a new level. Our model-making operation was already crucial to our success, but the extra space – and the greater headroom allowed by the new extension's very high ceiling – dramatically increased our capacity for creating models and prototypes on demand. No other independent designer in the UK could match this. We could take a car from concept to model to working prototype, and could be creatively flexible at any stage in the process. We could even build a full-size model of a double-decker bus – and soon did so. Later, we built a full-size aircraft fuselage, which you can see peeping out of the hangar in the illustration.

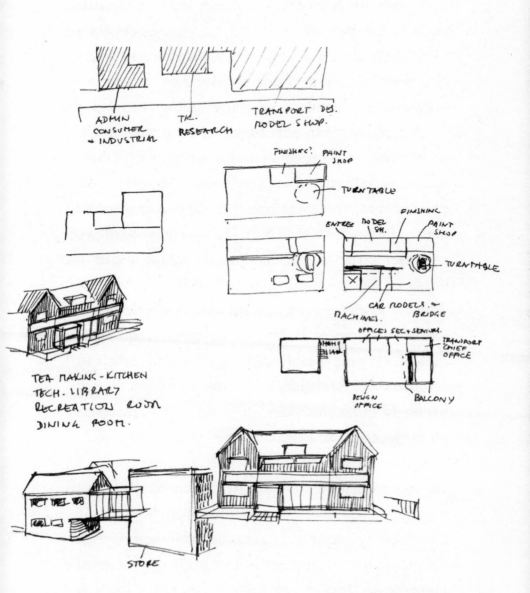

ADMIN
CONSUMER
+ INDUSTRIAL

TR.
RESEARCH

TRANSPORT DES.
MODEL SHOP.

FINISHING
PAINT SHOP

TURNTABLE

ENTREE   MODEL SH.   FINISHING   PAINT SHOP

TURNTABLE

MACHINES.   CAR MODELS & BRIDGE

OFFICES SEC + SENIOR.   TRANSPORT CHIEF OFFICE

DESIGN OFFICE   BALCONY

TEA MAKING - KITCHEN
TECH. LIBRARY
RECREATION ROOM
DINING ROOM.

STORE

273

Fears that we might be overstretching ourselves financially were offset by the knowledge that the increased value of the property balanced our investment; or so Christopher Pepper assured me. Meanwhile, there was a clear message, to the outside world and to everyone who worked on the site: Ogle was going places.

In fact, by 1980, this hardly needed saying. Ogle dominated the British design scene. In the motor industry, we were acclaimed for our work on cars, trucks, coaches, motor caravans and more. One journalist noted that, at the 1980 Motor Show, Ogle was represented on 13 different stands. But that was just one strand of our business. Our total portfolio included toys, furniture, printing machines, copying machines, wheelchairs for the Department of Health, earth-moving equipment, furniture for the disabled, an acclaimed pushchair (for Cindico), a child's slide, hi-fi units, a perfume bottle, a handheld microcomputer for Dataport Microsystems, an upright vacuum cleaner for Electrolux, an anchor winch for North Sea oil, a 'people mover' on rails for Hawker Siddeley Dynamics, an influential electric taxi for Lucas – not to mention various projects in what we called Design Research, creating large-scale systems for public use. (Our emergency escape system for the Hong Kong Mass Transit Railway was a much admired example of this.)

To keep this expanding show on the road, I relied increasingly on Christopher Pepper to build sound structures and a strong senior team. This sounds boring, but it was worth it. Over a period of three or four years, Ogle resolved itself into eight divisions: Transport Design; Product Design; Design Research; Prototypes; Model-making; Engineering Design; Dummy Manufacture; Human Factors (which would nowadays be called ergonomics).

I was lucky enough to have a strong and supportive board, and a wonderful Finnish lady called Sonya Pilcher who had a remarkable gift for financial analysis. I also had some great designers working for me, and some brilliant section heads (Charles Harvey, Keith Jacklin, Russell Mannoy, Stuart Mason, Jack Methrel, Carl Olsen, Geoff Platten, Ron Saunders, to name but a few). The more successful we became, of course, the more we became a magnet for talent – including one or two senior figures, such as Olsen and Saunders, who had left Ogle to seek bigger things but now realised that British design companies didn't come much bigger than us.

But our success wasn't just about great design. It also flowed from our unrivalled capacity for making models and prototypes; and, increasingly, from our unusually methodical approach to project management. Every stage of every project was obsessively tracked and logged. Every commission had a job number; every drawing had a drawing number. At any given time, you could tell who was working on what. All I had to do was consider the quality of the work they were doing.

Even that felt like a heavy responsibility. Maintaining quality, maintaining momentum, maintaining morale – the same mountainous challenges had to be confronted every day. Yet somehow I needed to maintain enough lightness of spirit to ensure that the inspiration kept flowing.

I usually woke very early and started planning my day, sometimes finding that a knotty design problem had solved itself in my head as I slept. I kept a tape recorder by my bed, so that I could record important thoughts in the night.

I would get up soon after waking, and the next few hours often represented my main daily contribution to family life. I would walk the dog, make tea for everyone, listen to the radio and, later, make breakfast; I would take Nicole hers while she was still in bed. Then around 8:15am I would drive off to work.

I was usually in my office by 8:30am. The model-shop staff would already be at work, but I usually had enough time to myself to deal with whatever thoughts had occurred to me overnight and to begin an important task or two. Often I recorded correspondence for Valerie to type up when it suited her. Then, typically, I would wander around, watching and talking, trying to catch up with what everyone was doing. There was a lot to keep track of, and a lot to be kept on track. I spent much of each morning wandering.

I tried to have a good meeting with Christopher Pepper every day, catching up with the administrative and business side of things. It was helpful for both of us to talk everything through and agree priorities, and because we trusted one another and shared a sense of humour, it helped keep us in a positive frame of mind. I felt very confident leaving things in Christopher's hands. I hate to think what I would have done without him.

Even with him, it was a struggle to keep on top of everything. I tried to find time each day for actual designing, but it was hard to forget that I was also running a business. I spent a lot of time in meetings with clients, either at Ogle or, all too often, at wherever they were based. We had clients in London, Coventry, Guildford, Wolverhampton, Walsall, Preston, Scarborough, Paris, Toulouse, Lyon, Sydney, Geneva, Frankfurt, Tokyo, Shanghai – pretty much anywhere – and in those days that meant endless travelling.

And all this time, I now realise, my children were growing up. By 1980, Nicolas was 15, Josephine 13, Max 12 and Eugenie 10. The first three had begun their education at a private school in Letchworth. Eugenie would have joined them there had she not been bitten, on her first exploratory visit, by the headmaster's dog. Thereafter, all four went to the state primary school in Ashwell, where they would, on reflection, have been better off all along. Secondary school, to which they were now progressing, proved more of a challenge. All four were initially sent to Roman Catholic schools in Stevenage: St Angela's for the girls, St Michael's for the boys, until the two merged to form John Henry Newman School. I don't think any of them thrived there. Nicolas was badly bullied, and Nicole spent a long time fighting to get him into a school where his dyslexia would be understood and taken seriously. She eventually found a school in Hampshire which had a unit for dyslexia, and he began to board there weekly. Max fell in with a bad crowd and came nowhere near achieving his academic potential. (He has done better since.) The girls fared slightly better, but I don't think any of them could be said to have enjoyed secondary education; or, I suspect, their teenage years. The whole family could probably have done with more support and guidance from their father, but there was no time.

I saw them at the beginning and end of each day; and at weekends we often messed around together – although occasionally I would go off alone to visit an exhibition instead if they didn't care to join me (or, at one point, to do pottery). I think we enjoyed one another's company. I tried to encourage them to be creative, playful people who were not afraid to express themselves, and I was always genuinely interested in their opinions and tastes. Eugenie, for example, had a good eye for car design, and on the whole shared my taste; but when she expressed a preference that baffled me – for example, she loved the Mercedes 190 – I took care not to criticise her judgement. I wanted my children to think for themselves.

But the fact remains that most of their growing up was done in my absence. Perhaps they missed me, but it was the only normality they knew, and it doesn't seem to have done them too much harm in the long run. As for Nicole, I think she simultaneously resented my lack of involvement and, as her sense of my uselessness grew, was happy for me to remain uninvolved. But I, like many fathers of my generation, realised too late that I hadn't made the most of the wonderful opportunities that parenthood offers.

I find it sad to think about all this today, but my plan of the Ogle site prompts a consoling thought. One bond between me and my children remained: a shared delight in Ogle's creative magic. In the days when I used to make things for them, I often used to do so in Ogle's model shop – the building in the top left-hand corner of the sketched site. My workshop at Ringstead was basically just the boiler room, in which I could do pottery and little else, whereas at Ogle I had all the materials and equipment I could possibly need, all the space I could need, no domestic distractions, and, above all, an atmosphere of unlimited creative possibility. If the model makers were there, I enjoyed their company: they were my favourite Ogle colleagues. And I loved the sense that, simply by being in their company, I was learning from them and absorbing their skills. The children, I think, experienced similar feelings themselves when they visited me, as they often did. Even when they became too old for me to be making them toys, they could sense that Ogle was no ordinary workplace. It wasn't just the model shop that delighted them, with its special cocktail of smells – glue, sawdust, paint – and its friendly, down-to-earth crafts-men. They were also fascinated by the product design studio (next building down to the left), where the design-ers, a slightly more rarefied breed, sat silently in their shirtsleeves at big, canary-yellow drawing boards, and the heady scent of Magic Markers filled the air.

Even my office (bottom left-hand corner) must have seemed more glamorous than most fathers' workplaces. There were pinboards on walls, festooned with photo-graphs showing the extraordinary range of products we made. On the windowsill, gleaming models of sophisticated vehicles for adults sat side by side with cheerful toy cars; on the bookshelves, technical reference books were juxtaposed with picture-books about toy-making. I myself was always dressed immaculately, just as I would have been had I been a banker or a lawyer, but my office was usually a mess. It probably felt as much like a playroom as a workplace.

Perhaps I am deceiving myself, but it seems to me that, in their different ways, all four children benefited from this; and that perhaps this compensates in some small way for my other shortcomings as a father. It was impossible to spend time at Ogle during our golden years without being caught up by a feeling that almost anything was possible. Sometimes the excitement came from coming into contact with exotic worlds far beyond the sleepy streets of Ashwell and Letchworth. For example, in 1977 Ogle was commissioned to create two vehicles for the first *Star Wars* film: the Y Wing Fighter, and Luke Skywalker's Landspeeder. The idea of Ogle being involved in the making of a film was thrilling for the whole family, even without foreknowledge of that film franchise's future success. Naturally, this made my work seem a great deal more interesting to the children, and my need to spend long hours at Ogle became altogether more understandable.

In fact, the commission was less exciting than it seemed. There was no actual design involved (although the Landspeeder did, as previously mentioned, use a Bond Bug base). Lucasfilm had already decided every detail. Our task was simply to convert their designs into full-size vehicles. The Y Wing had to be scaled up from about 18in to about 45ft. The end product had to be robust enough for repeated transport and use – and it all had to be done very fast. We made it mostly of wood, with big plywood surfaces subtly curved in two planes ('double curvature'). Our model shop sweated blood getting every detail right, not realising that most of their work would never be caught by the camera. The Land-speeder was easier: it seemed to have been designed around our Bond Bug. The studio provided draw-ings and we produced two fibreglass shells, one fitted to a Bug platform. Both were painted white; the film-makers applied a slightly more worn look after delivery. Overall, they seemed delighted with our collaboration and invited everyone who had worked on the project to a special screening of the finished film in a Soho cinema. My children, meanwhile, earned lifelong bragging rights to say that they had sat inside the actual Landspeeder and Y-wing Fighter that appeared in *Star Wars*.

Such magical brushes with show business and celebrity were exceptional, of course. But a more general kind of magic could be found at Ogle every day. Ours was a workplace powered by creativity and lit up by a sense of limitless possibility. No object was so big or so ambitious that we wouldn't have a go at making it; no design challenge was too daunting for us to try. If it wasn't immediately obvious how to do so, we'd just rub our heads together until we worked something out. What child could fail to be enriched by such an atmosphere – and what adult, for that matter?

There are many aspects of life at Ogle that I don't much miss, now that I am long retired. I don't miss the meetings, or the endless anxiety about things that might go wrong. But I do miss my daily prowls around the site, seeing who was doing what, discussing the merits of different designs and swapping ideas with some of the most brilliant creative talents in Britain.

Most of all, I think, I miss my quiet times in the model shop, when all of my life's discords seemed to vanish and I could lose myself in the processes of pure creation – and if I happened to notice a child watching me, I could be confident that he or she was happily absorbed in the same world. In fact, I think that these days I miss the old Ogle site even more than I miss our old home in Ashwell.

19

HOW I SAVED THE iPHONE

I DON'T use my iPhone much these days. I go out so rarely that I don't really need a mobile phone anymore, and if I do happen to need it the chances are I'll have forgotten to charge it. But I like having it handy, even so. It's such a beautiful object. I couldn't tell you what model it is (I suspect it's an iPhone 7) but I could talk to you for hours about the simple elegance of its design and its perfect balance of form and function. Every designer dreams of creating a product with such resonance; and few design buffs would dispute the iPhone's iconic status. Yet very few people realise that, without a crucial contribution from me, it would probably never have happened.

One of my sidelines, while I was at Ogle, was education. I think it was in 1967 that I helped Professor Misha Black to set up Europe's first automotive design course at the Royal College of Art. For the first couple of years I was the course's part-time tutor, but I had to give that up. Spending one day a week teaching in London simply wasn't compatible with running Ogle. But I did continue to give occasional lectures, and I also made regular visits to other colleges, giving talks, looking at portfolios and generally trying to make contact with the most gifted designers of the future.

This was crucial to Ogle's success. Only by spotting the most exciting talents and giving them guidance and opportunity could we ensure that we remained at the cutting edge of design. So I put a lot of time and thought into recruitment. I looked for students who could draw very well, because this suggested an instinctive appreciation of form. I was less concerned about engineering ability, which could be developed through experience. For many of those we hired, Ogle acted as a kind of finishing school. They would spend a few years being shaped and nurtured by us, and then, when they were fully fledged Ogle-trained designers, they would seek more lucrative employment elsewhere – usually in a more glamorous location than Letchworth. This was frustrating for me, but we hung on to enough of our designers for the process to be worthwhile, and the constant influx of fresh, ambitious talent made Ogle a consistently exciting place to work.

This was appreciated not just by the designers but by the model makers (whom we also trained) and by the administrative staff, most of whom lived locally. And although there were always some who thought the grass would be greener elsewhere, generally our staff were exceptionally committed to the company. I think this was partly because, self-evidently, we valued any staff member who had something to offer, and saw and encouraged potential that a more traditional company might have missed. For example, I remember helping one young applicant, who sent me the most appallingly written letter but also enclosed some excellent drawings, to get a place on a design course. And when a disabled Jamaican designer called Charles Harvey wrote to me seeking work in car design, I was so impressed by his potential that I immediately moved the transport department to the ground floor to accommodate his wheelchair (and, later, installed lifts). This was at a time when British employers still struggled to grasp the idea that ability and disability can coexist in the same person. I never for a moment regretted hiring Charles: he was a precious addition to the team.

Meanwhile, by the end of the 1970s, Ogle's involvement in education had become deeper. The catalyst was the tragic death, in September 1977, of Ogle's other founding father, John Ogier. Like David Ogle before him, he was killed in a car crash. He was 56. Unlike David, he was driving a Reliant Scimitar GTE, not an Ogle Mini, when he died. Like David, he habitually drove too fast, and there was a certain tragic inevitability about the head-on collision in a Sussex lane that killed him. That did not make his loss any easier, for his family, for Ogle or for me. For my first 15 years at Ogle, John had acted as a guiding influence on me, as well as being a wise, perceptive and encouraging chairman. Without his trust and nurturing, my aspirations as a designer might have come to nothing.

We appointed a successor as chairman in November 1978: Sam Alper, who as head of Caravans International had been a long-term client. Sam was a pleasant and competent man, but I missed John's enthusiasm. For him, Ogle had been an adventure, not just a business. It therefore seemed fitting that, in 1979, we established a design bursary in his memory with the Royal Society of Arts. The £1,400 award, co-sponsored by Pilkington and Lucas (and, later, Motor Panels), was supposed to be spent on travel but also brought with it the option of starting work at Ogle. Design students were invited to compete in a different competition each year: anything from designing a better bus to designing an environmentally friendly car that was fit for the 21st century.

The John Ogier Memorial Bursary made many headlines. Journalists were always interested in the entrants' futuristic designs. Ogle's relationship with academia – and, specifically, my relationship with academia – became more visible.

Every now and then, I'd do something that made a headline or two: helping set up a new course in modelmaking at Ogle's local polytechnic, North Hertfordshire College, for example. Most of my activities were below the radar: judging a competition here, handing out some prizes there. Local schools often asked me to give talks, and I tried to help out when I could. But that, of course, led to further invitations, as word spread that such things were possible.

It was worthwhile work, helping to cement Ogle's reputation as an asset to the local community and as the sort of blue-chip agency that an ambitious, up-and-coming designer might aspire to work for. But it sometimes felt more like a chore than a joy. I've always been driven by a sense that, conceivably, the next thing I create might be better than anything that has been done before. That's what makes me excited to wake up in the morning.

One of my activities was judging a design competition that BP organised in schools. Called the Build-a-Car competition, it was very well organised and made lots of headlines. I became a regular judge for it and, as a result, got to adjudicate alongside various interesting figures from the motoring and design worlds. One of these, one year, was an HMI (Her Majesty's Inspector of Schools) who was also a silversmith. We got on very well and seemed to see eye to eye about what constituted good design. We were both on the judging panel again the following year – I think it was 1985 – and, again, enjoyed one another's company.

A few weeks later, my new friend rang me at Ogle. He wanted to ask me a favour. His teenage son was studying design at Newcastle University but was not enjoying the course. In fact, he was struggling with it so much that he had more or less resolved to chuck it in. My fellow judge thought that this would be a terrible waste: his son had obvious talent and had barely begun the course. Hence his phone call: would I allow his son to visit me at Ogle and show him around, in the hope that perhaps this might make him think again?

I always feel sympathy for young people who are struggling to find a way forward in life. I remember how lost I once was. So I said yes. My friend, whose name was Michael Ive, came with his son down to Letchworth, and I spent some time showing him around the Ogle site. We had a long conversation in my office, in which I explained how fulfilling a career in design had been for me, and to what an extraordinary range of challenges a product designer's talents can be put. But I think what really persuaded him was the place itself. I can still remember his rapt, silent attention as we walked from building to building. The dummies department, the model shop, the ranks of the designers with their drawing boards, the vast hangars for transport design and prototypes: everywhere we went, you could see that he was absorbing the sounds, the smells, the bewildering range of different projects, and the bright, focused alertness on almost every face. He was like a child in a toyshop – just like my own children on their visits, but more intense. By the end of our tour, I didn't even need to ask him what he thought. I could tell that he couldn't wait to do whatever was necessary to become a designer himself.

Sir Jonathan Ive went on to become one of the most important designers of the modern world: the creator, for Apple, of the iPod, the iPhone, the iPad, the MacBook and much more.

Jonathan's co-creations epitomise what I mean by good product design. They are distinctive, but they are not self-conscious or gimmicky: they just marry form and function in a breathtakingly elegant and economical way. And, as a result, they have that crucial quality of 'rightness' – the sense that there's nothing you could add or take away without making it worse.

20

THE OGLE RECIPE

Tom Karen
OGLE DESIGN

13

ingredients of a successful piece of design

1. Sculptural quality
2. Colour
3. Structural logic
4. Respect for material
5. Simplicity
6. Theme
7. Solidity
8. Joins
9. Focal Centre
10. Detail
11. Handleability
12. Cleanability
13. Piquancy

THERE'S ANOTHER printed card from Ogle that's usually to be found on or above my desk. It's this list of ingredients, with a big, red '13' at the top. It's a bit like a menu, when you hold it, but a better analogy would be a recipe card. It's my statement of design principles, compiled, I think, in the mid-1980s, and used in lectures for design students. It's of limited use to me now, but I like having it around.

The card comes into my story because it is a distillation of the main ideas underpinning my work. You could almost call it my creed. Ogle was still growing in the mid-1980s, and the growth showed no signs of slowing down. We were constantly adding to our repertoire and widening our range of ideas. Yet our reputation for quality remained unquestioned. We became known for the depth and thoroughness of our processes as well as for the flair of our designs; and, increasingly, were engaged as consultants as well as designers.

Our 18-month project to help London Buses create a better kind of bus in 1985–86 had as much to do with intelligent research as with the kind of design skills you learn at art school. We recruited a large team of local people to get on and off our model of a No. 177 bus, using different configurations of entrance; but we also made heavy use of 'Sammie' – a pioneering computerised System for Aiding Man/Machine Interface Evaluation. Our resulting recommendations not only helped shave a second and a half off the 'stop time' at bus stops required for each passenger (a significant saving when you're carrying three million passengers a day) but significantly improved access for wheelchair users. And although the specific 'Superbus' project for which this work was commissioned was subsequently abandoned, our entrance design, using a drop-frame chassis, was adopted by a number of bus companies.

Meanwhile, we continued to design cars and, especially, big commercial vehicles; and the range of our other work seemed to broaden every month. Our Human Factors department, for example, did surprisingly well with a succession of health-related products, from orthopaedic chairs to hip callipers. In 1986, we expanded our model-making workshop again, by about 25 per cent. This was partly to accommodate state-of-the-art computer-controlled quality-control equipment, made by Ferranti; but it was also a symptom of growth. By the end of the decade our turnover was approaching £3 million, and the staff count was around 80.

The danger, when a company expands at such a rate, is that quality suffers, which for Ogle would have been disastrous. So I was keen to ensure that nothing came out of Ogle that I didn't feel proud of. But establishing and maintaining an appropriate degree of control wasn't easy.

Important projects mostly started off in my sketchbook. Once I felt that the broad concept was right, I would get others involved. I took care to choose and brief the right people, but once I was confident that they were heading in the right direction, I would leave them to it until the project was approaching completion. Additional creative input (from model makers as well as designers) was always considered sympathetically but not always adopted. The last word was always mine.

I tried, however, to avoid micro-management. Our brilliant designers would not grow or flourish (or even stay with the company) if I kept all the creative decision-making to myself. I had to give them the space and freedom to use their talents. Yet I also desperately wanted everything we produced to reflect my design values. How could I find the right balance?

I began to think in a more detached way about what my design values – Ogle's design values – actually were. Were there any definable qualities that our most successful products shared? Eventually, I came up with a list of what seemed to me to be the most important points, which I put down in writing. I suppose you could think of them as a kind of Ten Commandments of Ogle design, although there were more than ten of them and they weren't commandments. (When I discuss this list with design students, I always remind them that rules are made to be broken.) I thought of my points as the '13 Ingredients' – which is what I called them on this card. I had it printed up and distributed them freely. You can see for yourself what it says:

Tom Karen

OGLE DESIGN

- - -

13

ingredients of a successful piece of design

1 Sculptural quality

2 Colour

3 Structural logic

4 Respect for material

5 Simplicity

6 Theme

7 Solidity

8 Joins

9 Focal centre

10 Detail

11 Handleability

12 Cleanability

13 Piquancy

Some of the words mean little by themselves; others are self-explanatory. I would summarise them today as follows:

1 Sculptural quality

I worship good form, and I wanted everything that came out of Ogle to have that same sense of overall 'rightness' that you get from, for example, a Henry Moore sculpture. That means that every form and every line should have a logical beginning and end. A pleasing shape is typically a mix of soft and tight shapes that are inviting to touch.

Vehicle bodies, in particular, are pieces of sculpture – very challenging ones. One form runs into another; sharp shapes run out and merge into other shapes; there are twisted shapes that have to be dealt with. And in contrast to a normal product such as a food mixer, say, which sits indoors all the time, a car is usually seen outside, where shadows and reflections of its changing environment are constantly altering its appearance.

But any product, no matter how mundane, is a three-dimensional object, and will be improved if you approach its design with the values of a sculptor. That's why I was always happy to see Ogle's designers building a model from clay, then lovingly scraping it down to get the right shape. They were, essentially, making a sculpture.

2 Colour

This is not my strong point: I tend to notice and imagine shapes, not shades. It is, however, important: as with everything else in design, there are right and wrong answers. The wrong ones are usually obvious. Who would want to, for example, use brown toothpaste or drive a green Ferrari? Finding the right answers is trickier. I sometimes resorted to trial and error: I once had a model of a Xerox machine repainted three times, though I hated testing the patience of the painter in the model shop who had to do it. In my experience, women are much more sensitive to colour than men. They are never colour-blind, and when choosing products will often consider colour in ways that men don't (for example, how will it go with their home environment, or their usual style of dressing?). That's all the more reason for those of us who lack that sensitivity to take pains to get it right. With a car, colour is particularly tricky, because cars reflect things, and get dirty, and are constantly moving through different environments. But when you get the answer absolutely spot-on, as we did with the Bond Bug's orange, you know that you have done so.

3 Structural logic

For the design of a product to be satisfying, every aspect of it should be as it is for a reason. I have often talked about the need for each line to have a logical beginning and end, and for forms to balance softness with tightness. But there is also a relationship between form and function, which is what I mean by structural logic. A vehicle needs to be structurally sound, obviously – otherwise you have a problem. Ideally, it should also look sound. If it doesn't, it will make you uncomfortable. I dislike it when, for example, a car's wheels are aluminium castings, but you can't understand how the loads go through them. It's the same with buildings. I hate the 'Look, no hands!' approach beloved by some architects, who like to create improbable-looking structures with extreme cantilevers. Henry Moore said that he didn't want his sculptures to look as though they might take off – I shared his aversion. A giant steel cube standing on one corner (as Bernard Rosenthal's *Alamo* does in Manhattan) may look eye-catching, but you wouldn't want to lean against it. With product design, it is more important to inspire confidence than amazement.

4 Respect for material

Each material has its own mind and its own limits. Whether it is wood or metal or anything else, you can push it up to a certain point but no further. That's yet another lesson I shared with Henry Moore; but every craftsman recognises this. So you need to choose the right material – something that, for example, my boss at Hotpoint didn't do for that washing machine I redesigned for him – and, having chosen it, you need to respect it, even if it limits your room for manoeuvre. This is true whether you're working with wood or metal, or using injection-moulded plastic or die-casting, or manipulating sheet metal. Beyond a certain limit there is a cost-penalty involved: for example, you might need to introduce extra operations to the process. I always prefer to avoid sharp corners, whatever material I am working with, because they are a potential weakness, and loads don't like going round them.

5 *Simplicity*

I love simple designs. I was a great admirer (and early adopter) of the Swatch, the radically simplified analogue watch launched by Nicolas Hayek in 1983. (I wonder how much my red Swatch would be worth today, if I'd kept it.) And no one ever looked at an iPhone and thought how complicated it looked. Similarly, I can't think of anything good that came out of Ogle that felt complicated, while a favourite project – the Bond Bug – was a triumph of simplicity. Even the Chopper, with its gratuitous embellishments, was at heart just a few simple lines. I think this can be translated into a general principle: often, when an object doesn't look right, it's because it isn't simple enough. To make it better, you just need to take something away.

In particular, I advocate making just one change at a time – from one form to another, or one material to another, or one colour to another. One such change can have a powerful and positive impact, but that is usually enough. For example, on the famous West Front of Wells Cathedral there are dozens of figures of saints – in other words, many changes of form – but they are all in the same stone and the same colour; so there is, in effect, only one change. Similarly, the architect John Outram would use many different coloured stones for the facade of a building, but they would all be in the same plane, with the ground in front treated the same way. So, again, the viewer has to take in only one category of change.

But those are just two examples. The core point is simpler: when in doubt, simplify.

6 Theme

A well-designed object cannot just be a random collection of disparate elements, even if each looks nice in its own way. It needs to look as if it has come out of one mind, even if several people worked on it. This means trying to create a sense of a consistent, unifying theme. The Leyland T45 range of truck cabs are a good example of how you can achieve this through the way you treat small details: you can see that sausage-shaped theme running right through it – the door handle, the entry steps, the rubber floor, the pedals and the recesses around the controls.

7 Solidity

People like things to be solid – even quite small objects, like mobile phones, that you put in your pocket. Yes, we like things to be conveniently small, but if they feel too flimsy we don't trust them. The great American designer Henry Dreyfuss once designed a very elegant, lightweight clock and then observed shoppers' reaction to it in a store, where it was displayed alongside other clocks. He saw a lady pick up his clock and feel its weight in her hand, before weighing up a rival, heavier product. She preferred the heavier one. Dreyfuss concluded that this was because 'to some people weight can be a sign of quality'. Perhaps that is an oversimplification: there is obviously much more to design than just making everything as heavy as possible. But it underlines the importance of conveying a sense of solidity. Sometimes this can be achieved by weight; more often it can be achieved by visual means. For example, thin sheet metal bent to form a 'shutline' (the line around a door or other panel) can suggest solidity if the curve is folded to a bigger radius.

With household products, it sometimes helps to ask yourself: 'Can I imagine this being knocked over by a cat?' I'm convinced that the success of the Bush T130 radio was partly to do with the fact that, thanks to its nice solid die-cast top and that chunky lens instead of the usual flat glass, it didn't look too lightweight. The radio still felt convenient and portable, but it also seemed substantial and, as a result, desirable.

8 Joins

Many designs go wrong at the points where one material joins another, or where one line or plane joins another. Joins make lines, which can be more or less pleasing, and the detailing can make a big difference to, for example, the perceived solidity of a product. Even the smallest botched connections can destroy a nice design. Since most products are made from a number of components, getting this right is a huge part of the challenge that designers face. That's why, on a car for example, there are so many lines around doors, the bonnet and boot, and all the connections from one component of a product to another have to be treated with respect. This spells quality when correctly handled.

9 Focal centre

When people look at a product – or at a person, or at a painting – their gaze is initially drawn to a particular point. When John Constable painted his pictures of the East Anglian landscape, he liked to introduce a spot of red somewhere – perhaps as the colour of some character's waistcoat. That was the focal centre that drew the eye before the viewer took in the rest of the picture. As a designer, similarly, you have to ask: where, and what, is that entry point going to be?

If you don't have an answer, you don't really have a fully resolved design. A car's focal centre is usually the front end; but even a toaster can be given a focal point by a well-placed name badge. With the C40 cab, I wanted the focal centre to be the driver. Everything else flowed from that. You need that kind of visual starting point for every product.

10 Detail

You cannot design a product with broad brushstrokes and leave the finer points for a draughtsman to do. You need to care about every detail. All great designs have that in common: nothing has been left to chance. It's the sum of the little things that creates the sense of unity and thus of simplicity. At Ogle, even with the very biggest products, we would agonise over minutiae, whether it was the width of shutlines or the knurling on a control knob.

11 Handleability

Well-designed products appear inviting to use and easy to live with. With the best products, you look at them and think: yes, I'd like to handle that – operating it would be a pleasurable experience. This tactile appeal often has as much to do with what a product looks like as with what it feels like. It doesn't happen by chance, though: you need to design it in. Sometimes it's a question of materials. So, for example, with the Bush TR130 the leatherette on the body had an inviting softness (even before you touched it). In other cases it's more to do with form. With a domestic appliance, for example, the tactile appeal is largely determined by controls. Every product should be designed for use with one hand only, if possible, as not everyone has two free or able hands.

12 Cleanability

Being easy to clean is not a quality that usually gets mentioned when design awards are being dished out. Yet you'll rarely see a successful design that looks troublesome to clean. That's partly for practical reasons: people don't want to buy products that will accumulate dirt or that can be cleaned only with great difficulty. I once had a car whose cast aluminium wheels had spiky features that would bite at my knuckles whenever I tried to clean them. I cursed the designer responsible every time I washed the car. Designers who don't do much cleaning themselves often underestimate the importance of this factor. But anyone who spends a lot of time keeping their home clean is unlikely to choose a product that looks as though it will make that process harder.

It is possible that 'cleanability' also embodies a more general aesthetic quality. A product with lots of inaccessible areas or inappropriate materials will tend to seem impractical; but it may also give you a bad feeling at a less conscious level.

13 Piquancy

This is the hardest ingredient to define but also very important. It's that special something – often an extra something – that is, simply, inspired: the part of a design that makes other designers think: 'I wish I'd thought of that first.' It's like the little bit of mustard that makes a steak or sausage far more appetising. This subtle touch isn't necessarily a huge thing, and it may not be obvious to the customer. But that little touch – an unexpected change of line or form, or a detail that doesn't follow the usual rules – can release a deep sense of satisfaction. That curved lens over the scale of the Bush TR130 radio is a good example, or the gratuitous sissy bar on the Chopper bike. It's a little touch that adds flavour to the whole.

I'm not sure why I settled on 13 ingredients. I have never been superstitious. Perhaps that was all I could think of. Still, it was a distinctive number, and the idea that you had to 'remember the 13 ingredients' became embedded in Ogle's culture.

I am sure our sense of shared design values played a part in our success. The ingredients aren't rules, though. They're just points for designers to consider. I sometimes used them as the basis for talks to design students – most memorably, many years later, when I was invited to give some talks and workshops at Beijing's Central Academy for Art and Design (roughly equivalent to our Royal College of Art). I discussed my magic ingredients, and my words were translated into Mandarin. Sometimes I wonder what became of those translations. Perhaps, even now, on the other side of the world, there is a *Little Red Book of Tom Karen's Magic*

Design Ingredients, being used by the design students of 21st-century China.

If so, I wish them luck, and I think they will probably do well. Even now, I can't see anything on that list that I would particularly want to change.

21

SHOWING OFF

CARD NUMBER I · POPEMOBILE

Kate Pearson

One of the Popemobiles I designed for Pope John Paul II's 1982 visit to the UK, as recorded by a nine-year-old Ashwell neighbour, Kate Pearson.

LIKE MOST parents, I feel a sentimental attachment to the clumsy artworks my children made when they were small. It's the same with my grandchildren's creations. Yet this picture, which is one of my favourites, was created by a child who wasn't mine at all.

I cherish it partly because it evokes poignant memories. It was drawn at a time when what little family life I had was starting to slip away from me. It was 1982. I was 56, and the children were growing up with disconcerting speed. The three eldest were already teenagers. They had their own friends, their own priorities; they spent less time at home. Nicole continued to keep their lives on track, when necessary. My mind was full of other things.

If my thoughts ever did turn homewards, they always ran up against one dispiriting fact: my relationship with Nicole had deteriorated a good deal. We ended up sleeping at opposite ends of the house, and our paths barely crossed.

My working days became longer. When I did come home, I spent more time with my sketchbooks, or assembling model aeroplanes, or making pottery. I even took myself off, once or twice, for a solitary holiday. More often, I would take the dog on slow walks around the village: one when I got up, one when I got home, and another last thing at night. And occasionally it occurred to me, with a stab of startling pain, that my four dear children were no longer children.

Perhaps that is why I am always moved by this naive drawing of a Popemobile. It means much more to me than the beautifully carved wooden model of the vehicle that sits on a bookshelf near the window in my front room, one shelf below my wooden Scimitar GTE. (The same toymaker, David Plagerson, made both.) The picture takes me back vividly to that bittersweet summer when it was drawn: the last sunlit days of our age of imagined family innocence. It was May, and the verges of the Hertfordshire lanes were brimming with nettles and cow parsley. Eugenie had just begun her last term at Ashwell Junior School, and Pope John Paul II was coming to the end of the first ever pastoral visit to the UK by a sitting pontiff. There can't have been many British schoolchildren who were unaware of this. They certainly all knew about it in Ashwell. This was partly because there were a number of Roman Catholics in the village but mainly because of the Pope's distinctive transport, which, as everyone knew, had been designed by an Ashwell dweller.

I didn't invent Popemobiles: Pope Paul VI used custom-made vehicles for several pastoral visits in the 1960s and

1970s. But those were little more than open-topped cars. John Paul II (next pope but one after Paul VI) was more of a showman. His pastoral visits became events of huge political significance, and the modes of transport he chose for them became significant by association. When he visited Poland in 1979, a special white version of a Polish FSC Star truck was made for him; in Ireland, a local manufacturer, OBAM, built him a special version of the Ford D Series truck; in West Germany, Mercedes-Benz made him an open-topped G-Class 4×4. By the early 1980s, an element of worldly competition was unmistakable.

Then the goalposts moved again. On 13 May 1981, entering St Peter's Square in an open-topped Fiat Campagnola, the Pope almost died under a hail of would-be assassin's bullets. His visit to the UK in May 1982 was one of his first major excursions since recovering enough to resume his duties.

As the time drew near, public interest became intense. The arrival of the spiritual leader of 1.2 billion Roman Catholics in a nation whose self-image had for 450 years been assertively Protestant was obviously no small matter. Much of the interest focused on the Popemobile: we couldn't just offer him any vehicle. Concerns about security intensified that focus. Britain had to get this right. But how? Who would design the vehicle? How would they reconcile the apparently contradictory imperatives of the brief? Could the vehicle guarantee the pontiff's safety without compromising his visibility? And could it do so while demonstrating to the world the brilliance of British motor manufacture and design?

This was the kind of high-profile challenge I relished, and I was pleased – although not surprised – when Ogle was given the task of designing the vehicle. British Leyland and Land Rover had been chosen, as the national motor manufacturer, to make the vehicle, and I had telephoned them early in the year to suggest that we might design it for them. I am not sure if any rival agencies were smart or energetic enough to put in rival bids. Even if they had, I don't think any of them could match our record or our facilities. If you needed a big design project to be done well, on budget and on time, Ogle were the people to go to.

We had our first formal meetings in January. Representatives of the Vatican, British Leyland, Land Rover and nine different British police forces all expressed strong views about what should and shouldn't be done. There were obvious contradictions. For most people involved in discussions, the only priority that mattered was keeping the Pope safe. For the Pope himself, all that mattered was that his flock could see him and that he would be able to communicate with them. Too much security would render the visit pointless. Leyland were mainly concerned that the vehicle shouldn't break down – which meant that it couldn't be too ambitious, and that there should be enough time to make it and test it. I just wanted it to be something Ogle could be proud of.

We began work in earnest in February. By March we were ready to share our broad design plans with the media. The key to the project, as far as I was concerned, was that there was no need to overcomplicate it. There would be two different models, one based on the BL Range Rover and one based on the six-wheeled Leyland Constructor medium truck (part of the T45 Roadtrain family, whose C40 cab we had designed). The truck version would take the Pope through vast crowds at venues such as Coventry Airport, York, Manchester and Cardiff. The Range Rover version would be used for motorcades through towns. Leyland would supply the basic vehicles; Ogle would convert them.

In each case, the key to the design was balancing display with security. There is no point having a Pope-mobile if nobody can see the Pope within; but there could be no question of allowing the Pope to fall victim to another assassination attempt. The solution was obvious: lots of bulletproof glass.

Perhaps it seemed more obvious to me than it really was. This was because, without knowing it, I had been preparing for such a challenge for years. Look back through any strand of my work – lorries, coaches, luxury cars – and you'll find examples of my instinctive wish to give visual prominence to the driver or passenger. Ever since Triplex introduced me to the joys of safety glass when they commissioned the Glass Top Special in 1965, I had been exploring the potential of transparency.

The 1972 Aston Martin Special (Sotheby) and the 1978 Glassback were the two most spectacular examples, but they were not the only ones. Ogle's coach designs for Plaxtons had consistently emphasised the importance of giving passengers, as well as drivers, as much glass to look through as possible. And then there was our C40 cab for British Leyland's T45 Roadtrain, whose windscreen was artfully designed to highlight the presence of the driver within.

I think of it as 'framing', with the vehicle as the mere frame and the important element being the driver within. It had always baffled me that automotive designers paid so little attention to this. They barely seemed to care about what a vehicle's occupants would look like from outside. At Ford, for example, when they presented a new design they would put a full-size model on a turntable. Management would look at it from every possible angle and then deliver their verdict. But no one ever thought of putting a person inside and thinking about that as well. So you ended up with all sorts of designs in which the driver appears in an unflattering way – with only their head visible about the waistline, for example, or with half of them hidden by the B-post. Perhaps some people like that, but I'm sure most people don't. When you drive on the roads, or are driven on the roads, you are going out in public, being yourself, expressing your essence through your appearance and your behaviour and your choice of vehicle. Design should facilitate this, not obstruct it.

More than a decade later, I would contribute an even fuller expression of this way of thinking in a design I did for Renault, for their second generation Renault Trafic van. Patrick le Quément, their newly appointed director of design, had previously won a Design Award with his Cargo truck for Ford, in the same year that I won an award for my C40 cab for Leyland. He appears to have been so impressed by the C40 that he asked me to contribute concepts to his corporate design department for a redesign of the Trafic (which had first been launched in 1981). I contributed a design that was little short of revolutionary, with a distinctive dome above the driver, which when the van was loaded (and thus lower at the back) appeared to be made mostly of glass. An enormous side window, with a low bottom, added to the sense of putting those inside it on display. Everything was calculated to frame the driver – and passengers – in a flattering way. If you saw it, you wouldn't just think 'van'. You would think: 'a person in their van'. This seemed both fair and important, affecting in a positive way how people reacted to the vehicle. When you sat in the driver's seat, you didn't just enjoy the fantastic visibility it gave you. You also sensed how impressive you must appear – like a monarch on a high throne. You could look around at the cars below and feel yourself in command.

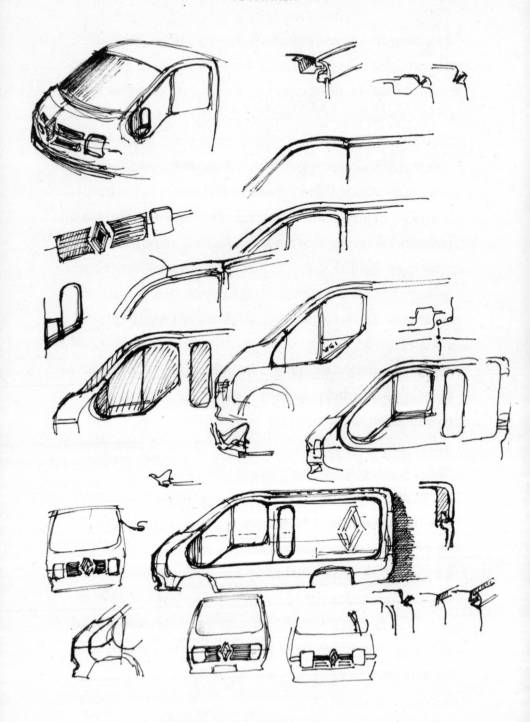

Perhaps that sounds fanciful, but Renault took the idea on board, and although it took them a long time to translate it into reality, it proved spectacularly successful when they finally launched the second generation van in 2001. The new Trafic became the bestselling van in Europe, and I am sure that this was because many van drivers welcomed the visibility it gave them. I know that a number of designers looked at my dome and kicked themselves for not having thought of it first. In fact, that is a good example of the ingredient that I call 'piquancy'. The dome is the slightest of bulges, mostly in front rather than above (so as not to breach what was then a two-metre legal height limit) until loading the van tilts the back downwards. It is barely noticeable if you're not specifically looking for it. Yet its effect is to turn an otherwise mostly conventional van into a design classic.

The challenge of the Popemobile, back in the early 1980s, was simple by comparison. All I had to do was to push the framing a little further, to make one of the most visible men in the world even more visible. You can probably recall the basics of my designs, so thoroughly have they been absorbed into collective consciousness. The truck version had a big central display area for the Pope to stand in, behind the cab, with its floor just above roof level and a raised greenhouse that protruded upwards with a trapeze-shaped profile. The Range Rover version rose up in a series of wedge-like steps: bonnet, windscreen, roof, secondary windscreen, secondary roof; the back came down almost vertically. Most of the back half, where the Pope stood, was made of glass – bulletproof glass – so you could see him in his entirety. In contrast to most vehicle designs, we knew the exact dimensions of the user, which meant that we could judge the framing exactly. The security personnel who accompanied him were, by contrast, barely visible. In both vehicles, there were big bulletproof windows on each side.

Altogether, we converted four vehicles into Popemobiles – two of each model. We converted the Range Rover version in our own workshops but the lorry conversion was done, under our direction, by another coachbuilder. There needed to be two of each vehicle to ensure that there would always be one in the right place at the right time. The Pope was doing much of his inter-city travelling by helicopter, and his schedule was too tight for our vehicles to keep up with him by road.

We had our Popemobiles ready before the end of April – less than four months after our first conceptual discussions. We handed them over, and that was the end of our involvement. There was, unfortunately, no prospect of taking one home for my children; but Josephine and Eugenie, 14 and 11 respectively, both contrived to visit the office at the right time and were thus able to stand in the finished version of one of the smaller Popemobiles – in the framed papal section – before it was taken away.

Thereafter, the vehicles proved a spectacular success. Millions of people saw them in person, and most of the rest of the nation saw them on television. From that point of view, it was the most unusual piece of transport design ever to come out of Ogle. The media loved it, and it certainly did our public profile no harm. What mattered more to me was that my Popemobiles fulfilled their function so perfectly. The papal visit was judged a triumph, and the Pope was so pleased with his vehicles that he asked to take one of the smaller ones back to Rome with him. (He subsequently used it on a pastoral visit to Poland.) The design has since been endlessly imitated. I don't think I've seen a single subsequent Popemobile that wasn't to some extent a copy of our design. I take that as evidence of a job well done.

Ironically, for all the papal visit's success, it failed to provoke any religious enthusiasm in the Karen family. On the contrary, the last traces of Roman Catholicism were rapidly fizzling out. I had been raised, notionally, as a Catholic, or at least sent to a Catholic school. So had Nicole, and, for that matter, my mother. None of us had shown the slightest personal interest in the religion to which we nominally subscribed. Our children, nonetheless, had been loosely brought up as Catholics. They were baptised as Catholics, had godparents, spent at least part of their education at a Catholic school, and, I dimly remember, usually ate fish on Fridays. And then, as soon as they were old enough to make their own decisions about which appearances to keep up, they stopped even going through the motions. One way or another, Roman Catholicism didn't work for them.

So, in short, I cannot pretend that my papal vehicles were a success from a spiritual point of view. Nor, I suppose, were my lacklustre attempts at parenting. But I do think that the vehicles, at least, helped brighten a lot of British lives that May. There was something about their form that conveyed cheerful optimism, as if they were some kind of giant, white, holy version of the Bond Bug. And they were certainly enjoyed by my children, who basked in the glorious fact that their father was the man who designed the famous Popemobile.

In fact, I think this relatively unsophisticated piece of design may have done more to win my fellow villagers' approval in Ashwell than all my other work combined. Ashwell Junior School held a competition to see who could draw the best picture of the pontiff's visit. The winning entry captured well the colour and excitement of the papal motorcade, and the frenzied interest in both the pontiff and his mode of transport.

I liked the picture so much that I had it printed up for use on one of the display cards that Ogle used for marketing purposes. I still have one of these cards, slightly worn at the corners, propped up on a shelf above my desk. It often catches my eye, and, when it does so, it tends to catch my heart as well. It depicts a moment of joy and celebration – and a triumph of Ogle design – but also reminds me of underlying themes of sadness and loss.

And when I glance at the artist's name, it isn't nine-year-old Kate Pearson who comes to mind. It is some other Ashwell schoolchildren, whose childhoods I wish I had cherished more: Nicolas, Josephine, Max and Eugenie Karen.

22

COMING UP FOR AIR

T HEY SAY that you never forget how to ride a bicycle. You tend to remember what you know about aeroplane design, too. Your knowledge may need a little updating when you try to reuse it, but the physical laws of flight are constant, while the habits of rigour you develop through aviation work are not easily unlearnt. I know this because, from the mid-1980s onwards, I returned repeatedly to the design of aeroplanes, with interesting results.

If you wander through my home today you'll keep seeing evidence of this enthusiasm. There's the shiny model box-winged passenger plane on my plan chest and supported in mid-take-off by a small wood-and-metal stand. There's the little white spy plane that dangles inconspicuously from my kitchen ceiling. And then there's the meticulous model of an aircraft interior at the back of my front room.

That model is my favourite. Barely 500mm long and perhaps 250mm high, it sits in a Perspex case on a small table, near the Chopper bike. Peer inside and you'll see furniture in the cheerful colours of a primary school reception classroom, with a comparably unthreatening sense of plentiful space. The passengers are little plaster figures, inscrutable as crash test dummies. There is a lot of pale blue carpet visible, and it all looks rather peaceful and relaxed.

This interior expresses a vision of air travel that has fascinated me for many years: one in which the passenger experience is comfortable and sympathetic rather than cramped and stressful. Many of my other aircraft proposals grew from this vision, and from the question it implies: if we wanted to make the experience of flight more pleasant for passengers, what adjustments would we make?

The model answers this question from the inside. You can see that my miniature travellers are not crammed into tight rows like bus passengers. Instead, they sit in comfortable spaces, apart from one another or in small groups, with plenty of legroom. They are already feeling relaxed when they sit down: windows in the ceiling by the wide entrance have turned boarding into a bright, optimistic experience. There are spacious, ceiling-to-floor luggage racks: none of those horrible overhead bins that intrude into the cabin space. The monotony of sitting is broken by an area with a coffee bar, allowing leg-stretching, socialising and refreshment. There are also areas with telephones and internet terminals. Even the toilets are a radical departure from the claustrophobic unisex cubicles most of us associate with air travel: there are separate, spacious conveniences for ladies and gents, appropriately designed for each. (The optimum floor design would allocate more cloakroom space to women, who would have wash-basins and mirrors outside the cubicles rather than inside.)

My model is a central cross-section of a cabin that could hold up to 300 passengers, yet would feel more like an upmarket hotel lobby than an overcrowded bus. Ridiculous? On the contrary, it is eminently achievable, for the simple reason that, compared with current aircraft interiors, this one has space to play with. And to see how *that* can be achieved, you need to look at my computer-generated picture of the same aircraft's exterior, which hangs on the wall just behind my model. It shows the plane cruising above big white clouds: shiny, silver and so obviously comfortable in its surroundings that it might take you a moment to notice something strange about the fuselage. Then it hits you. Instead of being a single elongated horizontal bubble or oval cigar shape like a conventional passenger plane (in which two thirds of the volume is under the floor), this one is a treble bubble, like a lilo, or three cigars strapped side by side. This makes the fuselage unusually wide, providing not only space within but – crucially – lift outside. In conventional aircraft, the wings provide lift to compensate for the fact that the fuselage contributes very little. If the fuselage did its share of the work, the lift from the fuselage would allow the wing-size to be smaller. This would reduce the overall weight, allowing a more efficient aircraft – and a much more passenger-friendly cabin. The aeroplane in my picture has elegant box wings like a staggered bi-plane, with two-thirds of the wing area at the back. This box-wing configuration is very tolerant of shifts in centre of gravity, but its key advantage is that it produces less drag and, as a result, greater economy. Everyone wins, in other words, and it all goes back to the simple idea of using a wide fuselage.

I completed this particular design in 2001, but I proposed an earlier version – which I now think of as *Aircruiser I* – in 1995, and the thinking behind it goes back decades earlier. Even in my sketchbooks from the late 1960s and early 1970s, unusual aircraft appear from time to time. But it was only in the 1980s that my early passion for flying, which had been largely ground out of me when I actually worked in the aviation industry, was reawakened.

One obvious catalyst was a commission from Saab, in 1982, to design the interior for their new Saab-Fairchild 340. I don't think they knew about my background in aviation, but once they had approached Ogle they quickly realised that I understood the basics of aeronautics, which seemed to please them. We made a full-size model of part of the cabin, and they were delighted with the interior.

Over the next few years, I became increasingly conscious that Ogle was uniquely well equipped and well qualified to provide design services to the aviation

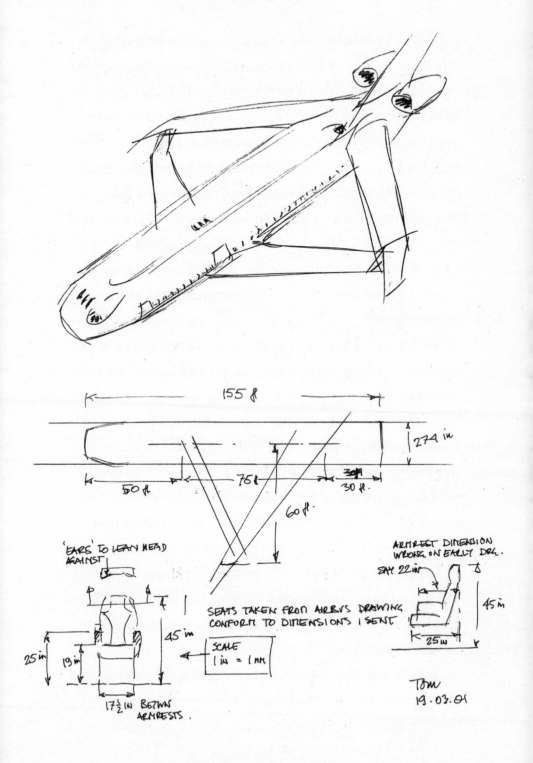

155 ft

274 in

50 ft

75 ft

30 ft

60 ft

'EARS' TO LEAN HEAD AGAINST

ARMREST DIMENSION
WRONG ON EARLY DRG.

SAY 22 in

45 in

25 in

SEATS TAKEN FROM AIRBUS DRAWING
CONFORM TO DIMENSIONS I SENT

45 in

19 in

25 in

SCALE
1 in = 1 MM

17½ IN BETWN
ARMRESTS.

Tom
19.03.01

industry. Eventually, we began to market ourselves in this field. In September 1988, we took one of our crash test dummies to the Farnborough International Air Show. This one was for testing ejector seats. It attracted great interest – our dummies always did – but I'm not sure that we sold any dummies as a result. What we did do was draw attention to Ogle's increased interest in aviation. As our stand at Farnborough made clear, we could also design cockpits and aircraft interiors – and were keen to do so. The message took time to spread, but gradually, as I had hoped, fresh commissions followed.

With hindsight, I think that my desire to find work for Ogle in the aviation industry was not just a business decision. There was also an emotional hunger involved. Perhaps that seems strange, given my relative misery when I had actually worked in the aeronautics industry. But even a grey decade in Luton and Croydon couldn't suck all the joy out of flying. In any case, life doesn't stand still. The world was changing; Ogle was changing; and I was changing.

It's hard to know where to start. At home, the late 1980s and early 1990s were mostly a time of pain. My children were no longer children and were beginning to leave home. Nicole, deprived of the role that had occupied her for two decades, turned her attention and energy to her marriage. This was not a positive development.

If we hadn't had a beautiful dog at the time – a Labrador-collie cross called Bon – I'm not sure I would have gone home at all. As it was, he would always be waiting at the door when I got back, and when we went off for our evening walk together the sense of calm and affection made me feel a little stronger. In other respects, home was a bleak and lonely place. For much of our marriage Nicole had performed traditional domestic duties such as washing and ironing my shirts and cooking my meals. (I know that sounds bad today, but most middle-class households were like that in those days.) Now she refused to do so, and, as pathetic as it seems, I had little idea how to perform such functions for myself. There was even a period when Josephine used to wash and iron my shirts for me – secretly, so as not to incur her mother's wrath. I spent a lot of time in my little 'work-shop' in the boiler-room, trying to escape through my pottery; but I could hardly spend my whole life in there.

Against that background, I wanted to explore the boundaries of the possible, not resign myself to the world as it then was. This emotional restlessness may have been exacerbated by the fact that, in 1986, my mother had died. She was 83, still barely absorbed into the village community, still bitter about the way her husband had (as she saw it) ruined her life; and still on sadly distant terms with her children. She and I had never got round to trying to establish a closer relationship, despite having lived in the same village for a decade and a half. This was partly Nicole's fault. She didn't even like having my mother round on Christmas Day (and several times limited her seasonal goodwill to sending her a Christmas hamper for one). But I never attempted to do anything to improve the situation myself.

Now, when it was too late, I began to wonder if I could have done. Maybe my habitual passivity and escapism had not been such clever strategies after all. And when I thought, sadly, about how my mother and I might have been closer, the woman I thought of was not the anxious, emotionally clumsy mother who had made such a mess of my upbringing, or the lonely, embittered creature of her later years, but the brave, adventurous woman who had found freedom and fulfilment in the skies of pre-war Czechoslovakia. Her domestic unhappiness made more sense to me now. So, perhaps, did her love of flying.

Meanwhile, in the background, Ogle itself was evolving. I had been there since 1962, and there was barely a facet of day-to-day consumer society to which I hadn't turned my designers' eye. I knew that my career was finite: in 1986, I had turned 60. The last few years of my career were approaching, and I wanted to use them well. I fancied less earthbound work.

In reality, I was feeling more earthbound than ever in my work. I got on well with Sam Alper, who had taken over as chairman following John Ogier's death in 1978, but by 1984 we both realised that he wanted to take the company in a very different direction to what I was comfortable with. So he stood down, and I stepped up temporarily to take his place. This was not in itself an onerous responsibility; nor was it a liberating one. More than ever, my time seemed to be taken up with management, or with being the public face of Ogle, but not with actually creating things. My diary was packed with meetings and presentations – and travelling. One day I would be in Paris, talking to the Société des Ingénieurs de l'Automobile about new trends in car design; a few days later I would be at the Geneva Motor Show; then I would be off to Shanghai to man Ogle's stand at the Automotive China show, before touting for new business at the Tokyo Motor Show. None of this was unpleasant work, but it was mostly mundane, and the lack of creativity wore me down. In one of my sketchbooks from this period, pages of careful designs for aircraft interiors are suddenly interrupted by a drawing of a monkey in business clothing, holding a mobile phone. I think I was trying to tell myself something.

For all the travelling, I felt that I was standing still – and that is a sensation I hate. It goes against my instincts as a creative person (always hungry to try something new) and as a refugee (always terrified of relaxing). Yet perhaps, from the mid-1980s onwards, standing still was necessary. Ogle had grown so big and successful that the main thing it needed now was for everything to keep working smoothly. The electric excitement of our golden years had faded: I no longer felt – as I had for two decades from the mid-1960s onwards – that I was at the centre of a unique convergence of exceptionally gifted people. Too many of our brightest designers had moved on – rightly, for they deserved bigger challenges. What remained was an atmosphere of quiet creativity and professional competence. And what was needed now was a leader who would consolidate: not a maverick, but someone whose priorities were conventional and prudent.

I didn't really fit that description. I wanted to make the business as innovative as possible, seeking new markets rather than trying to replicate past successes. When I thought of strategies for the future, my approach was creative and speculative. So, for example, in 1984 we created a 'Project 2000' car – our own prototype for a four-seater family car that would not look out of place in the 21st century. Exhibited at the Design Council's 'Drive Forward' exhibition that March, it was a bold 'one-box' design with a shallow V-shaped windscreen and an unusually aerodynamic profile that was obviously inspired by the aviation industry. Margaret Thatcher, keen to comment but not to listen, was among those who saw it. I don't think we made any money out of Project 2000, but I was and am proud of it.

Subsequent initiatives seemed (at the time) even more futuristic: an information terminal for Shell petrol stations; a film processing test unit for Kodak that could be used only in total darkness; a scanning electron microscope for Cambridge Instruments. These, at least, did pay their way for us, but they might not have done so: they hadn't been surefire bets. You could say much the same about our forays into aviation: they were part of a quest for growth that some might have considered too creative for comfort.

The trouble was, there weren't many easy pickings left. The design industry had grown spectacularly since 1962, but British manufacturing was in long-term decline. We were competing in a shrinking market against big, well-funded rivals, many employing designers who had learnt their trade at Ogle. Just knowing how to do things better than our rivals no longer guaranteed success, especially now that many of our long-term clients were struggling. British Leyland was in the process of corporate dissolution; Reliant was focusing its attention (disastrously) on property speculation. UK radio manufacture had more or less ceased, smothered by foreign competition. Even the leading toy companies – Matchbox, Lesney, Airfix, Kiddicraft – had little appetite for investing boldly in new designs. Sometimes I feared that Ogle itself was the problem: had we fallen out of fashion? But the truth was that companies had lost their appetite for innovation. They later paid a price for this failure of imagination, but that was scant comfort for us.

It was a great relief when I was finally able to shake off some of the chains of boardroom responsibility. John

Thompson, a former director of Smith Industries (who made car instruments), agreed to become Ogle's chairman on the strict condition that we found ourselves a managing director. After several false starts we eventually found the right person. John took over as chairman in June 1990 and Nigel Wemyss, who had previously held some very senior positions in the aviation industry, became acting managing director a few months later. Christopher Pepper remained company secretary, while I became creative director.

In my new role, I was free to do all the things I enjoyed most: guiding Ogle's long-term design strategy, giving lectures, and, when I felt like it, actually creating designs in my own sketchbook. I initially found the transition painful, even so. Perhaps that could have been predicted. I had been responsible for everything for so long – in charge of everything, answerable for everything – that to relinquish that total and unilateral control felt like losing a part of myself. Two things made that loss easier to bear. The first was that John and Nigel were able to take on the burden of worrying about things that might go wrong. Shortly before their appointment there had been a nightmarish episode in which we had hired a highly qualified engineer to help us design a big roller coaster for a client who supplied fairground rides across the UK. The project was completed – but failed to work properly. It was, I think, the only failure that Ogle had had under my leadership, but it was potentially a disastrous one. The client sued us, and for several months I barely slept with worry. My involvement in the actual project had been minimal, but the fallout threatened the whole company. In a worst-case scenario, it could ruin us – wiping out everything I had achieved. I used to pace up and down at home at night, literally banging my head against the wall as I wondered what to do. Eventually, miraculously, that situation was resolved, thanks to the magnanimity of a much bigger co-contractor which took part of the burden of settling the case. But the fear that something similar might occur haunted me, and knowing that the buck now stopped with John and Nigel did at least help me to sleep at night.

The other factor that eased the transition was the fact that, at around the same time, some interesting opportunities were opening up for me to indulge my reawakened interest in aviation design. The biggest of these came our way when Nigel introduced us to British Aerospace, who were making a new 29-seat regional airliner (a "feeder liner"), called the Jetstream 41. It was only a small plane but it was a new fuselage, and they were struggling to get it ready in time for the very important Paris Air Show that June at Le Bourget. We won the job of designing the interiors.

They already had a working design from a previous aircraft, but we completely redid it. I softened all the shapes in the cabin to make them less intrusive and applied lighter colours throughout. I also went to Switzerland to have a special fabric made for the seats. The colours echoed the company's logo, while the pattern was random, which minimised waste. I also rationalised the space around the entrance, along with many other obvious minutiae whose cumulative effect was transformational.

The 18-metre aluminium fuselage that we shipped over to Le Bourget, just in time, was correct in every detail, down to the smallest call button; we even did the cockpit. Many of the parts were models made by Ogle: accurate but non-functional. But some of the instruments were genuine. There was air conditioning; the passenger lights and ventilation units actually worked; the release panels were fully compliant with safety regulations.

An added feature was the boarding stairs. I knew from experience that it was often very hot at Le Bourget, and that when it wasn't it tended to rain, so I arranged for a canopy to be added to the steps. I also made them much wider at the bottom, so that they almost scooped people in. It seemed to work: that sort of attention to detail usually does. Swarms of people entered the aircraft, all in a positive frame of mind and not feeling hot and bothered before they started. Our design was widely praised for the feeling of 'space, airiness and luxury' it created. Better still, relatively little attention was paid to the new Dornier model nearby, which I thought was a much more interesting design. Indeed, one senior figure at Dornier visited our aircraft and exclaimed: 'Why couldn't we have an interior like this?'.

The project was not a financial success. The need to complete it in less than six months forced us to pay huge amounts of overtime, and we ended up making a loss on it. But it was a *succès d'estime* which led to further aviation commissions, from BAe and others. We did some helicopter interiors for Westland, and in 1995 we built a cockpit-orientation trainer for the Royal Navy Air School in Yeovilton, to help students acclimatise themselves to the experience of flying a Sea Harrier. We also designed interiors for some Saab 2000s ordered by the Swiss air carrier, Crossair. (I discovered that their aircraft were due to be delivered on the birthday of Crossair's CEO, Maurice Saulter, so I suggested to him that we give them some special touches inside. The results delighted him.)

Best of all, we attracted the attention of Bob Lange, the marketing director of Airbus, who invited us to comment on the proposed cabin design of what would become the Airbus 380 (which was supposed to be the successor to the Boeing 747). I went to a series of meetings in Toulouse and suggested numerous innovations to distinguish the 380 from its rival, the 747. These included providing a lift to the top deck for passengers with mobility problems; having separate, purpose-designed Ladies' and Gents' toilets; and moving the stairs to the upper deck backwards to reduce dead space while airborne. Unfortunately, the conservatism of the engineers involved, combined with an understandable desire to play safe with such a big and important project, meant that all these opportunities were missed. Instead, they ended up with a cabin with all the usual design features, applied to a larger-than-usual cabin.

This was frustrating, but it didn't dim my enthusiasm. I began to take my advocacy for better cabin design to various conferences – in Cannes, in Hamburg, in Florida. But still people's minds seemed to be closed to my proposals, so I took my ideas back to Ogle to develop them there. The first model we built had a fuselage comprising twin horizontal bubbles, with a canard wing arrangement with main wings at the back and winglets at the front. I knew that Airbus had considered a double bubble structure, and I felt confident that this was an idea worth exploring.

Over time, however, I began to feel that what we should be looking at was a successor to existing 200-seater passenger aircraft such as the Boeing 737 and the Airbus A230. My design, which I decided to call Aircruiser (to distinguish it from the less comfortable-sounding Airbus), would seat anything up to 300 people. I therefore created something that no one had thought of before: a flat fuselage made of three intersecting bubbles.

I have already mentioned the multiple advantages that this provides: more lift from the fuselage, allowing smaller, lighter wings, which, if a box-wing configuration is used, produce less drag and, as a result, greater economy. The design has huge and obvious potential for a world that's increasingly concerned to minimise the environmental costs of air travel.

Yet I think what excited me most was the passenger-friendly cabin, which I felt could radically improve the experience of flying.

Because of the relative flatness of the wide fuselage, nearly all the space inside is available to passengers (in contrast to a conventional fuselage). A wider-than-usual entrance allows passengers to bring on board larger pieces of luggage (which can be stored in a central spine of floor-to-ceiling racks running down the length of the aircraft). Windows in the ceiling above the door create a sense of light and space, in contrast to that claustrophobic sense that you usually get when you board an aircraft. The coffee bar and the leisure area are the first sights that greet them. Another big bonus is that the wide treble bubble allows the cockpit to off-set to one side, which means that, for the first time on any aircraft, passengers can look through windows facing forward. It's a completely different kind of air travel, reducing passenger stress and making long-haul flight something to be enjoyed rather than merely endured.

I continued to refine this design, even after I retired from Ogle in 1999 (an episode I will deal with in the next chapter). I never like abandoning what I know is a good idea, just because other people can't see its merits. By 2000 I had developed a fairly detailed proposal for what I called *Aircruiser II,* and this is the design that you can see in my front room. It's a shame that the model is on a tiny scale – but of course if it were bigger I wouldn't have anywhere to put it. In any case, the key features on the inside weren't hugely different from the *Aircruiser I*, although the seating plan was more free-form. The key conceptual development was the form of fuselage itself, and that can be seen only in the picture on the wall.

Would it work? I see no reason why not. It's a win-win design (more space, more lift, less drag), which could make long-haul flight more affordable, more comfortable and more sustainable. I subsequently discussed the proposal with Lockheed, who confirmed that the box wing worked well, because it would be very tolerant of shifts in centre of gravity. Even then, however, it was always unlikely that a giant corporation would totally rethink its approach to aircraft manufacture on the say-so of a designer in his seventies who by then was retired from full-time work. The status quo won out, and the nearest I ever got to getting my *Aircruiser II* off the ground was to propose it to a conference in Cannes in 2001. *Design Week* then published a feature about it in May 2002.

But good ideas never entirely die. The aviation industry still needs to face up to the challenge of making long-haul flight more economical, and, even now, manufacturers are still flirting with ideas for wider fuselages. So far, their natural conservatism has held them back, but they are increasingly aware that, if they want to survive in these challenging times, they must adapt and evolve. I remain quietly confident that, one day, many larger aircraft will incorporate elements of my *Aircruiser* design. It's just a shame that I never persuaded a major manufacturer to embrace this way of thinking while I was still at Ogle. It would have been a marvellous swansong for my career in industrial design. I could have flown off into the sunset proudly, trailing clouds of glory. It is possible, however, to be a little bit too far ahead of your time.

23

FRESH START

I'M SURE you've noticed the birds in my home. Visitors often remark on them. They're in every room: clay birds, cane birds, papier-mâché birds; birds made of bronze, wood or wire. I made most of them myself, including this plump, long-legged, brightly painted creature who usually shares a shelf in my front room with three other long-legged birds.

This is Henry. He's about 25 years old – I think I finished him in 1995 – and although I have made a lot more birds since, Henry is my special favourite. He embodies a turning point in my life.

To an outside observer, it might not be obvious why. The 1990s were full of personal landmarks for me. Why would I focus on a zoologically implausible papier-mâché bird? The answer, I think, is that those other landmarks were about endings. Henry marked a beginning.

Let's start with the endings. Henry came into the world at a time when, for the first time in decades, I was adrift. I no longer lived in Ashwell. I had just got divorced. Even Ogle's days were numbered – at least in the form that I knew it. Most of what happened was inevitable and expected and, as far as I was concerned, welcome. Nonetheless, it was a startling contrast to the predictability of the previous three decades.

John Thompson and Nigel Wemyss had been exploring ways of rearranging Ogle since shortly after they arrived. The details need not detain us. It is enough to observe that, when the process was eventually completed, in 1999, the Ogle that I had led had been superseded by three successor companies. The dummy division, already a separate operation, became Ogle/TNO (merging with its Dutch partners) in 1997; in 1999 this was bought by the US company First Technology and became First Technology Safety Systems Europe (FTSS Europe). The rest of Ogle split in two the same year. The design side of the business was sold to a Norwegian company that recast itself as Ogle Noor. Our model-making operation did a buyout and became Ogle Models and Prototypes, which continues to operate, very successfully, from our old Letchworth site.

I retired the same year, aged 73. My role had been dwindling anyway, through much of the 1990s, and it was clearly the right thing to do. Part of the corporate rationale for the break-up had been to prepare for a post-Tom Karen future. Now we had gone our separate ways.

You might expect me to have been traumatised by the separation. Ogle had been the focus of my existence for nearly 40 years. But I had seen it coming, and I was ready for change. I had also been preoccupied, for a long time, by other, more personal matters. By 1990, the misery of my marriage had become impossible to ignore. The only thing that Nicole and I could agree on was that we had no future together – and even that didn't unite us. She began divorce proceedings. I thought this would be a relief. In the short term, it made things worse. I was advised to carry on living at Ringstead until the divorce settlement had been agreed. This wasn't much fun, to put it mildly. The process went on for years and made several lawyers rich. The children had left home by then, but I don't think any of them were left unscathed by this outcome.

I will not speak badly now of Nicole, who died in 2016. I know that there must be a way of telling this story in which I was the villain. At the time, I felt very much like a victim. Nicole was a forceful character, who liked to get her own way. That made her an effective mother. It also made her an implacable enemy.

On the bright side, those painful years allowed me plenty of time to find myself a new home. I settled on Cambridge, which was just a short drive from Letchworth and which I already knew quite well. I thought the future might offer me more if I lived in a lively, cosmopolitan city full of culture and restaurants and shops and stim-ulating people; isolated villages had lost their appeal for me. After much searching, I found and fell in love with a little terraced Victorian house in a quiet cul-de-sac. It needed improvement, but there was time for that, too. I had it extended at the back, on the south-facing side (later on I extended it further, for more space, height and light).

Where a wall had been removed I had an exposed steel RSJ put in, painted orange (with fire retardant paint); this would soon double up as an elevated shelf for objects I liked. I had the garage at the end of the garden done up as well, so that I would have a workshop. Our divorce was finalised in March 1994, and by the end of the year I was happily installed in the home I still live in today.

At first, I continued to devote time and attention to Ogle. But the force of that habit was weakening. Away from the familiar boundaries of my family and my old home, I felt as though my life was starting again, and I began, for the first time in years, to think freely about what I wanted from life. The sense of liberation was startling.

There was sadness as well, of course, and a sense of waste. A 35-year chapter of my life had closed, and on a personal level it was a chapter of failure. I hadn't been a brilliant husband, but what bothered me more was the knowledge that I had made a bad choice. I had selected my life's partner with my head, not my heart. Desperate to avoid the mistake my father had made, I had married Nicole mainly because I thought she would be practical, reliable and a good mother. Perhaps I saw her as the opposite of my own mother. The one consideration I had neglected was whether or not I was in love with her. I don't think I ever was; and, as a result, our marriage ended up much like my parents' marriage: a union of two people who, whatever their individual strengths and weaknesses, didn't much enjoy one another's company.

Nicole had a house built for herself in the vegetable garden at Ringstead, then sold the main house in, I think, 1996. All sorts of memories, happy and unhappy, slipped away with it. I took barely any furniture with me to Cambridge, although I did bring my pottery with me. The really sad thing was that I had no way of keeping Bon. Losing him almost broke my heart. He was such a kind, devoted friend: he had never needed a lead – he just did as I asked him. He loved me, and now I had deserted him. I can hardly bring myself to imagine how miserable he must have been, pining away for me after I had vanished from his life.

But I couldn't have kept him in Cambridge, alone all day in the middle of a city. There was nothing for it but to forget him, along with any other happy memories from my decades of family life, and to look forward. This proved therapeutic. The more I thought about the future, the more I realised how much I had been missing out on in the past. For most of my adult life, I had lived for my work, looking neither left nor right. Everything else I had neglected, partly because I never developed the skills to be good at anything else. Now my work was vanishing. My family had gone; so had my home. What friends I had were mostly former colleagues who, like me, had retired and gone their separate ways. I didn't even have a dog to take for walks.

But one of the great benefits of having a creative mind is that new beginnings come naturally. The urge to make new things ensures that your gaze is always drawn to the future, where new ideas are found and made real. In Cambridge, I realised, I could build a new life that suited me.

I spent time and money turning the building at the end of the garden into a workshop. When I got here it was just a decaying garage. I had it renovated in brick, with two roof lights, and kitted it out. It had electricity, a concrete floor, plenty of elbow room and a lovely big window on the garden side. I equipped it with a workbench, shelves and tools, and accumulated other equipment and materials as the need arose. It wasn't the Ogle model shop, but it was good enough for me.

Meanwhile, I started trying to put down roots in the local community. I sensed that Cambridge was full of like-minded people, and I was keen to meet them. The other residents of my cul-de-sac proved remarkably friendly, which was a great help. I also got in touch with a local organisation called Cambridge Open Studios (COS). Founded in the 1960s by a group of community-minded artists, this was one of the earliest examples of an idea that has since been replicated in many cities. Once a year, usually over four weekends in July, members of the group invite the general public to wander into their studios and look around. Visitors see a wide range of finished work; if they wish, they can buy any items that are for sale. They also get to see the environments, methods and materials from which all those works grew; and to meet, watch and talk to the artists who made them.

I met one of the organisers, talked about what I did, showed her some of the many pieces of pottery I had brought with me from Ashwell, and was invited to take part. That was when I started to make Henry. I'm not sure why he took the form he did, but I remember being keen to make a bird. My mind was already full of thoughts about flight, thanks to my work for BAe; and I had only to glance out of a window, from my workshop or from my kitchen, to see a garden fluttering with birds. I loved watching them. The cleverness of their flight fascinated me; so did the delicacy with which they hopped about on the grass.

Henry was my tribute to them. He is about 18 inches tall, including a relatively heavy base, made from scraps of MDF that I have painted to look like marble. Two thin, straight legs, made from coat-hanger wire; above them sits a roundish body whose puffed-up form somehow suggests both cartoon sparrow and plump cartoon chicken. The body started out as a two-dimensional cardboard cut-out. I turned this into a skeleton by adding other cardboard shapes at right angles to it, a bit like ribs. When I was happy with this structure, I draped it with strips of newspaper that I had soaked with PVA and water. It was a slow, laborious process, but patience is one virtue that the craftsman learns early on. Eventually, as a final surface layer, I coated this papier mâché with tissue paper, which is smoother. Then came the paint – white emulsion for the base coat, poster paints for the colours – and then, finally, a coat of varnish.

The strange thing was, I had never done anything like this before. But I have always had a strange confidence where crafts are concerned. Whenever I come across a new technique or a new material or tool, I just assume that I'll be able to do it; and, as a result, I usually can.

In Henry's case, I was rather pleased with the outcome. I still am. The three-dimensional caricature somehow seems to evoke the essence of 'birdness'. This isn't a soaring bird, with a mighty wingspan; it is the kind of ordinary bird that hops around your garden – with the exaggerated length of the legs somehow focusing your mind on the idea that his next movement will be a hop.

What pleases me most is his plumage. All that paint and varnish gives him a bright vibrancy that seems almost alive. His green crest and tail feathers are crudely sculpted: they stick out straight like stubby gloved fingers. A few dozen scratches and dots of complementary blue convert those fingers into wings. The blue echoes the background shade of Henry's torso, which, again, is animated by a few deft stripes and dots, in brown and beige respectively. These shades are picked up in his chest, which, again, is enlivened with orange, and that in turn is echoed in his beak and legs. It's the same with the shapes: the dots and the curved lines pick up from other dots and lines, just as the toe-like crest feathers pick up from the finger-like tail feathers. The colours all overlap, so that no shade is isolated. It is simultaneously sophisticated and simple. The patterns hug Henry's form so closely, and harmonise so sweetly, that he almost feels like something from the natural world. And that was precisely the effect that I wanted to achieve. Nature understands form better than any designer. If you look at the face of a tiger, or the wings of a butterfly, there are never any surprises in the markings: just inexhaustible complexity and harmony. Everything moves in accordance with some unseen formula; each part of each shape or pattern flows logically from all the other parts; everything is resolved.

Obviously I was never going to create something truly comparable in my workshop, but I hoped at least to create an illusion of nature, and I think that perhaps with Henry I succeeded. There was a sense of rightness about his form; almost a sense of necessity. I was pleased with him, and he became the centrepiece of my first contribution to Cambridge cultural life.

That summer – in July 1995 – I opened my studio to the public for one weekend (some people did it for four in a row). The Open Studios organisers produced postcards for the participants to use. Some of mine, which featured Henry, escaped and went viral. The effect was spectacular. In the course of one weekend, at least 300 people passed through my home. Between them they bought around £1,000 worth of my artworks – mostly items I had brought with me from Ashwell, which I was ready to part with.

But the one item that everyone really wanted to buy was Henry, who, I insisted, was not for sale.

Despite that, all my visitors seemed to enjoy themselves, and so did I. All those decades of discussing designs with Ogle clients had left me very comfortable with the idea of discussing creative matters with non-specialists, and I found it particularly stimulating to discuss my work with ordinary members of the public, who had fewer preconceptions than many clients but more curiosity – and, in many cases, a much greater understanding of art and craft. Talking about my work to such clued-up people, sharing the practical backstory of each creation, was and is a real pleasure for me – not least because such discussions usually leave me with a clearer sense of how I might achieve my aims more successfully the next time.

I have done Open Studios several times since. More importantly, I have been making things ever since. Some of the results are still littered through my house and garden. Others are scattered through the homes of my children and my friends. I've sold a few, too – but my favourites I can't bear to be parted from. Henry the Bird isn't the only one of my creations that means a lot to me. Rusty the Dog is another example – although he has the advantage that he can easily be replicated. I had been drawing such dogs for decades before I finally got round to bringing Rusty into the world for the first time (in 2013, I think). He's a simple folded silhouette – laser-cut from a steel sheet, folded into a three-dimensional shape and left to rust – who now sits like a 3D cartoon dog in my garden. But he's also a simple topographical idea: a way of conveying the benign essence of 'dog' through a few well-chosen lines. Having found the formula, I find that it gives me pleasure each time I contemplate it. And the joy of Rusty is that I can keep reproducing him. I have sold several Rustys over the years and have often exhibited him, too. I keep two versions of him in my garden, one bigger than the other; and there is an even smaller one indoors. The medium-sized one works best for me: he feels more like a real dog. In fact, he reminds me of my beloved Bon.

But Henry was the turning point. His creation, and his success with the public, confirmed to me that I did have a future as a craftsman or artist of a kind. He helped me to forge links with like-minded people in my new city, as a result of which my work has been exhibited at many local venues, including Kettle's Yard, Clare Hall and the Old Examination Hall. I was particularly proud of the one at Clare Hall, whose director wrote to me afterwards to say that it was one of the best exhibitions they had ever had. I presented my work in three sections: one devoted to Ogle, one to art and craft items and one to toys and games. Wherever possible I had 'please touch' notes added, and one Saturday morning children were invited to come and play with my toys. They had a wild morning, but nothing was broken; and I was touched by the warmth of the subsequent feedback. One mother told me that, for a long time afterwards, her son kept trying to rush back into the building 'to play' whenever they passed it.

Some galleries have also sold my pieces: notably the Broughton House Gallery in Cambridge and what was then the Pam Schomberg Gallery in Colchester. And that brings me to another layer of Henry's significance – because it was while visiting Pam Schomberg that I met a new romantic partner: a fellow crafts enthusiast, younger than me, called Annette Stewart. She lived in Colchester and, like me, had just emerged painfully from a failed marriage. We instantly hit it off, began to see one another regularly, and found that we could help one another to be happy again. It was an unusual time of life to embark on a new romance: I turned 70 in 1996. But it worked for us. I don't think either of us saw the other as the great love of their life, but that was part of the attraction. There was no pressure. We spent a few happy years together and then parted amicably. There is no need to say more than that: we are still in friendly contact.

But those few happy years helped me to achieve a personal transformation. After all those decades of strained married life, I learnt how to see life as a delight that could be enjoyed, not merely hidden from. It was a bit late to be learning such a basic lesson in being human, but better late than never.

For much of our time together, Annette and I travelled. I remember wonderful holidays in Sri Lanka and Thailand.

I had travelled widely before – endlessly, it sometimes seemed – as head of Ogle. But this was a different kind of travel. Then, I had been focused all the time on achieving objectives. Now I learnt to look around me, mind open, without actively looking for anything. In other words, I learnt to live.

This was a big breakthrough, and back in the UK the sense of liberation filtered through to other areas of my life. My craft became more adventurous. I made pieces from driftwood, from wire, from spare bits of wood or cardboard. There were no rules. I didn't entirely lose my interest in product design and transport design (I was still discussing my *Aircruiser* design in mid-2001), but in the absence of tight practical briefs from demanding clients, I became more accustomed to following my own inclinations. My work became more personal, and the more it did so, the more human I felt.

Towards the end of 2001, I spent three weeks in Africa. I visited Max, who had moved to Botswana; then went on to Malawi, where I did a pottery course. It was a magical place, with a beautiful lake that I swam in three times a day to cool down. There were some brilliant potters there, and I loved working with them. I suggested that we invite some children from a nearby village to join us. I can still remember their excitement as we let them draw, make tiles and model in clay.

It hardly needs saying that my horizons were broadened by such experiences. (I have happy memories of a similar course in Tuscany, too.) But it was more than a broadening. It was a liberation. By teaching me to enjoy myself, Annette had empowered me to throw off psychological chains that had shackled me all my adult life.

I'm always reminded of this when I look at the panel of painted bathroom tiles in the corner of my front room. There are 28 tiles in all, hanging from a wooden board, and together they create quite a pleasing pattern, so visitors don't always examine them closely. Those who do are sometimes taken aback when they realise that each tile is painted to depict a different animal's bottom. There's a short, animal-specific message on each one: 'Giraffes have high-up bottoms'; 'Snails have slimy bottoms'; 'Skunks have stinky bottoms', 'Baboons have very red bottoms', and so on. Children find them hilarious. They came into existence because Annette had two lovely grandchildren, Jessica and Victoria, with whom I got on very well. My first grandchild had yet to arrive (in 2005), and so while I was with Annette I found myself almost 'adopting' hers: playing with them, making things for them and encouraging them in their own creative activities. One Christmas, I made each of them a ceramic plate and decorated them with my first two bottom pictures. One showed the backside of an elephant with the message: 'Elephants have huge bottoms'; the other one showed a bumblebee with a 'buzzy bottom'. They liked them so much that I then started decorating tiles left over from my bathroom with more bottoms. Eventually – years later – a small publisher, Happy Cat Books, decided to do a small collection. It was called *A Little Look at Bottoms* and came out in 2004. It did very well, until the publisher ran into problems and was taken over. I'd love to see someone bring out a new edition, or a follow-up. It was a great way to show young children that reading books could be fun: they laughed at the bottoms, and they absorbed all sorts of information and vocabulary while they were doing so. Meanwhile, at least I still have my collection of 28 bottoms, all lovingly hand-painted by me. I've seen them thousands of times, but they still make me smile, reminding me of a happy time when, in some important way, I learnt to enjoy myself again.

Even when Annette was no longer on the scene, my personal renaissance continued. I continued to make friends; and I realised that, among like-minded people, I enjoy being in company. Creative traces of some of these friendships can be found in my home. The blackbird in my front window was made by the potter Rosemary Wren. The badger was made by another potter, Jennie Hale (who also does wonderful nature tours for children in the woods and fields around her pottery). The toymaker David Plagerson, another friend, made the beautiful wooden Noah's Ark and its carved animals, as well as carving my two wooden Popemobiles and, as previously mentioned, my wooden Reliant Scimitar GTE. Then there's a lovely lino cut by Eileen Cooper, showing a couple having a friendly tête-à-tête with a tiger; and a wire crow by Jenny Goater; and some figures by the automaton-maker Peter Markey;

and, of course, my beautiful wooden kitchen table, made by the craftsman Paul Anderson, whom I discovered when potting in Devon.

There's not enough space to list every example, but two other works definitely deserve a mention. One is the giant bird with floral plumage that stands on the floor near the kitchen door; the other is that big colourful street painting at the back of my plan chest. Both are souvenirs of parties I have held here. In both cases, I made the basic artwork myself, then asked the guests to embellish it. For the bird, I had made a large plaster bird, then painted the blue background colour of the plumage. All the flowers – in every imaginable shape and shade – were added by guests. With the street, similarly, I did the basic picture: the street, the sky, the road and the structure of the houses. Then I put out paints and brushes and asked each guest to contribute something. Everyone added a detail: a cobble or two from the shyest; from the others, trees, window boxes, washing lines, passers-by, birds, cats, dogs, traffic, an aeroplane, even a couple of suns.

Both of these artworks are actually rather nice to look at. There are some pretty creative people in Cambridge. But the quality of the finished works isn't the point. They are souvenirs of two moments of shared happiness; and a reminder, for me, this home is a place where happiness happens easily. It is the first such home that I have had.

All this is somehow associated in my mind with Henry and his fellow birds. They represent the moment when

I found my place in the Cambridge creative community – and, more importantly, the moment when I began to evolve from successful designer to proper Mensch: a flesh-and-blood human being who isn't afraid of the emotions that make us human.

I have made large numbers of other birds since: models, drawings, sculptures, in many sizes. Many seem to belong to the same family as Henry. I have made a Mexican bird, an African bird, a Squire bird (who obviously likes a tipple), a Madam bird (with fishnet stockings), a bird made from the Yellow Pages and a bird that's a Senior Fellow at a Cambridge college (he is covered in lots of 'R's – not just the standard educational three).

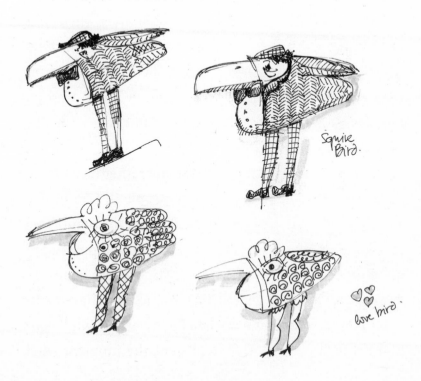

Sometimes I sell my birds. Sometimes I give them away. A series of little ones are sold through galleries, with all the proceeds going to the children's unit at Addenbrooke's, our local hospital. But my urge to make new ones tends to outstrip my enthusiasm for getting rid of them.

One way or another, I expect that some of the birds you see around me today will eventually find new homes, if only to make room for new creations. But I would really hate to be parted from Henry. Like all my favourite works, he is precious to me.

24

TOMORROW'S
WORLD

I HAVE two versions of this illustration. I'm proud of them both, even though I didn't do them myself and even though they bear only a loose resemblance to the simple sketches, in my own hand, on which they are based. The one shown here was first published in *Blueprint* magazine in 2006; there's a simpler version, by the same artist, in my front room, next to the Bush T130 radio. Both are in colour, but the essence of the idea comes across equally well in black and white.

The illustrations depict what I have tended to call a 'floating city', although 'floating urban settlement' might be more accurate. It's an artificial structure that could be inhabited by around 10,000 people. I designed it in my retirement, and *Blueprint* published the article – or perhaps you should call it a manifesto – that I wrote to explain it. Mark Wearne, an architectural illustrator, was commissioned to illustrate my piece. I started the crazily exuberant interpretation, inspired by the fantastical drawings of Friedensreich Hundertwasser, the Austrian-born artist and architect who died in 2000. I share Mark's admiration for Hundertwasser, an early advocate of self-sufficient communities and environmentally friendly architecture, and I am happy for my very practical vision to be presented with a little of his free-spirited panache.

But I don't want anyone to assume from this that my proposal for a floating settlement is just a far-fetched fancy. On the contrary, like my wide-fuselage aircraft designs, it is a serious idea that I believe in deeply. No one in a position to make such a thing happen has shown more than a passing interest in exploring it, but the idea itself is watertight, and the arguments for taking it seriously have never been more pressing. What I like about Mark's illustrations is that, precisely because of their playful approach, people tend to linger over them, poring over the details curiously. For this kind of design, that is often half the battle. Usually, when you propose an idea that involves significant change, people will snatch at any excuse to think about something else instead. Persuading them of the merits of your idea may be easier than persuading them to consider it in the first place – which is where an enjoyable illustration comes in useful.

The underlying logic of a floating settlement is simple and persuasive. Urban populations are growing. Demand for living space and infrastructure is outstripping supply. Climate change promises a future of volatile weather and rising sea levels. Major metropolises need to expand but have no land on which they can do so in a desirable way. So, what if they were to expand in a different direction, into the areas of sheltered water that so many of them adjoin? It hardly seems like a crazy question to ask.

In the early years of my retirement, with all those decades of success in the design industry behind me and all this time unexpectedly on my hands, I felt empowered to take the question a step further, and to try to imagine how cities could act on this logic. What would a floating urban settlement actually look like, in the real world? How would it work? Every bright idea has strengths and weaknesses. The key to making bright ideas happen is to work out the details.

The more I thought through my proposal, the more robust it seemed. Most of the construction techniques that would be required have been well developed, by the shipbuilding industry. The main platform could be built in prefabricated sections, then pulled together – like slices being reassembled into a cake – and joined together on-site; the prefabricated superstructure would be added later. We know already that enormous, habitable floating constructions are possible: there are ocean-going liners that carry 5,000–6,000 people and are hard to distinguish, when you're on them, from a dry-land holiday resort; the next generation of liners will take nearer 9,000. A large, self-contained, tethered settlement in sheltered waters would in many ways be simple by comparison – and it would certainly be massively simpler and cheaper than building a similarly sized settlement on land near a city centre.

The rest of the concept is flexible. That's the joy of this kind of development: few of the traditional constraints of town planning apply. I've proposed a 10,000-person settlement because that's a good size to produce a kind of social self-sufficiency, whereby most people spend most of their time working and socialising within the settlement. But there is no reason why you couldn't make a smaller settlement as well: a university campus, say, or a hospital.

Each floating settlement you made could be a world within a world; its architecture would need to harmonise only with itself. In my design, the mini-city is constructed in a big ring, with accommodation, shops, schools and other facilities dotted around the circumference. These buildings form a big, solid protective wall, like the outside of a stadium. The structurally efficient doughnut shape provides overall stability: even in high winds any rocking motion would be gentle and predictable. It also gives the architecture an underlying connectedness that liberates it to be varied in other respects. An internal corridor allows easy circulation, and there is also a promenade along the top. The area in the middle of the island is free to be a big green space for recreation and entertainment.

Inhabitants who wished to do so could spend all of their time in (or on) the settlement, but I'm assuming that a connection to dry land would be necessary, in addition to moorings. That connection could be achieved easily enough with a flexible bridge or tunnel, although boats could be used as well. My design envisages a population of around 10,000 people. If you needed to accommodate more, you would build more islands.

Roughly a fifth of the construction would be under-water. If the island was sited in a tidal estuary, this substructure could include a system of propellers and turbines to harness the power of the moving water.

In Mark Wearne's more fantastical version of the design, the verdant central park was supplemented by abundant plants and trees on the upper part of the super-structure. There is no reason why a floating settlement could not incorporate this. Once you have escaped the constraints of land scarcity and existing development, almost anything is possible.

But the point of my concept is not to create a green paradise – although one might as well aim high – but to respond to real and present dangers. The idea came to me after I saw the devastating impact of Hurricane Katrina on New Orleans in 2005. What if something similar happened in the UK – or, for that matter, somewhere else? It might not affect me, but I also had children and, from 2005, grandchildren to think about. Might there not be something to be said for a more forward-thinking, environment-conscious approach to development – in contrast to the traditional approach of planning for the short term, crossing our fingers and hoping for the best?

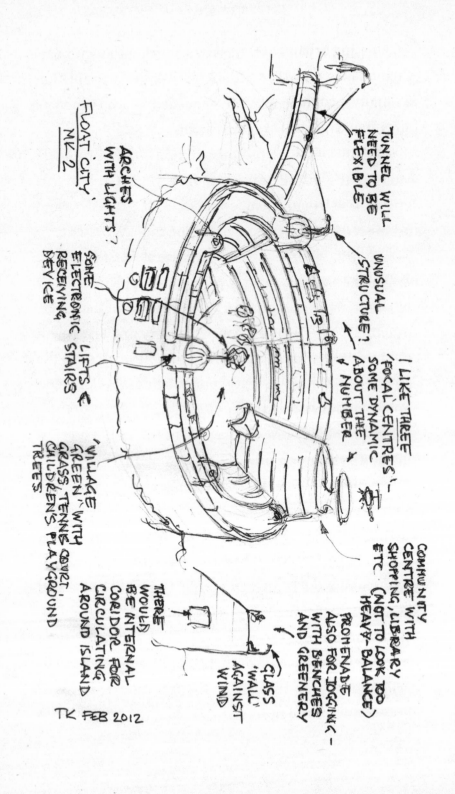

Floating urban settlements would be safe from floods, earthquakes and rising sea levels: imagine their value to many people around the world. But their obvious advantages go further than that. They would not use up precious land – an important consideration in parts of the world that are densely populated. They could be constructed with little disruption to existing settlements. And they could be sited where they were needed, rather than being built where the land happened to be available.

There is clearly an appetite for maritime construction in many parts of the world. But most of the artificial islands built so far (in the Persian Gulf, Hong Kong, the South China Sea) have actually been built on the seabed, at huge financial and environmental cost. In the Netherlands, by contrast, they have built whole communities of floating houses on their extensive inland sea. There's little room for doubt as to which approach is more affordable and achievable – or, in an age of rising sea levels, sustainable.

If you're still tempted to dismiss the idea, imagine trying to build desirable new accommodation for 10,000 people in central London. How would you go about it? Where would you get the land from? Would you undertake a programme of mass demolition? And what would happen to life in the capital during the period – years, presumably – when the development was taking place? The logistics would be a nightmare; so would the cost.

To build on water instead wouldn't be crazy: it would be common sense.

You can of course build significant structures on water that are significantly smaller and simpler than a 10,000-person settlement. Imagine, for example, a floating park in the Thames: a fresh green paradise in the heart of London for people to escape to, at a small fraction of the cost of the ill-conceived 'Garden Bridge'. Imagine, if it comes to that, a floating Houses of Parliament, moored alongside the crumbling Palace of Westminster. Perhaps that would be a good place to start, if only as a temporary solution while MPs' traditional workplace is being refurbished. (I'm not the only person to have thought of this. The US architects Gensler published a speculative proposal for such a structure in 2016. Needless to say, it wasn't taken up.)

You would have thought that the concept had enough going for it to be worth considering, at least. Unfortunately, we live in a world in which the merits of an idea are not the only things that determine whether anything comes of it or not. Talk to an architect or a politician or a town planner or a developer about floating cities, and the one thing that you can be sure of is that you will yourself be pigeonholed as a maverick or eccentric. These are the great flattering put-downs with which British complacency neutralises radical thinking. A floating city? Yes, that's a delightful thought, but, er, it's not how things are usually done. It's just blue-sky thinking.

Well, blue-sky thinking is what I do. At Ogle, many of my most successful designs defied received wisdom – yet we still converted them into commercially viable reality, and some were spectacularly successful. Since retiring, I have continued to think in much the same way: outside the box, but not beyond the bounds of feasibility. There is, however, a difference. Now that I have no commissions to fulfil, my objectives are slightly different. I no longer aim to make clients happy. Instead, I want to make the world a better place. I live alone, but I am still on good terms with my four children and – at the last count – my seven grandchildren. I see less than I would like of Max and his family, who now live in Zambia; generally, however, it is a rare week when I'm not visited by at least one of my direct descendants. What sort of person would I be if I didn't think about the kind of world they will live in after I am gone?

Long before my grandchildren are my age, people will be worrying about the problems of keeping civilised life going in the 22nd century. First, however, there is a terrifying range of potential 21st-century catastrophes to negotiate: climate change, pandemics, over-population, air pollution, environmental degradation, nuclear escalation, social and political breakdown. Flooding alone threatens more than 500 coastal cities around the world, potentially affecting up to 1.5 billion people by 2100. What could be a more appropriate response than to ask the time-honoured designer's question: how could we do things *better*?

I had been thinking about such big issues while I was still at Ogle, especially in those final years. My 'Project 2000' car, my *Aircruiser* designs, our various electric and hybrid vehicles for Lucas: these were all created with half an eye on the thought that industrialised civilisation could not carry on as it was indefinitely. So is my (never-realised) Smarter Than Smart (STS) car: a proposal I made after my retirement for a compact, tubular-framed, fabric-bodied, three-seater electric vehicle that would achieve unprecedented levels of economy and sustainability through clever minimalist design. I saw the STS as a three-and-a-half wheeler, with two wheels at the front and a single wheel at the back. An electric motor driving these twin wheels provided a power 'pod': the only technological component needed. The driver would sit centrally, almost like a motorcycle rider, with room on either side for the legs of two passengers or three children behind. A brilliantly ergonomic 'swivel and kneel' chair made it easy to get in and out; it was ideal for disabled drivers, too. The boot at the front could take an entire trolley-load of shopping. And although the STS would not be exactly fast, it had more than enough speed for safe driving in built-up areas.

The body envelope would be a sandwich of renewable materials: a weatherproof outer layer, a firmer filling to provide the form made possibly from bamboo, and an inner layer similar to the outer one. An unlimited range of colours and patterns would be available; in theory, the status-conscious could, if they chose, pay a premium for a design from someone like Chanel or Louis Vuitton.

Construction would be easy. The tubular design meant that the car could be manufactured anywhere in the world, creating local employment as well as convenience. The fabric body would be made at minimal environmental cost. The (removable) electric power-pack at the back could be relatively small, completing a virtuous circle of minimalism.

As with the Bond Bug, I devised a distinctive 'fun' shape for the vehicle. Perhaps potential manufacturers are not ready to take it seriously. Yet the thinking behind the STS car was serious. It was aimed at all those motorists who use vehicles mainly for local errands: shopping, taking children to school, making visits, going to the gym. It's incredibly wasteful, and environmentally unfriendly, to use a normal car for such purposes. But the SMART car, launched in 1998, failed to offer a real alternative: it had an internal combustion engine, over-engineered body, minimal luggage space, and seating for only two people. This struck me as a major missed opportunity, and it bothered me. Even in the late 1990s, it was obvious that manufacturers needed to adapt for a world of dwindling resources and growing human vulnerability. To thrive in future, their products needed fuel economy, flexibility, sustainability. My STS car showed what a real alternative would look like. It saddens me that motorists may never have the chance to consider buying it.

To be fair, much of the car industry has now begun to explore ways of adapting their products to make them more suitable to the world's needs. It's a bit late, but at least it shows that they are capable of grasping (belatedly) the need for change, and of altering course accordingly.

But that illustrates another point about my 'floating cities' idea. It seems far-fetched because we are used to the idea that, when it comes to the built environment, only a very limited range of options is available to us. We build homes using much the same materials, methods, styles and ideas as our ancestors did in the 19th century; and we have a chronic housing crisis. Yet imagine what would happen if we approached housebuilding with the skill, energy and competitiveness of the modern motor industry. Carmakers innovate constantly. They manufacture in huge quantities yet maintain extraordinary consistency of quality. Their products are attractive, comfortable and effective – otherwise people wouldn't buy them – yet they conform to a vast range of safety regulations and high-performance specifications; and, when necessary, they adapt. Our housebuilders, by contrast, seem mostly content to churn out the same bland little boxes as cheaply as possible, as shoddily as they can get away with.

Increasingly, therefore, I have been turning my attention to those aspects of the future that I can influence: that is, to children. I have already talked about my affinity for children: an ability, which most adults seem to lack, to see the world as they do. I hope that, all through my life, there have been children who have benefited from this – including my own children.

But retirement has added something to this gift, by giving me the time to use it. The main beneficiaries have been my grandchildren. I love it when they come to visit, and they seem to love visiting. The house is a treasure trove of interesting things for them to pick up, play with and mess around with. Many of the objects were made specifically for them: the abacus-like object, for example, is also a set of brightly painted fruit that you sort by colour, shape or names. Louis – Josephine's youngest – loved playing with it. I've got a picture somewhere of him making a big tower out of the parts. There's also a beautiful transporter aircraft somewhere here that I'm very proud of. That took a long time to make – you can put motor vehicles inside, and there's a ramp and a loading mechanism – and so the young ones were able to watch it develop. It works beautifully, and the fact that they saw me making it makes it all the more fascinating for them.

But there are other things that weren't really made for anyone. I just felt an urge to make them. Otto the Blue Dog, for example: I made him a long time ago. I'm not even sure that any of the grandchildren were old enough to play with him, although many have done so since. He has a handle that you crank to make his tail wag and his jaws open and close to snap at a ball. He's basically a canine automaton – one of several automata that I've made.

A lot of time and effort went into making some of these objects, yet I'm curiously relaxed about the risk that an over-enthusiastic child might break one. Objects are made to be handled, and toys are made to be played with. And the great thing about watching children messing around with my creations is the feedback I get. It fascinates me to see what interests them and what doesn't, what works for them, what aspects of the experience please them most. It was this kind of observation that led to the Marble Run. Sadly, I feel that some of today's toy manufacturers don't give much thought to what children might actually want, or how a toy might give them lasting pleasure. Of course, a toy that carries on giving satisfaction for a whole childhood is likely to generate less profit than a whole series of plastic toys that you can't do anything with – but that's not much comfort for the children who are fobbed off with them.

Children are born with an urge to build and create. Toys that allow them to explore this urge fascinate them. That's why brands like Lego and Meccano are so successful. But modern toys often leave little for the child to actually do, and much of the smart thinking has gone into the packaging instead. I've tried getting in touch with toymakers to suggest how they could make products that children would find more satisfying. For example, I tried to tell Hornby about what I had learnt from watching Theo, who is fascinated by trains, but they weren't interested. All my decades of successful product design counted for nothing. Instead, Hornby turned in a new direction: making items for mostly adult collectors.

The rejection doesn't bother me: you can't have a successful career as a designer without growing a thick skin. What saddens me is the waste, and the fact that children are missing out. Have you been to a museum recently, or an art gallery? Almost anywhere you go, the prevailing message to children is 'Don't touch'. It's enough to dampen any child's enthusiasm. But imagine if you turned Tate Modern into a giant experience hall for children – a place where children could plan and feel and touch and learn. That's what I'd like to do. It would be a dream: the world's most stimulating place for children; and every museum in the world would consider following suit. My guess is that adults would love it too.

I'm pretty sure that I understand children better than most people do – and certainly better than most people who work in the toy industry. I'm basically still a child myself. I make toys partly because I love children, but also because I love toys. Before my grandchildren came along, I exhibited some of my work locally, and, perhaps because some of the exhibits were toys, or toy-like objects, this led to my being asked to give a workshop at Meldreth Primary School, just outside Cambridge. My brief was to talk about design, so I showed the children work by architects I admired and then spent a day there while they built houses from cardboard and painted them. They clearly loved it, and wanted me to come back to do weekly craft sessions with them. Best of all, their teacher, a brilliant and inspirational lady called Dawn Moffat, got them all to write thank-you letters. I treasured the one from a little girl who wrote to say that I would be famous one day. I was 70 then.

All this gradually evolved into a wider, regular activity. I've done workshops with children in a number of schools, not just in Cambridge, and in galleries too: at Kettle's Yard, for example, and at the Sainsbury Centre in Norwich.

The interesting thing about these workshops is that children love them – yet you don't need to bring along any ready-made toys to get their interest. It's making things that engages them. The practical details fascinate them: sometimes it's almost as good as a science lesson – as when we made hot-air balloons from tissue paper powered by hairdryers; or, on another occasion, using white spirit. That balloon, which was released well clear of children, was spectacular. It floated upwards, as predicted, then it burst into flames and crashed. I'm sure no child who was present has forgotten the experience. Since then, I have often asked schoolchildren to bring along old cardboard boxes to my workshops – before encouraging them to turn them into the objects they want. It isn't difficult: the children do all the work. But I'm obviously felt to be offering something unusual, because I keep being asked back.

Deep down, in some sense, I have never fully grown up. I find it easy to relate to children because I think like a child. That's why I enjoy my grandchildren's company so much: we see the world in much the same way. For them, as for me, play is an adventure: the toys they find at my house are designed to challenge them, not just pacify them.

But it's not just my grandchildren who like the 'real' toys I make for them. I think most modern children are grateful for any plaything that offers them a role that isn't just passive. They get so many opportunities to be spectators, whether it's watching screens or looking at elaborate plastic models that come into the world fully formed from a factory mould. One of the most popular playthings I have created recently consists of little more than big blocks of wood. I call them Big Brix. They're about six inches long with the same proportions as ordinary bricks, but of course they're wooden: I went to a local wood yard to buy some big lengths to cut down. The idea is that you see how big a tower you can make with the Brix, and part of the fun is the horrendous racket they make when the tower collapses. They're always the first thing the younger grandchildren run to. I'd like to market Big Brix commercially, as I think they'd be a huge success.

I still think about designs for adults too, but the adults I have in mind are basically today's children. I'm concerned about the kind of world they'll live in, and from time to time I publish grown-up ideas about how that world could be made better. For example, I'd like to see a travel tax on employers: I've been arguing for that for years. Companies should be taxed according to the distance their staff travel on their behalf. It would ease the UK's transport problems considerably. I also did a detailed proposal for making Regent Street into a pedestrianised zone, with a central moving walkway and a glass roof. The bad-tempered droning and choking of traffic jams would cease, and you'd be left with a street that was spectacular, beautiful and pleasant for walking and shopping. It could be a wonder of the world.

More recently, when they were refurbishing Cambridge station, I proposed some really good ideas for them, suggesting how they could create a transport interchange that would work for everyone. I did detailed drawings for them; but of course they took no notice whatsoever. Why would they? Who cares about the unsolicited views of one old man? So they went ahead in the usual way and wasted an opportunity. It pains me whenever I see it: people dragging luggage long distances from one part of their journey to another; people queueing for taxis in the rain. It would be so easy to set things right.

If there is hope for constructive change, it comes from our children themselves. I feel so much admiration for the young people who take part in those Extinction Rebellion demonstrations. I just wish they had the politicians they deserve. Look, have you seen the logo I designed for the Green Party? It's as simple as it could possibly be: a solid green circle with the words 'Save Our World' reversed out of it in white. It's so much more powerful than that bizarrely overcomplicated thing they have at the moment.

But adults rarely do see the need for change. That's why I made some T-shirts for my grandchildren. They're just simple black and white, with slogans such as 'We are the future'. That's the message that the grown-ups running the country ought to be listening to. Less and less money gets spent on helping children to realise their potential, and yet somehow we still have millions of pounds to spend on things like nuclear submarines.

If we could liberate the creative potential that lies within each child, we could empower a new generation of innovative thinkers who could transform the world for the better. And I suspect that, if floating towns of the kind I proposed ever do become a familiar feature of urbanised civilisations, it is today's children who will make it happen.

I might not personally be able to make for my grandchildren and their friends a trouble-free world full of eco-friendly cars, sustainable floating settlements, pedestrianised streets and other beautifully designed things. But I can bequeath them the gifts with which to create such a world for themselves.

25

GROWING OLD GRATEFULLY

Y OU'RE NOT leaving, are you? Already? There's still so much to show you. Look at this, for example. It's called *The Queen's Flight*. I made it years ago: around 2001 or 2002, I think. A newspaper historian could probably date it from the font used for the words on the aeroplane. I cut the letters out of the *Guardian*, and I don't think they use that font anymore. The rest of it is made from the insides of envelopes – now you know why those wavy blue patterns look familiar – and from stamps. The second class queens are bunched together on the bottom deck, the first class ones on the top. It's a simple conceit, yet it seems to say a lot about our strange, hierarchical society.

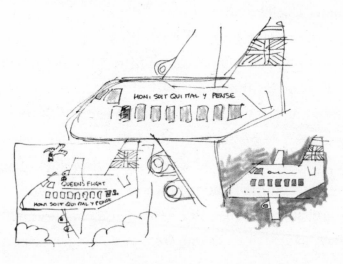

I like making art that makes a point simply. You can see something similar in the screen print over there, with the cut-out female figures queueing outside a toilet. It's called *Ladies in Waiting* and pokes fun at the way that the men who design toilets for public use never provide enough for women. It could hardly have been simpler, yet it somehow captures all the stress and absurdity of those female queues that you still see outside the toilets at almost every public building or event. I showed the print at the Royal Academy's Summer Exhibition in 2010, and the whole edition of 60 sold out instantly. I imagine that many of the purchasers were women who had just been queueing outside the RA's toilets. No doubt some of the prints ended up on toilet doors.

It's the same with *The Queen's Flight*. It's a clever idea, simply expressed – or perhaps a simple idea, cleverly expressed – and it sticks in your mind because it's so accessible. I suppose that's something that being a designer teaches you: to create accessibly.

I've printed many postcards of *The Queen's Flight*. It captures my ambivalence about British life and how I fit into it. It pokes fun at an absurdity, but it is also affectionate. The last time I used it was in early 2019, when it appeared in edible form. I think it went down well. My daughter Josephine held a small party for me, to celebrate the fact that I had just been awarded an OBE. This was arguably a strange thing to celebrate: a meaningless trinket, named after an empire that no longer exists. Yet the award meant a lot to me. Seventy-seven years after first setting foot in this country, I felt that my contribution to British life was finally being recognised.

Josephine asked a young friend, Nikki Lindsay, to make a cake, and Nikki created a beautiful one with my picture of *The Queen's Flight* on the icing. She uses a brilliant technique where she basically prints out images on to rice paper. I'm fascinated by that kind of thing – and it looked remarkably similar to the original.

I was forced to make a short speech, but the cake spoke louder than any words I could find. The British establishment, ridiculously class-bound and traditionalist, had taken me, a maverick designer, to its heart – and had made me very happy by doing so.

Perhaps it seems odd that, after so much success, I should still have felt the need for the reassurance of an official accolade. But that's what happens when you've been a refugee. You never quite feel safe enough to relax. I know that, no matter what comforts and luxuries I possess today, they can all be taken away from me tomorrow. My continuing capacity for hard, creative work is the best security I have – and public recognition reassures me that my work still has some value.

My gratification may also have had something to do with a sense that, as an outsider, I had for many years felt somewhat shunned by the design establishment. In the 1970s and 1980s, London's big design names tended to rub shoulders at the same fashionable parties, associations and clubs. I was rarely asked to join them, and sometimes I felt that I was specifically excluded. During my time at Ogle, the RSA gave more than 50 designers its special honour, the Royal Designer for Industry award, but it never gave one to me.

I think the first time I was honoured for my oeuvre as a whole was in 2001, when Loughborough University gave me an honorary degree. The following year I was awarded the Prince Philip Designers Prize – the citation said I was responsible for some of the most iconic British products of the 20th century. This prompted a feature about my work in *Top Gear* magazine: the headline described me as 'the greatest designer you've never heard of'. But more fashionable bodies have remained resistant to the idea that my career as a whole merits recognition. As far as I am aware, neither the Design Museum nor the V&A has ever shown any of my work.

Yet interest in my output has been growing recently, at least in some quarters. My work has featured in exhibitions not just in Cambridge galleries but at, for example, the Jewish Museum in Camden (for their big 'Designs on Britain' exhibition in 2017–18). The film-maker Martin Mortimore made a short film about my life to coincide with that show.

All this is welcome, not because it glorifies me but because I think the designs we created at Ogle deserve to be remembered. It was an amazing company, with amazing people working for it. We made so many beautiful things, improving the quality of day-to-day life in countless ways. We never created a product without trying to make it better than anything that had gone before. I really do think that our work made the world a better place.

I feel so proud of Ogle: not just the designs I did there, but the people who worked for me and all that talent and enthusiasm that they put at my disposal. Looking back, I realise that I've been incredibly lucky.

Yet the truth is, I don't look back very often. Even now, when interest in my life and work is increasing, there doesn't seem to be much point in dwelling on the past. A company like Ogle could never thrive today: we were part of an age in which the UK still manufactured things, and the quality of British product design really made a difference. Those days are long gone. Now there are different challenges to face.

I have given my archive to the V&A, who will do with it what they will. With this book I have set down those elements of my life that I think are worth remembering. As for my designs, they will all become obsolete sooner or later. Why cling to them?

A journalist once asked me which of my creations was my favourite. I thought about this, then responded, honestly, 'The next one.' It wasn't my line: I think it was first used by an elderly female painter who was asked a similar question. But it perfectly expressed – and expresses – my own feelings. I still feel a special pride in some of my designs: the Marble Run, the Reliant Scimitar GTE, the Hemitech truck cab, the Bond Bug. But my favourite piece of work from a lifetime of creation is the one I will make tomorrow.

Perhaps I will even start on it today, after you've gone. Making things takes me longer than it did. It's irritating, but I can't always get things right first time these days. I recently turned 94, and my craftsmanship isn't what it used to be. But I'll have to adjust: it's just one more challenge, and in its way it's quite an interesting one.

Most of the time, I barely notice my age. But the years keep on going by, and I want to make good use of the time remaining to me. Already, most of my grandchildren have grown too old for the toys I used to make for them, so I am making new challenges for myself. For example, I want to make a large car model not unlike the Bugatti we used to have in Brno. But that's just one project. Every day brings new ideas and new possibilities. I am always creating things and, as a result, I am never bored. I get tired sometimes, but there is still so much that I want to do.

I would like to redesign the world to banish cruelty and misery and to preserve it so that my grandchildren have a future in 50 years' time. If I cannot complete the task, I would at least like to teach them – and as many other children as possible – to carry on seeking better ways of doing things after I've gone. That's why everything I create these days seems to me to be important and urgent. Have you seen that little blue-and-yellow aeroplane I made – the one underneath the kitchen clock? It has a bomb underneath it, which you can release by pressing the pilot's head. The bomb has 'big fat peace bomb' written on it, in large letters. I imagined it releasing a mist of love and goodwill, to end all conflict. It's a bit battered, because it's been dropped so often, but I hope the message has sunk in.

This kind of work strikes me as just as important, in its own way, as the cars, lorries, radios and washing machines I designed earlier in life. Every child is born with creative tendencies and destructive tendencies. I am reminded of this every time children play with my Big Brix. If we made more effort as a society to nurture the creativity, there might be a little less destruction in the world, and a little more hope for the future.

Anyway, I mustn't keep you. Can you show yourself out? It takes me a while to get to the door. Thank you for letting me share my memories with you. It's been a strange experience, looking back on my life. I am proud of what I achieved, and of the hard work that enabled me to achieve it. But I have also realised an uncomfortable truth. If I hadn't made a success of my career as a designer, my life would have been mostly a disaster.

I feel wiser now than when I first arrived in Britain. I am more at peace with myself and my family. I think my two decades of retirement have been the happiest of my life. I may even have found a role in family life – being a grandfather – at which I am not completely hopeless. But the lessons in living that I have learnt have been very late coming, and I still have much to learn. Luckily, I still have my workshop to retreat to.

And that, in a nutshell, has been my life. Designing things was a doddle. It was everything else that was difficult.

ACKNOWLEDGEMENTS

This book came about because some of my work was featured in an exhibition at the Jewish Museum in London. I was in the company of refugees who had made an important contribution to design in the UK.

My family managed to escape from Czechoslovakia after the German occupation in March 1939 because of a wonderful Belgian lady named Tante Rose, who managed to get us our visas. I owe my life to her.

When I was still working in the Aircraft industry and based in Chipstead, a lovely Surrey village, thanks to the artist Christine Waddicor and her boys I was able to build a little vehicle which was the first step towards my career in industrial design.

I was lucky to be in digs with the Pepper family whose son, Christopher, later became the Director for Admin and Finance at Ogle. His contribution to the success of the company was priceless. So was that of Valerie Murray, a PA we shared. Christopher was instrumental in recruiting Sonja Pilcher, a Finnish lady as our Financial

Controller, who offered valued human touches beyond her professional expertise.

I went to Central Saint Martins to train as an product designer where a Mrs Tomrley from the Council of Industrial Design took an interest in my career. She became a kind of Fairy Godmother to me, I never failed to take her advice and it was a proud moment when I was able to invite her to Ogle when I became Chief Designer and MD there.

I owed my job to John Ogier who invited me to Ogle after the death of David Ogle. As Chairman, he was endlessly supportive with his enthusiasm and skill in steering the company through a difficult reorganisation. I was lucky to have the help of later chairman, Sam Alper, who became a good friend, and John Thompson who helped the company through a difficult period. He was also instrumental in introducing us to Nigel Wemyss, who helped us to get important work in the Aerospace industry.

Ogle was a design company and it goes without saying that its success was based on the quality and motivation of its design, engineering and model making personnel. Dedication to the company was exemplary and I knew I could depend on them to produce high quality work on time.

My mother showed great courage through our refugee trials and beyond and I regret not showing her more appreciation for this. I loved my father, but circumstances kept us apart for much of our lives. I would have loved him to know how I succeeded.

I am grateful to my children, Nicolas, Josephine, Max and Eugenie for their unfailing support, with special thanks to the latter for her diligent work on this book.

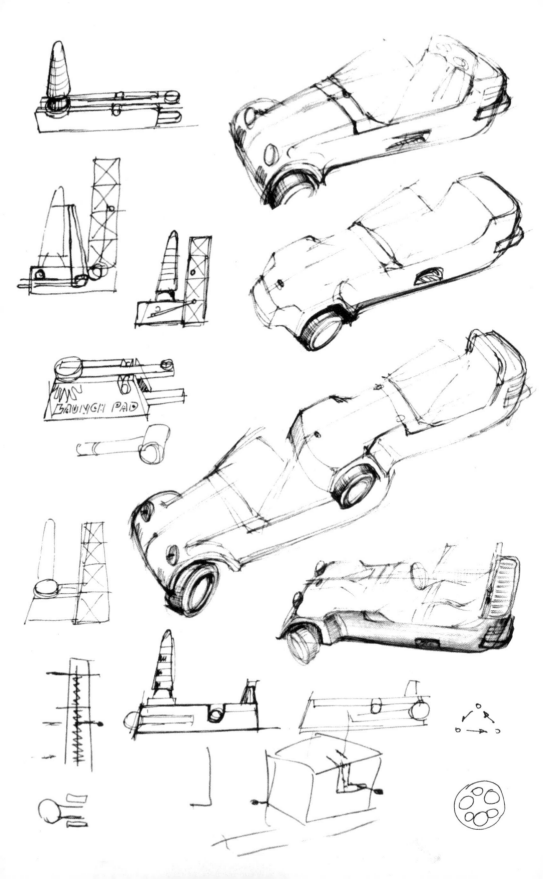

LAUNCH PAD